The American Journalists

VIEWS AND INTERVIEWS ON JOURNALISM

Charles F. Wingate, Editor

ARNO
&
The New York Times

Collection Created and Selected
by Charles Gregg of Gregg Press

Reprint edition 1970 by Arno Press Inc.

LC# 78-125724
ISBN 0-405-01707-3

The American Journalists
ISBN for complete set: 0-405-01650-6

Reprinted from a copy in
The Columbia University Library

Manufactured in the United States of America

VIEWS AND INTERVIEWS

ON

JOURNALISM,

EDITED BY

CHARLES F. WINGATE.

(CARLFRIED.)

NEW YORK:
F. B. PATTERSON, No. 32 CEDAR STREET.
1875

Copyrighted by F. B. PATTERSON, in 1875.

Press of KILBOURNE TOMPKINS, 10 Cedar St. New York.

To

GEORGE RIPLEY,

LITERARY EDITOR OF THE *Tribune*,

Who has truly been to me

A GUIDE, PHILOSOPHER, AND FRIEND,

I dedicate this little book,

As a proof of

grateful remembrance.

TABLE OF CONTENTS.

	PAGE.
Introduction,	7
Henry Watterson,	11
Whitelaw Reid,	25
Samuel Bowles,	41
William Cullen Bryant,	49
Charles A Dana,	52
Henry J. Raymond,	64
Horace White,	77
David G. Croly,	84
J. C. Goldsmith,	102
Murat Halstead,	113
Frederic Hudson,	130
George W. Curtis,	139
Mrs. Jennie C. Croly (Jennie June),	146
Horace Greeley,	151
R. R. Bowker,	183
William Hyde,	195
Theodore Tilton,	203
E. L. Godkin,	208
Manton Marble,	216
Parke Godwin,	222
Henry Ward Beecher,	227
F. B. Sanborn,	235
Mary L. Booth,	253
George W. Smalley,	260
James Gordon Bennett,	275
James Gordon Bennett, Jr.,	287
George P. Rowell,	296
SUPPLEMENT.—	
Illustrated Journalism,	317
The Motive and Method of Journalism,	325
APPENDIX.—	
College Training for Journalism,	359
Newspaper Nom de Plumes,	361
INDEX,	365

INTRODUCTION.

DURING the last twenty years journalism has become prominent, if not pre-eminent, as a profession. The press is to-day the most potent agency for good or evil; and editors, far more than statesmen, are the guides of current opinion. Already a distinct branch of literature has been created, relating to newspapers. Nearly every leading writer of the past half century has formulated his opinions upon the influence of the press, while several bulky works have been written upon the history of newspapers, the most notable being those of Eugene Hatin, James Grant and Frederic Hudson, treating respectively of French, English and American journalism.

Many biographies of famous editors have also been written, among them lives of Daniel Defoe, William Cobbett, Douglass Jerrold, and Charles Dickens, the autobiography of Leigh Hunt, Parton's "Life of Horace Greeley," the "Recollections of a Busy Life," Pratt's "Bennett and his Times," Maverick's "Life of H. J. Raymond," the "Life of William Seaton," and the "Life of Gerard Hallock."

There have also been published several selections of newspaper articles by individual journalists, beginning with the controversial writings of Swift, the Letters of Junius, "Peter Porcupine," the disquisitions of Samuel and John Adams, Hamilton, Jay, Madison, and other political writers previous to the Revolution and during the discussions prior to the adoption of the Federal Constitution; two volumes of articles by William Leggett, which appeared in the *Evening Post* during his editorship; a volume of Theodore Tilton's leading articles in the *Independent* entitled "Sanctum Studies," "Tribune Essays," by Charles T. Congdon, a volume of letters and articles written for *The World* by Wm. H. Bogart, its "Sentinel" under the title "Who Goes There"; another volume of "World Essays" entitled "Among my Books," by Wm. B. Read; one or two volumes of Essays on scientific and philosophical topics contributed to the same journal by John Fiske; and a volume of letters about publishing, by Wm. Henry Hurlbert, of its regular staff

These are exclusive of the innumerable reprints of reviews, critiques, and sketches from various newspapers, which belong more to pure literature than to journalism.

Finally, a number of articles on journalism have appeared in the reviews and magazines, some of which displayed much acumen.

The English quarterlies have contained more than a score of notable disquisitions of this class, a list of which will be found in Poole's "Index to Periodical Literature. Mr. Parton's article on the *Herald* in the *North American Review*, D. G. Croly's prophetic sketch of "The Newspaper of the Future" in *Putnam's Monthly*, L. J. Jennings' obituary of H. J. Raymond in the *Galaxy*, with characterizations of Messrs. Godkin, Curtis, Tilton and Parke Godwin in the same magazine, by Eugene Benson, besides Richard Grant White's disquisitions upon the ethics of editing, Whitelaw Reid's lecture on schools of journalism before the New York University, and F. B. Sanborn's address on journalism and journalists before the Boston Radical Club, and Parke Godwin's paper upon journalism in *Putnam's Monthly*, reprinted in his volume— "Out of the Past"—are among the American periodical contributions to this class of discussion.

Much valuable material relating to the history and prime functions of our national press may be found in De Tocqueville's great work on Democracy in America, and in Hildreth's History of the United States. The opinions of both these writers, on the broader principles of the subject, are especially valuable on account of the known reputation of the former as a philosophical observer, and the sound judgment and long experience of the latter as a practical journalist.

The present work differs from all of those just named. It does not treat directly of the history of the press, nor does it contain the opinions of certain editors upon general subjects. Its prime object is to give the views of the most representative men in a special profession, regarding the practice of that profession. As fulfilling such an object, it appeals not only to the members of the Newspaper Guild, and to those who aspire to master its principles, but also to the general public, who naturally feel a keen interest in the inner workings of that great agency—the press—by which their opinions are regulated, and who already hold the chief editors of the great journals of the country in high·estimation.

Thus it is at once a technical treatise and a general statement, and it appeals both to the professional reader and to the public at large.

Several of the interviews here presented have already appeared in print in the now defunct New York *Leader*, whose literary editor, Mr. J. C. Goldsmith, was an enthusiastic student of journalism as a science and as a trade, and who reported and published the interviews with Messrs. Croly and Reid. Mr. Hudson's interview in the *Leader* I did myself, as well as those since reported with Messrs. Watterson, White, Dana, Bowker and Goldsmith.

The summaries of Messrs. Godkin's, Curtis, and Marble's opinions have been compiled from the journals which they severally edit, and have had their approval.

Mr. Bowles' views first appeared in the twenty-fifth anniversary number of the *Independent*, and are acute and tersely expressed, like all that he writes. The other statements of opinion will be found credited to the sources from which they have been taken.

The business side of journalism is clearly set forth in Mr. George P. Rowell's essay.

Lastly, the sketches of Messrs. Bennett, Raymond and Greeley, aim to bring together authentic information regarding their methods and motives as journalists. The views of these eminent editors in regard to the practice of their profession were never formulated during their life-time, and in view of their representative position in the press, the present work would be very deficient without some presentation, however imperfect, of their opinions and practice. Fortunately, I have been able to gather considerable material suitable to this end, and while it is to be regretted that the results obtained are not more complete, yet they are worth reading.

Since the interview with Mr. Croly took place, that gentleman has thought a good deal further upon the scope and method of journalism. This new matter has been incorporated as a supplement to the present work. As Mr. Croly began the late discussion of journalism in his article in *Putnam's Monthly*, these latest expressions of his thoughts on the subject, are especially deserving of attention.

In an appendix will be found a list of newspaper *nom de plumes*, and two valuable communications relating to college training for journalists.

Due prominence has been given to women journalists, who are ably represented by Miss Mary L. Booth and Mrs. Croly (Jennie June).

In conclusion, I desire to thank the many original contributors to this volume for their aid and encouragement toward its execution, and to express a hope that they, as well as the public, for whose benefit it is published, will excuse its shortcomings.

C. F. W.

HENRY WATTERSON,

EDITOR OF THE " LOUISVILLE COURIER-JOURNAL."

QUESTION.—What do you think of the foreign papers?

ANSWER.—I can speak only of the English and French press, which I have had some opportunities to study. The German papers are a sealed book to me; though Senator Schurz tells me they are edited somewhat on the American plan. I dare say, like most German publications, they have merit. There is but one thoroughly readable London daily, and that is the one the critics attack most savagely. I mean the *Telegraph*. It is not particularly wise or weighty, but it is full of raciness and variety; that is to say, it is less dull, pompous and able than the *Times*. Your "able journal is like your novel with a "moral purpose." It may be very fine, after its fashion, but it produces few effects and gives no pleasure. It is not the business of the editor to affect the functions and characteristics of the statesman. Imitation in journalism, as in all things else, implies something more than mediocrity; it involves just that sort of insincerity which discredits the whole tenor and direction of useful effort. The English papers are over-dignified, and therefore pretentious, not because the English are incapable of brilliant journalism, but because the journalists of England regard the conventional ponderosity of the *Times*—which was at the first, and now is, an affectation—with the servility which all of us, more or less, pay to extraordinary success. The London *Times* has certainly been an extraordinary success. But so the New York *Herald* has been; and it would be as unfair to set up the success of the

Times and the *Herald* as standards in journalism as it would be to set up the late Borie as a standard in seamanship, or the late James Fisk, Jr., as a standard in financiering. Mr. Lincoln offered the French mission to Mr. Bennett. What manner of diplomatist do you think Mr. Bennett would have made? He would have produced a sensation—perhaps many sensations—in Paris; and so he did in the *Herald*. But journalism does not consist in a series of sensations any more than diplomacy. The London press goes to the opposite extreme, and in seeking for wisdom and accuracy, falls into the magniloquent commonplaces of the parliamentary debates, which are the models set before every aspiring English cub. There is a deal of stately gabble in the newspapers of London; and very little of the pith, marrow and earnestness—the originality and the vitality—which once made Mr. Greeley, in spite of his personal oddities, so great a power in the journalism of this country. The truth is, the London press is ruled by coarse, third-rate men, who engage the services of clever—sometimes brilliant—literary hacks. These latter have neither inspirations nor force—except of a verbal kind. The journals themselves, therefore, lack the modest individuality—*the glow*—of genuine conviction.

Q. Do you believe in "personal journalism?"

A. By no means. Let me illustrate what I mean by the "individuality" which ought to enter into the conduct of a newspaper. If a man thrusts himself upon your notice—if he says by his act or by his word, "See, what a great man I am"—*being*, mind you, a person of consequence or parts—you will give him credit for perhaps all that he assumes, reduced in its effect upon your respect by the drawback of an obtrusive vanity. *That* is personal journalism—abounding in forcibleness, but abounding also in conceit. There is a power greater than this, and that is the power of the brave, earnest and thoroughly equipped mind, which forgets itself, which ignores itself, and goes in to accomplish results not in its own exaltation, but for purposes cherished beyond its exterior belongings, conscious at all times of an assured position, and wasting none of its energies and its time upon "the fever and the worry and the fret" of aspirations which, like water, are pretty sure to settle themselves, and like fire, won't do to be tampered with. There is a pretense of this sort of "impersonality" in the London press; but only a pretense. The reality, which is a power in every walk of life, is rarely found anywhere. Mr. Schurz, as a statesman, seems to me to have it. Mr. Jefferson, the comedian, has it. Gen. Lee, as a soldier, had it, Mr. Lincoln had it.

Q. Do you know of many newspaper examples of it?

A. Not many. Horace White, of Chicago, has it. I think William Hyde has it. I have a newspaper friend in Tennessee, Albert Roberts, who has it very decidedly. Indeed, it is less rare among us than it is in England, where it is chiefly developed among scientific men. Old Michael Faraday was a great example. Huxley and Herbert Spencer and Tyndall—all of whom I have had the pleasure of meeting—suggest it.

Q. You do not think so highly, then, of the English journalists?

A. We surpass the English in journalism as the English surpass us in fiction. The English are born novelists. The born journalist is a Yankee product. Halstead and I set out in life as writers of romance; he emulated Cooper, and I worshiped Thackeray; and both of us at this moment have a sneaking notion that two great literary persons were destroyed by the exigency which forced two gushing youths out of fiction and into the beautiful, picturesque and varied reality of journalism. To be sure neither of us believes in this literary phantom—as an actual fact—anywhere before the second or third bottle of champagne; and I can't answer for Halstead even after the fourth bottle. He's a sturdy buck, and keeps his head better than I do. But as for me—just ask our friend Harper—" Joe, Brooklyn "—how it is; and he'll tell you its very " bad " about the times the dessert comes on.

Q. What about the French press?

A. I begin, latterly, to think better of the Paris papers. Their mechanical deficiencies are great. They are unimposing, being small and carelessly made up. But they are sinewy and cultured. Their matter, as a rule, is admirable. Many of Prevost-Paradol's editorials have never been surpassed. Saint Beuve was only one of a great school of social writers, of whom, in England, Andrew Halliday is a solitary example. In this country we have not one. The Paris critics, too, are the best in the world. All in all, I think the French press—with many drawbacks—realizes the mission of journalism—whilst falling far short of it—more nearly than the English press. Both the French and English press are inferior to our American press. The difference is about that which exists between the foreign railway carriages—models of neatness and deficiency—and our sleeping coaches, which might be cleaner, but are immensely complete.

Q. To what do you attribute this?

A. Mere lack of enterprise and a very natural unwillingness to take lessons in civil economy from a race of half educated pioneers, whose necessities, joined to national characteristics, have driven the entering wedge into the true secret of the future—producing by the process many hurtful splinters and much discomfort—but, in the main, driving home at the real work of revolution, that needs to be accomplished before we can hope to arrive at the perfection of public and private life, which, thus far, the Germans seem to have approached more nearly than any of us.

Q. How is a good paper made?

A. That is a good paper which is best fitted to its place. It depends on the man, rather than the locality. Mr. Prentice made the old Louisville *Journal* the most famous newspaper in America, though when he began it Louisville was a village. Mr. Bowles has given the *Republican* a repute which is national; yet Springfield is hardly more than a village. There is room even in New York, in spite of the crowd of newspapers that now block the way, for still another, if a man can be found with the practical sense to strike out a new idea—open it up like an avenue—grade it and pave it and light it. You may rely upon this, that the result of every newspaper enterprise depends upon the character of the man who engages in it, his capacity to discern correctly and to adapt his paper to the wants and needs of the audience it is meant to serve.

Q. What is the best method of newspaper training?

A. There is but one school of journalism, and that is a well conducted newspaper office. To be sure this may be preceded by a certain special course of study in political economy and *belles-lettres*. But versatility of talent and accomplishments—which, as a rule, is a drawback—is, in journalism, a prime necessity, and this cannot be acquired within the narrow compass of an editorial college. I don't believe a journalist can be made to order. I have tried it under favorable conditions and failed; whilst, on the other hand, I have seen some most unpromising beginners come out amazingly. Severity of culture, involving logical distinctness and accuracy, is needed to make a good leader-writer. But I never knew a good leader writer, except Mr. Raymond, who was a good journalist. Mr. Whitelaw Reid is a good journalist, and has shown himself a good leader-writer. But just as he gains in the one character he will lose in the other. The two are very nearly incompatible. Their functions are totally at odds and constantly interfering the one set of duties with the other.

Q What is your opinion of a young man's chance for newspaper advancement?

A. It is with newspapers as it is with every pursuit in life—availability is always at a premium. If a man can do a certain thing—that needs to be done—better than any other man within ready reach, he will be pretty sure to be engaged to do it. There are perhaps more chuckleheads in journalism than in any of the professions, and therefore the openings for real talent are more numerous.

Q. Do you believe in confining men to special departments of newspaper work?

A. No, I do not, except upon compulsion. If a man is to become a journalist, he must begin at the bottom and go by each round of the ladder to the top, familiarizing himself with each round as he passes. It is neither healthful nor profitable to allow an editorial staff to grow stiff, to crystallize in set and changeless duties. Men easily fall into ruts. You want your staff so made up that any one member can at a moment's notice fill another's place. This gives each a *general* view of the business, qualifying him, if he has brains enough, for leading work. A good managing editor must be able to fill, by having filled, every subordinate place. In the education of a journalist frequent changes about are essential. Special instructions in artillery does not make a man a soldier.

Nor will special knowledge of one department, merely, make a man an editor. Certainly, when a man fills a post acceptably it may be inconvenient to transfer him to a post he may not fill so well. But, in the long run, it is best to accept temporary inconvenience in order to secure that universalism in the working capacity of an editorial force, which, when once obtained, is beyond all price.

Q. Is there much favoritism in editorial life?

A. I think not. An editor must be an autocrat, but a wise editor will be a moderate autocrat; and the autocrat of a pure democracy. He has no time for favoritism. He must use the most available material he can get. A well-trained editorial force—a force in which every man is able, by reason of the changes I have mentioned, to do the work of every other—suggests regular promotions where vacancies occur. Thus strangers are not brought in for lucrative places and put over the heads of those who have been waiting to be advanced. I have tried this system thoroughly, and know that its moral effect is very great.

Q. What do you think of anonymous journalism?

A. Letters ought to be signed by the name of the writer in full. So should literary reviews and art criticisms; for the fidelity of these is referable, in a great measure, to the writer. Personal responsibility in such matters, joined to the chance of individual character, elevates the aim and purifies the tone, to say nothing of its direct mechanical effect upon the work itself. Editorials should be impersonal in every way. The power of the editorial "we" is not a one-man power; it is the power of the ten, twenty or fifty thousand readers, who are supposed to be represented by their chosen paper.

Q. You believe in representative journalism?

A. To be sure I do. An editor is nothing if not representative. He must be the type of a class, and will be great or small according to his class.

Q. Should he have convictions?

A. Intuitions rather than convictions; too often convictions imply obduracy, a dangerous newspaper quality. He should certainly be honest. Technical consistency is impossible in journalism. But if a man sticks to his intuitions, and is faithful to them, his conduct will display a spiritual consistency—a sincerity of purpose—which, if he be a man of sense and popular sympathies, is pretty sure to hit the masses of the people somewhere not very far from taw.

Q. You are credited with having organized the famous "newspaper syndicate" at Cincinnati; what did it amount to?

A. It organized itself, and it amounted to several excellent suppers at the St. Nicholas Restaurant. They called it "a mutual admiration society," and I suppose it was. Nothing is more natural than that ten or a dozen members of the same profession, who have succeeded in a common line of work, should nob and hob-nob over a square meal of victuals, and that, sopping the gravy out of the same dish, they should beam each upon each and love one another. For my part—being a little gushy and caring little for appearances within the limits of good behavior—I have a dreadful infatuation for my own guild, for the guild as a corporosity, and for each of its particles. I never knew a first-class journalist who was not a "devilish good fellow," and "a devilish good fellow" with brains and work in him is a rare compound. Usually your "devilish good fellow" is a cheat and vagabond. There were in our mutual admiration society a dozen men of exceptional strength and geniality. It was, in fact, the oddest combination that ever gathered about a supper-table, and, as it fairly illustrates the journalism of the country, I may as well tell you about it. There was, to begin on, Hyde, of the St. Louis *Republican*, a square-shouldered, open-faced man, who looks like the pictures of Mirabeau, only he is not pitted with the small-pox. He has a bucket-full of brains, is a newspaper counter-part of Robinson, the well-known Congressman of Illinois, and considers himself the inferior of everybody; a shy, strong, warm-hearted man, who has passed his life in hard work, and cares nothing at all for notoriety. There was Murat Halstead, another and very different character; a queer cross between a country belle and a field marshal; as showy a fellow as John Breckinridge and as bashful as "a poor boy at a frolic," conscious of assured position and power, and assuming a curious school-girl bravado to cover up a constitutional shyness. There was Sam. Bowles—whose head is uncommonly level—the typical New Englander, ready, genial and shrewd—the most representative Yankee alive—and, *per consequence*, the *fac simile* of your live Mississippi planter, who wears a Panama hat, keeps "open house," and can, if need be, ride a race, make an oration, fight a duel, or trade for a horse, and all with equal powers of adaptability. There was Horace White—a quiet, resolute man—severely cultured—who would be a scholarly recluse if he were not a journalist, but who, being a journalist, is, in spite of his apparent coldness, which is simply composure, a most genial and entertaining man among his peers,—an earnest, brave fellow, full of convictions, and, by odds, the most incisive writer of terse leaders in this country. There was Whitelaw Reid—who, at the age of thirty-two or three, finds himself at the head of the most thoroughly journalistic journal in the world—an extremely polished, comely man of the world—with rare tact and judgment, who played Horace Greeley's hand for him in a way that some of us "despised." There was Bromley, of Hartford, a most observant, quietly witty, cultivated and traveled man; and Theodore Tilton, who ought to edit the home-organ of St. Paul in Paradise; and Don Piatt, who is the most sensitive, provoking, genial satirist in America; and George Alfred Townsend, a Yankee Dickens with the head of a prize-fighter and the manners of a Philadelphia *Bourgeoise*, a brilliant, somewhat exclusive man of society, who has taken some of his points, unhappily, from John Forney, and others from old Shelton Mackenzie, but who, in spite of his Dickensism, Forneyism, and Mackenzieism, is a dashing fellow, with a vast working capacity.

Q. You speak with enthusiasm?

A. I don't think I draw the sketches, rough as they are, beyond the permission of nature. Do you wonder that a set of this sort, with no professional or business conflicts, without the sense of rivalry or jealousy, should admire itself? It had a good time at Cincinnati—certainly. It enjoyed itself. It was felt as a power. It was a power. Its *bonhomie*, its resources, its journalistic freedom from petty and unworldly envies—for journalism broadens a man's knowledge of life to that degree that he begins to understand what a genuine ass he is if he does not recognize the law that every tub stands on its own bottom—its vitality, its ready wit, its muscle, made it what Spenser calls "a goodlie companie." The most cosmopolite class in the world are "the roughs." Imagine a company of educated, scholarly, able, hard-working, wealthy "roughs," and you have the Syndicate to a dot. Now, go on with your questions, and we'll come back to business.

Q. How far should a newspaper practice independence of party organization?

A. I can only answer out of my own experience. For ten or a dozen years I have practiced perfect independence, consulting only my inner consciousness and my partners in business. Because a paper is the organ of a political idea does not imply that it must be the mouthpiece of the party leaders who do the work of that idea, and are paid to do it, being the servants of the people, not the masters of the press. Three times in my life I have had to wage an uncompromising war on my own organization; at Nashville, in 1861, where I was opposed to the Harris Government; at Chattanooga, in 1862-'3, where, as editor of the *Rebel*, I had to assail the many and fatal short-comings of the military establishment of the time; and, in Kentucky, where my own party had, somehow, gotten miserably out of joint. In these several controversies, which included a great deal of personal bitterness, my faith was strong because I felt that I had the right of it. In the last of these fights I was the more confident because of the backing I received from Mr. Haldeman, who is surpassed in newspaper acumen and judgment by no member of the profession. Neither his mind nor his heart misgave him during a long and trying ordeal, a fight for life, on which the fortune of both of us absolutely depended. His experience in independent journalism is very great, and its lessons correspond to my own. There was a time when he, and the late Mr. Potter, of Cincinnati, were the only independent journalists in the West. For twenty-five years he held his own against Prentice and Harney, personal journalism and the party drill, and never lost a battle. The sum of it is that where independence does not degenerate into factious obstinacy, where it is animated by a good purpose and guided by sound, common sense, it is the one sole method of journalism which will bear investigation. When the people feel that in their newspaper they have a watch set on their politicians whose fidelity to their principles can not be suspected, they give to the paper, thus situated, vast confidence and power. I consult my partners, and my subordinates, constantly; and am often instructed by their suggestions. I believe Mr. Haldeman and I never had a difference of opinion, and I am often laid under obligations to him for valuable hints. I think two minds are better than one if they can be made to go the same way. My habit of discussing matters with my subordinates has another advantage. They get, somehow, into my own way of thinking, because they know very well that I allow the largest freedom of opinion, and wish to avail myself of individual peculiarities of thought, where they do not conflict with the general harmony of the paper. In this way many things appear in the COURIER JOURNAL which are not precisely what I should say on the same subject. But if it is not my fight, and does not interfere with other matters, I let them go; conceiving variety of treatment, and the play of many minds, properly organized and kept within bounds, to be one great element of newspaper strength.

Q. What are your habits?

A. I usually waken about ten in the morning. Take a cup of coffee in bed. Write two hours. Go into a plunge-bath, dress and breakfast at 1 o'clock, when my family have their midday lunch. I go to the office at 3 P. M. to see company, hear complaints, look after my people, and, in short, to set the machine going. At 10 at night I am back again, and run the paper through to press. I believe, with Halstead, that the last two hours are the most important of all. I personally overlook the making-up of the forms. My health is good, and my capacity for sustained endurance very great; during the first three months after I took hold of the journal I did not average exceeding four hours of sleep in the four-and-twenty; and I have often gone two entire days without any sleep at all. I rarely go to the theatre, but I am fond of music, and seldom miss any that is worth hearing. I got my fill of the sock and buskin when I was a yonng fellow and made dramatic criticism my *metier*. Sometimes I play draw-poker, which is to Kentucky what whist is to England. Do I play it well? No; there is but one worse poker-player in the world, and he has recently joined the church. At night I use an amanuensis altogether. I can write in the forenoon for an hour or two, but I can not read a column of matter, and all my reading is done for me. It is not such a drawback as it seems to be. I contrive by the aid of another's eyes to get through a deal of work.

Q. What do you think of the telegraph as a conveyancer?

A. It ought to be used to the full extent of a newspaper's capacity to make it commercially profitable, no farther. It can be over-used, and is often neglected. Letters, as a rule, are valueless as vehicles for news. They are valuable where they are made to depend on their own specialty. Picturesque writing, like that of Townsend, and racy writing, like that of Piatt and McCullagh, is very valuable. But, short of this, the mails are slow, and the wires the better reliance. They have cut down the ascendency of the New York press. After four-and-twenty hours of travel a daily—no matter how good—meets a competitor it can not hope to rival. The New York papers have no circulation in the West, and before the pneumatic tube is perfected we shall be rich enough to keep them out though they should be delivered on time with us. Mr. Parton's prediction is that of a clever observer, not a practical journalist.

Q. Do you think editors should accept office?

A. The journalist who wants office mistakes his calling. An editor is himself an official, occupying a very enviable position; and his consequence is to be measured by that of his journal, great or small, as it may be. He should desire preferment only in his profession, which is a branch of the public service. But in order to be a good journalist he must eschew caucuses, committees and conventions, he must hold himself aloof from cliques; he must beware of intrigue. His road lies straight before him. He must not become a party to personal, local and party struggles, to be advised as to what is going on; and the more isolated he keeps himself, and the more disinterested he is, the better will he fulfill his mission as a faithful servant of the people. All the editors who have gone into politics have made mistakes, because journalism and office are at odds, and a man must violate the one or the other if he attempts to join the two.

WHITELAW REID.
EDITOR OF THE "NEW YORK TRIBUNE."

After some preliminary conversation, in which Mr. Reid expressed his unwillingness to be made prominent in connection with whatever he might say on the subject of journalism, or to be put forward as having any special theories or system to air, save as every thoughtful man must have notions about the business that occupies him, he proceeded to answer the questions, as follows:

Question.—What, then, is your idea of the modern daily newspaper?

Answer.—I should say that it is exactly what its its name expresses: a *news*paper, with the promptest and best attainable elucidation and discussion of the news to attend it. I know there is another idea urged by men who are anxious to become propagandists; but whenever such men have obtained exclusive control of a daily newspaper they have ruined it. The essence, the life-blood of the daily paper of to-day, is the *news*. The paper which most thoroughly, accurately and systematically, every day, collects and attractively publishes all the news of the world for the day before, best worth the attention of the average men of intellect—whatever be its fancied or real drawbacks in other directions—will inevitably be the leading journal.

Q. But do not readers, and especially readers of the *Tribune*, require their favorite paper to express certain lines of opinion, and do they not object to a wavering from those lines of opinion?

A. Theodore Tilton said to me not long ago that the *Tribune* is no longer a newspaper for which he can cherish such regard as formerly, because it doesn't represent anything, He was good enough to pronounce it "better for *mere* news" than it had ever been, but maintained that it was wasn't "a representative journal." Passing over the folly of this charge, my answer was, "Will you take ten thousand dollars for the single share of stock you own in it, for which a few years ago you gave less than half that sum?" He was not ready to accept the offer. He didn't like the paper, but he considered it more valuable—the best proof that it was fulfilling the functions for which the public wanted it.

Q. Well, all editors will claim that their journals are newspapers?

A. I might add that "THE NEWS" is, of course, a thing hard to define. I mean by the term not merely accounts of political matters, accidents, movements of great individuals, accounts of public demonstrations, and the like, but would include every attainable fact of sufficient significance, affecting the social, political, intellectual and moral movements of the world. Here, in truth, is one of the points in which it seems to me journalism is likely to make the most progress. When we comprehend that, as a matter of news, Herbert Spencer's great ideas are as important, because likely to affect future philosophy, as George H. Pendleton's plan of paying the national debt in greenbacks was, because likely to affect the action of the Democratic party; that the fact that a small number of the thoughtful people in London have certain ideas of the powers of municipal government over property, is as important as that some of their disciples have made monstrous troubles in Paris, we shall better understand the true significance of "News," and better adjust what *The Nation* has aptly called the "Perspective of Journalism." To-day many of us attach more importance to an accident in Chatham Street than we do to the greatest advancement made in physical science—especially if we do not see where the money is coming from out of the latter. A few years ago our average New York newspaper gave longer accounts of clam-bakes on Long Island than of the meetings of the American Society for the Advancement of Science. There are now in progress in the West a series of experiments looking to the use of petroleum in locomotives, and wherever it is necessary to have a portable and convenient fuel, a scheme very practical in its bearings on travelling, and very important to human life, and yet this scheme has hardly been mentioned in the newspapers. In one of our suburbs is an engine driven by electricity, which it is claimed will generate all the power needed at only a fraction of the cost of steam. Men of great penetration have been willing to put their money into it, and yet I don't remember seeing more than a dozen lines in any newspaper about it. How immeasurably less is the notice given to other things of higher importance, but of less obviously immediate practical interest, every journalist knows.

It is a mistake, of course, to suppose that the fountain is going to rise higher than its head. Newspapers print what people want.

Each newspaper caters to its own constituency, and its success depends on reading with the utmost promptness every indication of what that constituency wants, and looking out for fresh subjects which are likely, while retaining the old set, to attract recruits.

Q. But do these endeavors not concern some active but

perhaps unheeded set of principles that are more scientific in their scope than we generally know of?

A. I remember seeing an account of some of Mr. Croly's views, wherein use was made of something in Herbert Spencer. It was the application of the theory of differentiation to various kinds of development. It seems to me that the progress of journalism is a progress by differentiation, and that the idea just hinted at will explain its method. Newspapers gather about them different constituencies with different wants. One wishes more politics, news, earnest controversial discussion; another elegant writing for gentlemen, and agreeable general reading; another the fullest market and shipping news. The result is a *Tribune*, an *Evening Post*, a *Journal of Commerce*,—each going far beyond these fields, but just filling these.

The relation between the newspaper and its constituency, from the moment the paper becomes firmly established, is a reciprocal one. Each acts on the other. I don't think newspapers very largely lead public sentiment or create it.

On the other hand, I do think that public sentiment is very often developed and increased by newspapers which have first caught it from the people, and which could not have existed, indeed, but by virtue of the fact that they first discovered a popular want, developed, and supplied it.

The *Tribune* did not create the Anti-Slavery sentiment of the country; but without the *Tribune*, or some such agency, it would not have been developed half so rapidly—might, in fact, have remained latent indefinitely. The *Tribune* never could have been a success if it had kept up to the unattainable high-water mark of Anti-Slavery sentiment as expressed by William Lloyd Garrison and Wendell Phillips. Those gentlemen were constantly dissatisfied with the "halting conservative tone" of the *Tribune*. But that sentiment owes much of its success to the fact that the *Tribune* fairly gave voice to the best utterance of its average constituency on the subject, and applied it, with tremendous force, to practical plans in politics. It believed in the adaptation of means to ends; while Phillips and Garrison seemed for a time to prefer rejecting the means altogether. Exactly the same sort of complaint is made now against the *Tribune*, from another generation of malcontents, inheriting all the querulousness, but less of the ability, of their predecessors, who insist that it is false to the "cause" they have styled Woman's Emancipation. The *Tribune*, it seems to me, may fairly claim leadership in the matter of promoting the extension of women's employments, and the growth of a healthy sentiment that women have the same right to equal pay that men have, and that the question of wages for work is to be decided by the worth of the work, and not by the sex of the worker. So the *Tribune* may fairly claim leadership in the matter of extending educational facilities for women, both in building up colleges for themselves and in securing their admission to colleges for men. It has urged the admission of women to the professions, and notably to that of medicine; has made the fight and won. These have seemed practical questions. But the editor of the *Tribune* did not believe woman's best interests would be subserved by crowding upon them the severer and already too-much neglected duties of political contests—just as he didn't join in Garrison's cry that the Constitution was "a covenant with death and a league with hell," as the best means for abolishing slavery.

Q. In regard to the *status* of the profession. How do you rate it?

A. It seems to me that the average grade of the profession is growing higher. There is certainly abundant room for advancement yet. Men now more rarely succeed (though as many try it as ever) in getting into journalism because they have nothing else to do. Our greatest newspapers are carried on rigorously upon the idea that journalism is a profession, and that they are not anxious to use 'prentice hands in any except its less responsible branches. The preliminary education of the mass of journalists in New York is much better now, I fancy, than that of the corresponding classes in the profession ten or twenty years ago. I know in the *Tribune*, about which there has been a popular idea, once falsely attributed to its editor, that " of all horned cattle he least liked to see a college graduate in his office," there is scarcely a writer who is not a college graduate; while, indeed, two-thirds or more of its reporters are, to use the vague phrase, men of liberal education. I presume the same thing is largely true of the other leading papers. Certainly it is of the *World*, which has many brilliant men in its service; and of the leading men of the *Times* staff; and it has always been true of the *Evening Post*. The *Herald*, I believe, is conducted on the theory always attributed to Mr. Bennett—that his own paper is the best school for the journalist (a theory which, if not carried too far, must work admirably), and it certainly gives them a journalistic training which, on his ideas and for his purposes, is perfect. But we shall see the time when the strictly professional education of journalists will be far better than it is now. We shall see, too, a better appreciation of journalistic honor; and a professional *esprit du corps* that will discourage the habit of perpetual personal attack upon individual editors rather than upon the newspapers they conduct and the principles they advocate. Why should it not be a universally accepted rule—we try to make it so in the *Tribune*—that public discussion has nothing to do with the editor, known or unknown, but only with the paper—unless, indeed, the editor should voluntarily connect his name with his article, or should hold an office which makes such connection by others a necessity?

Every great newspaper represents an intellectual, a moral, and a material growth; the accretion of successful efforts from year to year until it has become an institution and a power. It is not, then, Gen. Butler's poor Bohemian in a back garret who speaks; it is the voice of the power that ten, twenty, or thirty years of honest dealing with the public and just discussion of current question have given. That this power is for the time in the hands of this man or that only shows that its conductors have reason to trust him. If they commit in this a mistake, they are soon made to learn it. If they do not, the power only increases and the man increases with it.

Q. Do you not think the present state of journalism, and especially the compact organization and rigid discipline of the great offices, discouraging to young men who want to rise?

A. No; there is always room for those who do things. Joaquin Miller said to me the other night, that the thing which struck him about newspaper men here was their extreme youth. Yet in the very company about which he made the remark were several holding the most responsible positions in New York journalism. One of his hearers replied that it probably arose from the fact that successful men in journalism generally begin it in early life and added: "You think that man young, but he has been just half his lifetime in his profession."

When I wanted to leave country editing (on a country weekly newspaper) and become connected with some city press, I hinted to my friend and namesake, Henry Reed, now of Chicago, and one of the most trenchant writers in the journalism of the West, or of the country, that I didn't want to do reporting. "Youngster," was the consolatory reply, "if anybody wants to succeed he must do whatever work he can get to do, and do it better than it has been done. Report the law courts, fires, prize fights, anything they set you at, and do your very best every time. That's what I did, and you have no right to expect anything else!" His own success was certainly a brilliant illustration of his theory.

It seems to me an utterly false idea that there isn't room here, or anywhere, for young men in journalism to rise. The best work cannot be kept from commanding recognition; for mediocre work there will always be the stifling competition of an over-crowded city. But surely many young men have come up rapidly enough in New York. The owner of the recognized leading journal of the Democracy of the Union, Mr. Marble, has made his position within a few years. One manager of the *Evening Post*, Mr. Charles Nordhoff, made his way to the front in half a dozen years. The two young journalists who have aided so largely in making the signal success of the *Sun*, Mr. Amos Cummings and Dr. John Wood, were a few years ago occupying comparatively subordinate positions in the *Tribune*. Mr. Louis Jennings, the editor of the *Times*, made a brilliant success, under peculiar difficulties, in two years. His immediate predecessor, Mr. S. S. Conant, though still young, came up from the ranks of the reporters in the *Times* office, and is now the manager of *Harper's Weekly*. Major J. M. Bundy, the editor of the *Evening Mail*, has made his place in a few years, and is still young. At the West, Horace White, a few years ago a poorly-paid Washington corrrespondent, rose to be the head of the most profitable, if not the most influential, newspaper west of the Alleghanies. In Louisville, Henry Watterson has made a reputation far more solid and better deserved for thorough general editorial work than his great predecessor Prentice ever was entitled to, though he came out of the confederacy a broken down rebel soldier with scarcely clothes enough to make him presentable when he sought the humblest employment in the office of the Cincinnati *Times*. The editor of the Chicago *Republican* is yet so young a man that I can remember when we sat at adjacent desks as local reporters on the same paper.

Q. Do you think the relative standing of reporters in New York newspaper offices is what it should be?

A. No; partly because of a false idea of the nature of their work, and partly because of their own failure, sometimes, to respect it. Somebody once called James Parton "an inspired reporter." It was a compliment to Parton, and a deserved recognition of what the business of reporting in its higher branches may be made. All Parton's wonderful power of story-telling, of entrancing the reader's attention, of seizing and making lucid the essential facts of a case, exhibits the precise sort of capacity that reporters have a chance to display. Curtis, in one of his most graceful speeches, called Dickens "the great Reporter," and Dickens took it as a rare and high compliment. Reporters are vexed sometimes at Grant White's slashing criticisms of "newspaper English," and the truth is, we all deserve far more than he has said of our sins in this regard; but if we had more of Parton's English, or Dickens', in the city columns, although purists might find other faults, they wouldn't find that one.

Q. You have spoken of the course of the *Tribune* and

its business. What do you think is the true relation of a publisher to his paper?

A. I think that the natural and almost inevitable tendency of the publisher is to consider the most important part of the newspaper the advertising department. That brings him money more directly, and in larger sums, than does the profit on circulation. Among most of the publishers I have known, the greatest delight is to report the procurement of advertisements, and the danger is of coming to believe these the most essential part of the paper, to which and for which its course should be shaped. This seems to me inherently unwise The one thing to get circulation is news, judiciously gathered ahead of other papers, or presented in a more attractive shape than any other journal gives it. The paper that does this, necessarily has the greatest circulation among the classes which it serves.

Given circulation, and advertisements follow as a necessity, while the power of the paper is enormously increased, and the value of its advertising space more and more enhanced.

True policy, it seems to me, would dictate that advertisements should therefore occupy as limited a space as possible. When they encroach too much on the paper, instead of enlarging the paper, and thus weary the reader with a dreary mass of unattractive printed matter, the price of advertising should be increased, so that where an advertisement before took a stickfull, it may now be reduced to half the space and pay the same money.

Murat Halstead has insisted, with a zeal which cannot be too much commended, on the policy of utterly refusing to permit any part of the reading matter of his paper to have any relation to his advertisements, except where they are of public concern and warrant notice. There are very few papers which peremptorily refuse, under any circumstances, to sell their space for the publication (in the guise of general news) of advertisements that have some general interest, but far more to the advertisers than to the general public, and far less than the matter they exclude.

I believe it would be better for journalism if every newspaper utterly refused to permit any single line of reading matter to be shaped by any advertising interest. Everything an advertiser offers should be charged for at so much a word, and put in the advertising columns. I would like even to see the day when we could refuse to call attention to any advertisement, under any circumstances, believing that the advertising columns may be made so attractive and interesting that they would always call attention for themselves. As it is now, too many newspapers depreciate the value of their own wares by admitting that it is necessary to give editorial notice to an advertisement to make people see it—an idea too much encouraged, also, by the horribly tasteless way in which advertisers are often allowed to convert the advertising pages into a jumble of show-bills.

Courtesy is the Trojan Horse, inside of which the enemies of independent journalism are conveyed to its citadel. A great actor has friends who would like the courtesy of a " pleasant notice " for him. A great musician is surrounded by fashionable admirers, who ask the courtesy of "something kind for the next concert." A great lecturer would like the courtesy of an " editorial paragraph calling attention to the lecture, lest the advertisement be overlooked." Each of these seems in itself a perfectly legitimate thing to do, yet when the fortifications are once carried there is no stopping the rabble of camp-followers and scum that drift on behind. Why should not this matter of notices be reduced to a business basis, conducted rigidly on business principles? If the editor thinks the thing of public interest on its news merits, let him say so; but let the person interested have the decency not to go to him to suggest it. If he does not think this, let the editorial columns contain no reference to it. If a theatrical manager or opera agent wants to contribute a notice, let him pay for it over the counter, and let it go into the advertising columns. Then, if the *attache* of the newspaper wants to go to the theatre or the opera, let him pay for his ticket at their box office, and go into the seat he pays for. If a point were once vigorously made of refusing news notices in advance to advertisers, the advertising columns would double their attractiveness, since people would be compelled to go to them for the news about amusements, lectures, events of any sort whatsoever, in which pay was involved and advertisements were required,

Q. This brings up the question whether you think journalists are really well paid?

A. I do not. One of the things which seems to me sure to come, with a definite understanding of the scope of journalism and its business, social, political and moral attitude of command, will be the appreciation of the value of first-class journalists, and payment proportionate to that value. I believe you and I will both live to see the time when the editor of the *World*, the *Herald*, the *Times*, or the *Tribune* will not only regard his own position as higher, but will find it held in the common estimation of any man he meets as higher, than that of the highest executive officer of the Government, with the advantage of a tenure for life or good behavior; and when the position of an editorial writer on any of the leading journals will rank with that of a Cabinet minister, while being better paid and more permanent, harder to get, and an object of more general ambition.

You cannot admire them as I do; but you will let me speak of my chief and my associates, because I know them better than others of like standing on other papers.

Horace Greeley seems to me to have an indisputable title, whether on the score of ability, of wide power, or of actual influence in the control of events, to a higher standing than any President we have had for a generation. Why shall we not all regard such a journalistic station then as outranking the political one? Ripley, Hassard, Hay, George W. Smalley, Bromley, Winter, Congdon, Shanks, *White*—either one of these men holds to-day, at the end of his steel pen, equal preparation for his work with, and more force, than any Government officer, of whatever station, in the city where he lives. Some day the pay for such men and their equals on other journals will correspond, measurably at least, with the power; and much sooner the rank will.

At present, the business men say the average pay on New York journals is nearly as high as they can afford. I doubt this, as to the higher grades of work; but it is undeniable that the enormous competition in the lower grades, and particularly the yearly increasing influx of young men from high schools and colleges who want to adopt the profession, and so are willing to work for next to nothing, keeps salaries down. The business of making a newspaper is no more independent of the law of supply and demand than the business of running a railroad or selling dry goods. Higher considerations, of course, influence its application, but some application of it cannot be avoided, save at the peril of bankruptcy.

Some of the vastly increased expenses incurred by

newspapers during and since the war will never be reduced—correspondence, inland and ocean telegraphing, etc. But, as it seems to me, a great deal of the present collection of news is done in the most wasteful way possible. There are six or seven morning papers in New York which are morally certain to have more or less detailed accounts prepared for each, at great individual expense, of precisely the same events, very often of considerable importance in the city and outside of it, in America and in Europe. Yet these six or seven papers maintain six different sets of machinery for the collection of a large part of this same news. Most of the reports will be the same. Say, for instance, accounts of meetings, reports of city officials, stories of accidents in the coal regions, or of railroad collisions in New England. The Chamber of Commerce does not employ so wasteful a system for market returns. And yet the outlines of general news should be reported as impartially in journals of whatever political or social faith as are the market returns.

In ideal journalism news of any great event should be accepted as absolutely true, whether the reader belongs to the same political party with the paper in which he reads it or not.

The ambition of the director of every great political journal should be to make his reports, his election returns, every article and item of *news*, so impartial and truthful that his political opponents well accept them as unquestioningly as his political friends.

Still in all these theories of journalism it must be remembered that practice can never come up to theory. But we need not therefore keep from making our theory as perfect as possible. If we aim at the stars, there is no probability of our hitting them, but our arrows are sure to go higher and in a better direction than if we take a lower aim.

Q. This seems to hint at journalism as a science. But what do you believe is the true relation of a newspaper to the city in which it is published?

A. There are divergent theories as to the space which should be given to the affairs of that city. For instance, we have here a community, including the suburbs, of practically two million souls—enough to make a European nationality. The events within it can all be easily reached and chronicled. Many of them are of such consequence that if they occurred in Oregon, or an interior Canadian city, they would be thought worth very long and costly dispatches; but their occurrence in this focus of action, and their nearness to other events of equal importance, belittle them. To-day we give as much space to the arrest of the vagrant in a Long Island village for burning down a barn as we often do to a death by violence in Water Street. In the village this event is really as notable and as much talked about as in the New York community the other matter is. Now, should the news of this great city, this nationality in itself, as we may call it, be made up on the theory of compressing accounts of different events because their nearness and frequency belittle them, or on the theory that because they are immediately around us they are of more consequence than the overthrow of administrations in Europe or the destruction of whole provinces by the plague in Asia? If, on the first theory, you have news enough within a range of twenty miles of New York to fill with matter really of importance every column of our largest paper, and you utterly ruin it as a journal giving the general news of the world, whether for readers in the city or out of it. On the other hand, more interest is felt in the United States in events in New York than in any similar events anywhere else, as is proved in the perpetual extracts from New York local reports in the columns of every journal between the Alleghanies and the Pacific Coast. The problem is a perplexing one. Whether, as affecting the differentiation of journalism (to use this pretentious phrase again), metropolitan papers will be divided into two classes,—the one of purely local interest, confining itself almost exclusively to local affairs, and the other dealing in a large way with all the news of the world, and giving the news of its own city in the exact proportion to its worth to the nation, is a question which, I fancy, no journalist has been able to satisfactorily settle even for himself. The tendency now, in New York, certainly seems to be to give greater prominence to local affairs. More than one of the leading journals have received complaints from thousands of country readers for giving so much space to the frequent political conflicts in New York, and presenting the careful and intelligent discussion which such news always demand. Whether such management will ultimately cost country support is not clear.—Whether, if it does, it will secure compensating additional city support, is even more obscure. But surely, in the main, the greatest journal will be that which, dealing best with the world's news, shall best satisfy the wants of the largest number of the best people alike in and out of the city of its publication.

SAMUEL BOWLES,

EDITOR OF THE "SPRINGFIELD REPUBLICAN."

Thirty years ago American journalism was undergoing the greatest transformation and experiencing the deepest inspiration of its whole history. The telegraph and the Mexican war came together; and the years '46-'51 were the years of most marked growth known to the press of America. It was something more than progress; it was revolution. Then the old *Sun* was in its best estate; then Mr. Bennett was in the prime of his vigorous intellect, and his enterprise and independence were at the height of their audacity. He had as first lieutenant Mr. Frederick Hudson, the best organizer of a mere *newspaper* America has ever seen. Then Mr. Greeley and Mr. Dana were harmoniously and vigorously giving the *Tribune* that scope of treatment and that intellectual depth and breadth which have never departed wholly from it, and which are perhaps the greatest gifts that any single journal has made to the journalism of the country. Then Mr. Raymond commenced the *Times*, and won for it at once a prominent place among its rivals. And then began that horde of provincial daily journals, springing up like mushrooms all over the land. Hardly a town of 10,000 inhabitants but that essayed its diurnal issue in these fertile years. Walking with trembling steps and varying fortune, with graves thickly strewn along their way, yet these local dailies have been a powerful element in the growth of the American press; some of them are among its finest illustrations to-day, and have contributed greatly to make daily newspapers a household necessity all over the land, and to forbid that centralization of power in the press which for so long was the glory of English journalism, but the misfortune of the English people.

It is fair to say, that the religious press of America have, as a class, made greater improvements in all the essential elements of journalism than the so-called secular press. In enterprise, in scope of subject, in breadth of treatment, and in literary and mechanical execution, they are very much examples for their brethren of the world.

The growth of American journalism in this last quarter of a century is marked very much by the same characteristics that have accompanied our growth in other departments. It has been hot, feverish, material, often vulgar and coarse, and closely allied and illustrated with the individualities of its prominent conductors. Henceforth, I think, we shall note a different phase of progress. The soil has been broken up, the position gained, the John the Baptists have had their day. The telegraph has placed all journals substantially on an equality as to the great material element of newspaper life—that is, the news; and we have a right to look now for steady and large progress, in culture and conscientiousness, in candor and philosophy, in breadth and thoroughness and wisdom, in their treatment of the universal questions of life and civilization that come within their insatiate maws. As personalities will cease more and more to be their themes, so persons will seem less and less to be the instruments of their progress and their power. The ambition and aggressiveness, even the excrescences and eccentricities, of editors and proprietors have been valuable, perhaps necessary, elements in the past growth of American journalism; but the days in which a great paper is simply a great man, or an odd man, or an audacious man, are over. The journal has come to be greater than the individual. Henceforth, the latter must be subordinated to the former. The true paper should have a character and a conscience of its own. It must be fed, of course—led even—by the energy, the wisdom, and the culture of individuals, the savor of whose head and heart will necessarily be imparted to its pages; but it must, to be the journal of the future, rise comparatively above their weaknesses, their prejudices, and their merely personal ambitions.

It should be enough to satisfy any journalist to feel the responsibility of his position, the breadth of the audience which he addresses, and the width of the influence which he exerts. The reward, the flattery of power, I know, is not direct; there is no quickly following wave of incense flowing back to his soul, like that which comes to a preacher or orator from the audience that he addresses face to face. The journalist's work is very much as bread cast upon the waters; but the gratification of his work is of a higher, deeper, and nobler kind than that which comes with a more direct manipulation of the persons and things of life. To say to one man—or a dozen men—go, and he goeth, is a very barren power compared to that which flows out through the columns of a widely circulated and honorably conducted journal. Therefore, I look for these features to mark the future character and progress of American journalism.

First. An increased growth of impersonality in its conduct. There will be fewer Greeleys, Bennetts, Raymonds, and Weeds, in its future than in its past; fewer men of such marked and aggressive individuality as to absorb and override all their associates. Their mission has been a great and important one; but its work is essentially done. The future growth and ripening of the press will be better served by the agency of a different class of minds, far more evenly, and certainly more broadly developed, and with less ambition outside of pure journalism. Its workers will subordinate themselves to the great instruments they assist in making. The traditions of a journal will be more potent than the personality and prejudices, the ideals and the idiosyncracies, of its conductors. It was because Mr. Bigelow did not recognize this truth that he failed even of a fair opportunity in the *Times*. With this change comes greater impartiality and candor, greater courage and influence, on the whole, in the character of our journals. A journal will more surely be written for itself, and its highest purposes—to enlighten, represent, and lead public opinion, to restrain abuses, command reforms, elevate mankind—rather than to punish the enemies and flatter the friends of its conductors, or to make a governor or a congressman.

Second. An enlarged sense of the power and responsibility of journalism, and with it an increased dignity and self-respect. These are obvious results of what is now seen going on on every hand.

Third. A still greater independence of mere partisanship. In this the press of the country simply represents the growing tendencies of the people themselves. The caucus, the party nomination, the party policy, the rewards and punishments of party, are less and less to be respected, sought for, or feared. The press reflects, leads, and enforces this growth of freedom and independence; and the party which seek to gain power, or to hold it after it has gained it, must conform its policy, its measures, and its men, to the critical demands of the free-thinking, independent voters, who find their leadership and their expression through the daily and weekly journals. The press in this regard has already become the great political power of the country; but it is more as the voice than the creator of public opinion that it holds this position. The press cannot save a party, or successfully defend an administration, but with the sympathy of the people; nor can it destroy or condemn without the same power behind it. It may break their fall, it may delay their disgrace, as it may anticipate them both by its early intervention; but the real power is the public opinion behind it, which it detects, foresees, and voices. It is just here that is the test of a true journalist—the capacity to see quickly and to express correctly the tendencies of public opinion.

Fourth. A higher culture in all its departments. This is, also, the tendency and necessity of its growth. It will be hastened by the increase of impersonality. Where no one man is absorbing and trading upon the reputation of a journal, it will be easier than it has been to procure as editors, assistants, and reporters, men of the best ability and culture. We shall feel less the present great want of good journalists when it is seen that, within the range of a proper subordination to the character and the traditions of the paper itself, each one has a fair opportunity to make reputation for himself, and that he is not to contribute simply to the glory of a man who seeks a seat in the United States Senate or the worship of the multitude on the platform. More than anywhere else, perhaps, is improvement needed, and, being needed and seen, is sure to come, in the reportorial departments of our journals. Too much of the most important work of our daily papers is left to men of limited knowledge, imperfect comprehension, partial judgment. The results are superficial, unintelligent, and prejudiced. A paper should be well-written, not only in brevier, but in nonpareil—not only on its editorial page, but in its news compilations and its police reports.

The spirit and the power of the future journalism of America lay more, it seems to me, in the late Mr. Raymond than any other man of our time. No man was more its prophet. Had he contented himself with journalism, he would have made his paper far more conspicuous, far more representative of American journalism, even, than it has become. When he went out of it, he made mistakes, and often failures. In it, as editor alone, he rarely blundered; and his journalistic life was full of triumphs. His example and his traditions as a journalist will grow brighter and brighter with years; and he will be remembered as the best type of American journalism in his generation long after every other circumstance of his life is forgotten. The little fact, lately recalled, that he never would allow any reply in the *Times* to a personal attack upon himself, was characteristic of his best instincts, and is pregnant with wisdom for those who would follow in his footsteps in the profession. Few men were really more sensitive than he to criticism, to misunderstanding; but he had that great first gift of high journalism—a subordination of himself to his paper, He was superior to Henry J. Raymond, to Mr. Raymond's friends, and to Mr. Raymond's enemies. He could do justice to all three; and no paper can hope for the first position in American journalism until it has learned to recognize and enforce the truth of this example. A journal that can criticise the acts of the personal and party friends of its manager, that can praise the conduct of his personal and party enemies, and that can refrain from obtruding or vindicating him personally, has laid a sure foundation for the Journal of the Future.

Few can fail to see that journalism has already come to be the first power in this land—that the pulpit, the platform, and the schoolhouse are all subordinate to it, or of narrower inflences. But its responsibilities have grown with its power. They are of the largest and most delicate character. They appeal to it to rise above the coarseness, the personality, the wantonness, that have marked its past, and still mar its present. They invite it to the highest plane of moral elevation, of intellectual capacity, of conscientious courage. They encourage it to lead the people and the nation out of the toils of corrupt and selfish men, in government, in business, and in society; to recognize capacity, virtue, intelligence, in all places of trust and responsibility; and to make the brightest and highest dreams of America a proud realization and a permanent possession of mankind. The press of America is its hope, its prophet, and its guardian. Woe betide press, and nation, too, if the former fails of its opportunity and its trust.

THE NEW PROVINCE OF JOURNALISM.—The primal object of the newspaper is to give the news. But news differs in quality; there is news of fact and news of opinion, news of incident, and event, and news of policies, and of the administration of public affairs, news of men and of personal character, and news of society and of social movements and life. The development of journalism in the last decade in this country has made this qualitative analysis of news one of the most rigid necessities of the profession. Not to attempt a nice definition, we might say that was the most successful journal which lays before its readers the highest class of news, most intelligently discriminated and wisely set forth, and which cultivates a taste for such among its readers.

The *Republican* is a newspaper, and an independent newspaper. As its readers know, it has positive opinions and a positive way of stating them. Belonging to itself, and not having the fear of politician, caucus, or convention before its eyes, it is very much given to speaking out its mind. Making no pretension to infallibility, it does lay claim to an honest purpose. In discussing public measures and public men, it endeavors to know no favor, as it knows no fear, to speak the exact truth, no matter what party is benefited; to do justice though the political heavens fall and lark pie becomes a drug in the market. Duty is not the less duty because it happens to be painful. But as the universe is under a moral government, and consequently fidelity to duty is bound to bring its reward. The *Republican* finds perpetual satisfaction and delight in printing the news.

This is not the organ's way. But it is the *Republican's* way, as it is the way of all independent journals and true newspapers. They see the party pack-horses munching the party provender, and wish them a good appetite. But they do not envy them either their work or their diet.

Of course this printing of all the news and giving both sides a fair hearing is apt at times to rather bewilder the reader. He finds in his paper opposite statements, assertions and contradictions, charges and countercharges, a conflict of plausible arguments. He doesn't know what to think, nor which version to believe. It may be some consolation to him to know that we are not unseldom as puzzled as he is. It is confusing; it affords an illustration of the embarrassment of riches. But it is better than to hear only one side,—than to be daily lied to, and hoodwinked, and made a fool of. The honest reader may take our opinion on trust, if he chooses. But if he prefers, as he ought, to compare and weigh and strike the balance for himself, we are bound to furnish him the raw material. And that is the philosophy of independent journalism in a nut-shell.—*Springfield Republican.*

WILLIAM CULLEN BRYANT,

EDITOR OF THE "NEW YORK EVENING POST."

IN reply to an inquiry from a Western editor for his views about journalism. William Cullen Bryant, the Nestor of the American press, under date of March 10, 1870, wrote:

When I am asked my opinion of the aim of a public journal, I suppose that a newspaper is meant. The original purpose of such a journal was to give such of the news of the day as is of public interest, and that, I take it, is still the main purpose. It should be given, of course, with careful attention as to its accuracy, and an equal careful avoidance of indecent details, and attacks on private character, and intrusions into private life. Exaggerations, for the sake of attracting attention, are a kind of petty lying, and degrade the character of the journal in which they appear. The same conscientiousness should govern all the comments made on the events of the day and public measures. They should be fair and just, and look to the public good. The success of a party—for all newspapers will naturally support one party or another—should be rigidly subordinated to the good of the community, and when the party to which the journal belongs makes a wrong step it should be boldly rebuked.

In its selections for the entertainment of its readers, the journalist should be on his guard against publishing what is false in taste or exceptionable in morals; but whether he will follow this caution in regard to taste will of course depend upon his own intellectual culture.

At a Harvard Club dinner in New York, Mr. Bryant was called upon to respond to a toast to "The Press." The following is an extract from his remarks:

Let us go back to the time when there was no printing press, and of course no journals. When Cicero in ancient Rome launched his fiery invectives against Catiline and delivered his grand defence of the poet Archius, small indeed must have been the circle of those who had any conception of his eloquence. But let us suppose that by some inscrutable means a communication could have been established between the world of that day and the world of modern times, and that an accomplished reporter of our daily press and one of Hoe's steam printing presses could have been quietly smuggled into the Rome of Cicero's time.

We will suppose the stenographer silently to take down in his manuscript those noble examples of ancient eloquence as they were uttered, we will suppose the steam press to perform its office. We will suppose the reporter early the next morning to visit the orator with copies of his oration. He might say to him, "Mr. Cicero,"—for your genuine journalist is ever courteous, as is shown by some notable examples—"Mr. Cicero, here is your yesterday's speech. You suppose that the manuscript in one of the pockets of your toga is the only copy of it in existence, but here you see are several others. Here are your exordium, your arguments, your illustrations, your peroration, and not only those, but here are all your figures of speech, your exclamations, your rounded sentences, your well chosen words, every one as they fell from your eloquent lips, with notes of the applauses of the audience in their proper places. The boys are already hawking it in the streets, men are reading it in the wine shops, the patricians are conning it at their breakfast tables, groups of plebeians are assembled in the forum, where one reads it aloud for the benefit of the rest. To-morrow they will have it at Parthenope and Baiæ, and in the northern cities of Italy, and it will soon be read in our colonies in Gaul, in Spain, and in Africa. Read for yourself!" What would Cicero have said to such a phenomenon, or, rather, what would he have thought, for we may suppose amazement to take away the power of speech. What would he have thought save that there was the interposition of some divinity—Apollo or Minerva—working a miracle to astonish mankind, and confound those who disbelieve in the gods.

But the press, important as is its office, is but the servant of the human intellect, and its ministry is for good or for evil, according to the character of those who direct it. The press is a mill which grinds all that is put into its hopper. Fill the hopper with poisoned grain and it will grind it to meal, but there is death in the bread. How shall we be sure to feed these massive and ever humming millstones with only the product of wholesome harvests, the purest and finest wheat, unmingled with the seeds of any noxious weed? We must claim the aid of institutions of education like that whose glories we this evening celebrate, to diffuse among the community—both those who write for the press and those who read—the exact knowledge, the habits of careful thought, the high aims, the generous motives, the principles of justice and benevolence, which alone give dignity and usefulness to the newspaper press, and make it a benefit and blessing to the world.

CHAS. A. DANA.

"NEW YORK SUN."

A comprehensive statement of Mr. Dana's views of the duties, opportunities and requirements of the journalist of to-day are contained in the annexed terse sentences, taken from an editorial in the *Sun*, and the accompanying extracts from the same paper:

To know how to gratify the universal appetite for authentic news; to entertain and interest the public while giving instruction; to impress none but correct and elevated moral principles upon the popular mind; to fight against vice so as to do good and not mischief; to resist all forms of public robbery, and to exercise a wholesome terror over open villains and sneaking hypocrites; to deal equal justice to all parties and all men; to encourage the good that is in the world as ardently and as pertinaciously as he represses the evil; to have eye, mind and sympathy open to every honest manifesttation of human activity; to cherish tastes broad enough to cover the whole range of society, and to appreciate what is conservative as well as what is radical; what is eccentric as well as what is regular; to be powerful without being tedious, and earnest without being extravagant; to speak a language which all can understand, and yet to impart to every discussion a light from the highest truths —this is what it is to be a journalist such as the public culture and public appetite now require to be. To be all this is not enough to possess intellect, knowledge, and experience. There must be a moral endowment also.

Independence of mind, good nature, unpurchasable honesty and digestion, freedom from every sort of meanness, and, above all, a moral courage that quails before no man and no party, are all alike indispensable. He who has a reasonable share of these qualifications—no man is perfect enough to have them all—and is not prevented from showing them in his paper, need not fear a scarcity of readers, nor have any anxiety about wielding his due share of influence in every department of public affairs.

OUGHT EDITORS TO BE EXCLUDED FROM OFFICE?— The *Brooklyn Union* does not agree with us that George Wilke's services as a patriotic writer during the war and since might have been properly acknowledged by a prominent diplomatic appointment at the hands of President Grant. Why not? Are not the labors of such a writer as important to the country and to a party as the ability to make a speech, or skill in directing the mechanism of a caucus? It is universally admitted that a good speaker, or a shrewd politician, is justly entitled to the rewards of office when his party comes into power; and for that reason ought a patriotic writer, who has contributed perhaps a thousand times more to the party's success in the election than either of the others, to be excluded from such recognition?

The Independent Press is a great power in this country, which statesmen and rulers would do well to treat with at least as much consideration as they pay the wire-pullers and intriguers of corner groceries and ward elections.

The *Union* is also pleased to say that our "views on office-seeking as an occupation for editors are unsound, not to say dangerous, to the real independence of the press." This is rather premature, inasmuch as we have never expressed or exhibited any views at all on that subject. But since the topic is called up, let us say that we hold office-seeking to be a very poor, and even a very pitiable occupation, such as cannot be excused in any man, except by the direst pressure of poverty and want. But we don't see that it is any worse for editors than for other citizens. Indeed, is there any generic difference between a newspaper editor and other persons? He has the same nature, the same interests, the same wants, and the same faculties, and is under the same moral obligations. If he is elected to an office by the people, or appointed by the President, he may or may not discharge its duties successfully; but he has just the same right to accept it or decline it as if he were a tailor or a lawyer.

But we are told that the independence of the press will be in danger if an editor takes office. This, also, is beyond our comprehension. The independence of the press comes from the independence of its conductors in character and circumstances, and this will not be destroyed nor imperilled by office-holding. Does anybody suppose that if Mr. Bryant had become Minister of Austria, as Gen. Grant desired to have him, his manly uprightness would have been decreased? Or that if Mr. Bennett had accepted the French embassy, which Mr. Lincoln offered him, he would have lost his freedom of mind? Or that if Gen. Grant had appointed Mr. Greeley Minister to England, as we endeavored to persuade him to do, the independence of the great Radical journalist would have been broken down?

Finally, is cant of any more use in connection with this subject than elsewhere?

PERSONAL JOURNALISM.—A great deal of twaddle is uttered by some country newspapers just now over what they call personal journalism. They say that now that Mr. Bennett, Mr. Raymond and Mr. Greeley are dead, the day for personal journalism is gone by, and that impersonal journalism will take its place. That appears to mean a sort of journalism in which nobody will ask who is the editor of a paper or the writer of any class of article, and nobody will care.

Whenever in the newspaper profession a man rises up who is original, strong and bold enough to make his opinions a matter of consequence to the public, there will be personal journalism; and whenever newspapers are conducted only by common-place individuals whose views are of no interest to the world, and of no consequence to anybody, there will be nothing but impersonal journalism.

And this is the essence of—the whole question.

Mr. Dana's opinions of his great cotemporaries, Bennett, Raymond and Greeley, are given in an obituary notice of the founder of the *Tribune*, as follows: "These three men were exceedingly unlike each other, yet each of them possessed extraordinary professional talents. Mr. Raymond surpassed both Mr. Bennett and Mr. Greeley in the versatility of his accomplishments and in facility and smoothness as a writer. But he was less a journalist than either of the other two. Nature had rather intended him for a lawyer, and success as a legislative debater and presiding officer had directed his ambition toward that kind of life. Mr. Bennett was exclusively a newspaper man. He was equally great as a writer, a wit, and a purveyor of news; and he never showed any desire to leave a profession in which he had made himself rich and formidable. Mr. Greeley was not so much a journalist, in the proper meaning of the term, as a pamphleteer or writer of leading articles. In this sphere of effort he had scarcely an equal. His command of language was extraordinary, though he had little imagination, and his vocabulary was limited; but he possessed the faculty of expressing himself in a racy, virile manner, within the apprehension of every reader. As he treated every topic in a practical rather than a philosophical spirit, and with strong feeling rather than infallible logic, so he never wrote above the heads of the public. What he said was plain, clear, striking. His illustrations were quaint and homely, sometimes even vulgar, but they never failed to tell. He was gifted also with an excellent humor, which greatly enlivened his writing. In retort, especially when provoked, he was dangerous to his antagonist; and though his reasoning might be faulty, he would frequently gain his cause by a flash of wit that took the public, and as it were, hustled his adversary out of court. But he was not always a victorious polemic. His vehemence in controversy was sometimes too precipitate for his prudence; he would rush into a fight with his armor unfastened, and with only a part of the necessary weapons; and as the late Washington Hunt once expressed it, he could be more damaging to his friends than to his opponents.

NEW ERA IN JOURNALISM.—It is a somewhat singular coincidence that the death of Mr. Raymond, which leaves such a great blank in one direction in American journalism, has been followed by the demise of the *National Intelligencer*, which leaves a blank in another direction.

Judging from the gradual disappearance of these old landmarks, and the astonishing success of *The Sun*, which shines for all, we conclude that a new era is beginning in journalism. It will no doubt be a more brilliant era than that which has closed, infusing greater literary genius and artistic grace, and originality and rapidity of thought, and terseness and picturesqueness of expression into our newspapers, and relieving them of that ponderous prolixity, majestic prosiness, elephantine heaviness, and rhinoceros Bombastes Furioso style which contributed so much to envenom the disease that culminated in the venerable *Intelligencer's* death. And so peace to its old ashes.

THE JOURNAL OF THE FUTURE.—The *Sun* conceived the idea of a daily newspaper that should yield more satisfactory dividends from large circulation than had ever been declared by the journals that had looked to the organism of political parties and to enterprising advertisers for the bulk of their income. It saw in New York a city of sufficient population to warrant the experiment of a two-cent newspaper whose cost should equal that of the four-cent dailies in every respect, the cost of white paper alone excepted. Accordingly, we produced the *Sun* on a sheet that leaves a small margin for profit, and by restricting the space allotted to advertisers, and eliminating the verbiage in which the eight-page dailies hide the news, we made room in the *Sun* for not only all the real news of the day, but for interesting literature and current political discussion as well. It was an enterprise that the public encouraged with avidity. The edition rapidly rose to one hundred and twenty thousand copies daily, and it is now rising; while the small margin of profit on that enormous circulation makes the *Sun* able to exist without paying any special attention to advertising

—approaching very closely in fact to the condition of a daily newspaper able to support itself on the profits of its circulation alone.

Only a single further step remains to be taken. That step was recently foreshadowed in a leader in which the *Sun* intimated that the time was not far distant in which it might reject more advertising than it would accept. With a daily circulation of fifty or a hundred thousand more, there is little doubt that the *Sun* would find it necessary to limit the advertisers as the reporters and other writers for its columns are limited, each to a space to be determined solely by the public interest in his subject. It will be a long stride in the progress of intellectual as distinguished from commercial journalism, and the *Sun* will probably be the first to make it, thus distancing the successors of Raymond, Bennett and Greeley in this great sweepstakes for recognition as the Journal of the Future.

THE RIGHTS AND DUTIES OF NEWSPAPERS.—We are in the habit, in the *Sun*, of commenting freely, and often severely, on the acts of public officers, as it is our duty to do; but our rule is not to assail any man without sufficient reason, and not to bring any charges until they have been patiently and thoroughly explored and fortified with an abundance of solid evidence.

The *Nation* desires that the law of libel should be modified so that libel suits may be more speedily brought to trial, and newspapers held to a more prompt legal responsibility. As the law now stands, our contemporary thinks that great delays render it impracticable to obtain a real remedy by a prosecution for libel. But would the *Nation* apply to libel suits any different rule from that which applies to all litigation? Ought newspapers to be subjected to any methods of justice different from those which obtain in other cases? It is certainly desirable that there should be no delay in lawsuits, and that every controversy brought before the courts should be decided as promptly as possible. But it will not do to make an exception of any particular class of cases, and to subject one set of litigants to one process and another set to another.

The legal responsibility of newspapers is a reality, but their moral responsibility is, after all, greater and more important. A journal may not be brought to answer in a suit for damages for its failure to substantiate its charges; but it suffers quite as effectually in the loss of public consideration and confidence which its conduct entails.

JOURNALISM *vs.* LITERATURE.—Journalism does, without doubt, absorb a good share of the literary capacity and mental training of the country. It offers the readiest means of influencing the public mind, and the writer for it has the satisfaction of seeing the quick rebound of his thought. It also affords the best, almost the only, chance for using that powerful lever for moving public opinion: iteration. The idea or the principle, argument or appeal, which finds no rooting when only once cast abroad, however sound it may be and however vigorously imperilled, usually gets well planted in many directions, and ultimately brings forth abundant fruit when it is daily reiterated, so that it becomes at last a part of the thought of the people. Herein lies the great power of the daily press, a power which distinguishes it from all other engines for moving public opinion, and makes it, where wisely and ably conducted, the greatest influence in a free country.

We do not believe, however, that the daily journals have destroyed the book writer. The growth of journalism, and of its power, should rather prove an aid to him in his appointed task. The newspaper can celebrate his work, and bring it in a day to the knowledge of a whole continent, whereas, without it, the character of his volume would only slowly come within the notice of readers.

As to the best brains of the country being in journalism, that is another point open to great qualification. There are unquestionably many capable and disciplined minds who regularly contribute to the daily press, but there are more feeble and incapable ones actually in positions of editorial authority. The journalism of New York may be a little more decorous to-day than it was fifteen or twenty years ago, but it is not, as a whole, so powerful now as it was then. In fact, we see evidences of feebleness all about it. The *Herald* surely is not the paper it was in Bennett's and Hudson's day, nor does any one competent to judge find in the amateur utterances of the exuberant *Tribune* any compensation for real earnestness, manly vigor, and Cobbett-like style of Horace Greeley. In journalism as in government, and all movements for the direction of men, a large controlling mind is essential to power. It is not a trick of writing, nor dexterity in manipulating facts and types, that produces the effect, but a strong man at the head of the paper, with ideas and purposes clearly defined, in dead earnest about it, and marshalling all the literary forces at his command. This is a fact worthy the consideration of the fancy young editors who imagine that the world pivots on their editorial chairs. There is a plenty of work for men of brains and courage to lay their hands to, both in and out of journalism. The workers, however, will need to take off their gloves, and coats too; and they must not expect to be members of fancy clubs or welcome guests in fashionable houses.

These concrete statements of Mr. Dana's views may be supplemented by a few notes of his remarks in several informal conversations at different periods about newspaper matters, roughly jotted down at the time, and hence of a very disconnected and incomplete character.

Politics is still of supreme interest to newspaper readers, and demands precedence of other kind of reading matter no less than it did twenty years ago. In New York city there are probably fifty thousand persons interested directly or indirectly in local politics, and hence it will be seen what a field there is for the press to occupy in this direction.

It is all very well for an editor to inculcate philanthropic or reformatory ideas in his columns if his public care to read such discussions, but otherwise he should exclude such matter.

The influence of newspapers had not lessened, owing to their having been multiplied in number. Fully one-fourth of our population do not read any paper at all, and there is ample room for increased newspaper circulation.

Parton's views about the small value of editorial articles are not sound. The influence of such writing depends mainly upon its quality. It is better to have a few good editorials than many poor ones; but excellence in this, as in other departments, will inevitably "tell" upon the reading public. No man can write well in opposition to his fixed convictions. What tells in writing is the muscular strength of the writer's ideas; the weight and force, not of his personality, but of his convictions.

There is no chance of founding another *Herald*. It just suited the taste of the time, and hence its success; but the experiment could not be repeated.

There can be no model journal. The ideal newspaper is that which every one would want to read, and that all would feel the loss of if they missed seeing a copy of it. The test of a newspaper's excellence must in the end be the demand for it among the special class which it aims to please.

A journalist should cater to the largest interests in preference to the small and local ones. The choice of selecting news is to be decided not by its being local or cosmopolitan in character, but by its attractions to general humanity.

A journalist should have an educated instinct, and divine the drift of public opinion by intuition.

It is safer for an editor to trust wholly to his inner consciousness than to depend upon what a leading journalist calls the "gabble of the streets" in forming a judgment as to the course of events."

The publishing and editorial departments of a newspaper should always be in harmony, and not in conflict with each other, as was usually the case in the *Tribune* It is indispensable that there should be one head, whose decision is final in matters relating to either department. The effect of this will be to make the management harmonious, and this alone is a vital matter. No great newspaper can be conducted solely with a view to making money.

There is in reality no such thing as impersonal journalism, because if a writer has any eminence at all on the press his identity cannot fail to be known. All the leader-writers on the *London Times* are known, and their personality is discussed in the lobby of parliament the day their articles appear.

R. H. Hildreth was the most accomplished and valuable newspaper writer I ever knew, and would be just as useful now as when he wrote for the *Tribune*, though he was not exactly a journalist; but as the result of a peculiar combination of circumstances, he was admirably fitted for the work he did on the *Tribune*.

The ideal American newspaper of the future must be indigenous to the soil. We cannot have a *Saturday Review* here, nor a *London Times*. The *Nation*, in spite of its admirable paragraphs, is still too much like the *Spectator*, and is not an American journal.

Paragraphing has always been common on the American press. The best persons in this department that I ever knew were Major Noah and Elizur Wright. John Swinton was a pretty good paragrapher, but Horace Greeley surpassed him, and the best things of his in the *Tribune* were his short articles. Bennett was also a brilliant paragraphist, while Henry J. Raymond borrowed his "Minor Topics" from the *Tribune*. "The Week," in the *Nation*, is excellent, while the Boston *Advertiser*, the Springfield *Republican*, and the Chicago *Times*, have very good writing of this kind.

HENRY J. RAYMOND,

FOUNDER OF "THE NEW YORK TIMES."

Mr. RAYMOND's opinions upon journalism were never formulated during his life, but a fair conception of his practice may be gained from the critical opinions of those of his cotemporaries who were best fitted to estimate of his editorial labors at their true value.

Respecting his industry, Mr. Greeley, in his "Recollections of a Busy Life," gave him this high tribute:

"I had not much for him to do till the *Tribune* was started; then I had enough; and I never found another person, barely of age, and just from his studies, who evinced so signal and such versatile ability in jonrnalism as he did. Abler and stronger men I may have met; a cleverer, readier, more generally efficient journalist, I never saw. He remained with me nearly eight years, if my memory serves me, and is the only assistant with whom I ever felt required to remonstrate for doing more work than any human brain and frame could be expected to endure. His salary was, of course, gradually increased from time to time; but his services were more valuable in proportion to their cost than those of any one else who ever aided me on the *Tribune*."

The *Tribune* said editorially at the time of his death: "There were probably others who evinced greater ability in some special department, but regarding journalism in its broadest aspects, we doubt whether this country has known a journalist superior to Henry J. Raymond. He was an admirable reporter, a discerning critic, a skillful selecter and compiler of news, as well as an able and ready writer. There was nothing in the whole range of newspaper work that he could not do well, and (what is of equal importance) with unhesitating promptness. He was never too sick to work when work had to be done, and always able and willing to do any amount of labor that the exigency might require. Others may have evinced a rarer faculty, which some might term genius; but Mr. Raymond embodied talents that have rarely been surpassed."

The *Nation*, in its obituary, remarked that Mr. Raymond was an editor constantly trammelled by his sense of the necessities and limitations of his position as a politician, and the habit thus bred lasted after he had ceased to be a politician. But for this he would probably have been the most successful journalist that has ever been seen. As it was, it would be difficult if not impossible to find his equal—to say nothing of his superior. His ability in statement was always marvellous, and so were the skill and vigor with which he was able to crowd the points of a case into a column or two of a newspaper, and not the least of his virtues as a writer was his admirable English. The very vividness, however, with which he saw that side of any question which he had taken up for presentation seemed to alarm him after he saw his article in print; but it was not the alarm either of a "trimmer," or time-server, or demagogue, but of a sensitive, conscientious, and kind-hearted, and, let us add, very modest man. He feared, in the first place, doing opponents injustice; he doubted, in the next place, his own processes of argumentation, or, if he had full faith in his conclusions himself, doubted their acceptance by other people. Whatever there was of infirmity in this was intellectual infirmity, but it was atoned for twice over by a delicacy of the moral fibre not often found amongst editors."

Mr. Frederick Hudson's judgment upon Raymond, as given in his "History of Journalism," is, that he had a *forte* for controversy. "He was quick and smart in repartee. His mind was keen and bright; what he most lacked was persistency in journalism."

One of the most acute and discriminating estimates of Mr. Raymond as an editor was contained in a review of Maverick's "Life of Raymond," in the *World*, from the pen of Mr. Montgomery Schuyler. The following extracts will serve to show the tenor of the whole article:

"The distinction of the *Times* under Mr. Raymond's conduct, was its courtesy. It was always proper and respectable. It never called names, and very rarely swerved into political rancor or personal abuse. At its foundation it had almost a monopoly of decency.

"At the death of its founder, many other journals rivalled it in this regard. Nevertheless, the example of the pioneer of propriety undoubtedly had its effect upon all the rest. And, as Mr. Raymond founded and conducted the *Times*, he did much towards raising the standard of political controversy. His merit in this was eminent, and it behooves us to acknowledge it. But it behooves us also to discriminate. It is quite possible for a man to keep his temper in arguing points about which he has no earnestness of conviction. As he grows more and more tenacious of his tenets, and more confident of their truth, he is proportionally provoked at the man who assails them; and when he comes to be passionately in earnest, it is rarely indeed that he can treat his opponents with courtesy.

"Mr. Raymond's suavity is closely connected with that mental equilibrium which his admirers called comprehension and his detractors vacillation. He was not under the control of any deep conviction, or set of convictions, which determined his course upon any special occasion which might arise. And hence he acquired the habit of looking at both sides, which enabled him, even while espousing the one, to understand the other. Of course, he must have had positive force, or he would not have been able to win and hold his position. But it was a practical, and not a speculative force. That is, he was essentially a man of business rather than a thinker. Such a composition of mind would lead a man, as it did lead Mr. Raymond, to seek success by the methods he found in vogue, and to accept the formulas of the society he lived in without overhauling their pedigrees or endeavoring to forecast their future. He took existing institutions for granted, and, in spite of his nominal radicalism in politics, he was thoroughly conservative in his mental habitudes and tendencies. In the discussion which first brought him into notice, between himself and Mr. Greeley, upon socialism, it is curious to see how his temper illustrates itself, and how he attacks the new notions for being innovations. The fact of establishment estops him from trying the title of the thing established. He was ambitious, and the balance of his mind prescribed the path of his ambition, and prevented him from exorbitating from the beaten track. He aspired to conduct one of the leading newspapers of America, and his adroitness and his singular energy enabled him to realize his aspirations. But he did not revolutionize journalism, nor introduce into it any other change than the improvement in tone we have already remarked upon. That improvement was due, as we have said, to that characteristic which made Mr. Raymond regard all public questions as quite open questions, and prevented him from being put in a passion by political strife. When he, himself, or the *Times*, which was himself, was assailed, his interest was more intense, and, of course, his feelings were warmer. The only dispute in which he ever was betrayed into such a derogation of the usual decency of the *Times* as made it really disreputable, was one with the *Herald* about the respective circulation of the two papers. But Mr. Raymond's character, while it forbids us to regard him with the feeling due a man who moulds the opinions of his readers into conformity with his own by sheer force of passionate conviction, or to regard him as a revolutionist in his profession, at the same time makes his life all the more accurate a counterpart to the progress of that profession. His career was almost coeval with journalism in New York, in the sense which we now understand the word journalism to bear. He rose from the lowest round of the ladder to its highest place, growing with the growth, reflecting always the opinions, and hitting with admirable nicety the temper of the most influential section of the community in which he lived. His extreme susceptibility to changes in opinion make his life more decided and positive. It was a sheet of sensitized and saturated paper from which we can detect the composition of the substance in which it has been steeped."

The following extracts from a sketch of Mr. Raymond, written by his successor, Mr. Jennings, for the *Galaxy*, contains much interesting information about his habits and character, both as an editor and a man. Respecting his theory that the members of an editorial force should change position at stated intervals, an old newspaper man once remonstrated with Raymond, insisting that it was bad policy to make such frequent changes; and that men worked to better advantage when thoroughly conversant with the exact duty required of them. "But men get to running in ruts," Raymond replied. He had a horror of adhering strictly to one line. "I never yet felt satisfied with anything I had done," he used frequently to say; and he showed the feeling still more plainly in his acts. He pushed aside the work of the day before as if glad to get it out of his sight. The one purpose in which he never lost his interest was that of placing his paper in the very front rank of journalism. He was always trying to recruit his staff—the great secret of keeping a journal at an even standard of excellence; and he was always ready to pay the highest price for the best work. This latter practice tended greatly to raise journalism towards the position which he was anxious to see it occupy. It could never become what he wished it to be unless workmen of a high class were tempted by liberal rewards to enter the field. The time has gone by when an able man could be found to write regularly in a newspaper for eight dollars a week—the wages which Mr. Raymond first received. It is greatly owing to him that journalists are now more justly treated. "I attribute a very large share of the early success of the *Times*," said he, "to the ability and the industry of the gentlemen engaged in the editorial department;" forgetting, in his self-abnegation, that every man in his employ was happy in the conviction that good work was certain to receive appreciation and reward.

Amid all the trials of editorial life he never lost his suavity of disposition. To all his associates and subordinates, he was invariably amiable and considerate. So even and perfect was his temper, that one day he referred, as though it were a serious fault, to the fact that he was "never in a passion in his life, and never had seen anything in the world that it was worth while to get angry about." Mr. Maverick relates, that "the sole indication that 'something had happened' was his occasional rapid transit through the outer editorial room to his private office, with an emphatic clink of his boot-heel upon the floor, but utter silence of the tongue. 'What's up?' one man would whisper to his neighbor; and the answer came within the hour, when some derelict person, who had made a blunder, or disregarded an order, was seen emerging from the presence to which he had been summoned—chopfallen and discomfitted. Raymond understood better than most men the art of controlling his temper. This was a part of the tact for which he was distinguished, and to which he owed a great part of his success in life. 'All men have sharp points,' he once said; 'what is the use of running against them?'"

Mr. Raymond had that peculiarly valuable knowledge of affairs which is only acquired by intimate relations with them. Though, of late years, he occasionally showed some impatience with metaphysical speculations, he always sought to grasp the principle that lay at the foundation of the actual or the apparent, and his logical habit demanded the reason and the sequence of whatever presented itself. Hence his conversation was singularly rich and attractive.

As a journalist no man ever dared approach him with a corrupt or dishonest proposition. He was as incapable of being reached by the temptations of place and power as by the vulgar temptation of lucre. In journalism he sought success only by the ways of honesty and justice. He was utterly incapable of even conceiving anything in the shape of what is called a *scheme*, either political or personal; and he often smiled at hearing that he had set in motion the intricate machinery that had brought about results of whose origin and very existence he was unconscious.

Mr. Raymond's experience in journalism prior to the establishment of the New York *Times* was a rough but effective course of training. He acquired a habit of working hard, which never afterwards failed him until his health and spirits were both breaking down. His new journal opened up an adequate field for his ambition. He had to create it, and he brought to his task an intensity of purpose and a capacity for sustained exertion in which few men have been his equal. Night and day he was at his post. His facility for composition was at all times remarkable. There are some men to whom the production of an article is an exhausting task; they rise from the desk nerveless and prostrated. Mr. Raymond was not one of these. His work was congenial to him, and it well suited the cast of his mind. It consequently never distressed him. He had the immense consolation of knowing that freedom from pecuniary cares would be an assured compensation for his labors.

When a storm of obloquy was beating about his ears, in 1866, an article appeared in the *Tribune* commenting upon him with some severity. He smiled when he laid it down, and said to me, " Horace Greeley may attack me as much as he thinks proper, but I shall never be able to get over my old liking for him." He was pleased when, one day in the House of Representatives at Washington, Mr. Greeley came up to him and shook hands cordially, and entered into friendly conversation.

Another of Mr. Raymond's intimate associates in the *Times* says, that during the latter years of his life he gave but little attention to the details of editing, but left the principal charge of everything to his assistants, reserving to himself the general control and tone of the paper.

He did not possess the suggestive faculty to any special degree, and seldom gave topics for other persons to write on. He was rather reserved in his manner, except toward his intimate friends, and it took years to gain his confidence. He allowed the members of his editorial staff to express their opinions freely on minor matters in the columns of the *Times* even when they differed somewhat from himself. This was one cause of the charge of inconsistency made against Mr. Raymond. On all important questions of the day, however, from abolition to reconstruction, his own views were fixed and unchangable, and it would be difficult to find another political editor whose record is so consistent. With time his mind expanded and deepened, and he was a much stronger thinker in later years. He was a very witty talker, and a delightful companion. His failure in Congress nearly broke his heart. He used to say in private that he ought to have studied law, and he should prefer to have been a judge.

He often wrote four columns in an evening, and once wrote twenty columns in a week, but he would always have a period of idleness after these spurts.

Mr. Raymond did not believe in paying by the yard. He would let one of his staff go on for a long while without noticing whether he was writing at all, and, in fact, he did not seem to care so long as the person in question would occasionally do some very good piece of work. He has been known to pay William Swinton five hundred dollars for a single article, and he often gave this gentleman high compensation in addition to his regular salary, yet William Swinton would frequently go for months or weeks without writing anything for the paper, and then come out with a tremendous review, or letter, or article of some kind, which would delight Raymond. The highest pay that he ever gave was seven hundred and fifty dollars for an account of the battle of Nashville, when the *Times* correspondent killed three horses in carrying the news.

Some of Mr. Raymond's theoretical views about journalism are set forth in the following paragraphs:

EDITORIAL OFFICE-SEEKERS.—Whatever may be said of it in other respects, there is one particular in which General Grant's distribution of official patronage meets our unqualified approbation; we mean *its ostentatious neglect of the public press.* No editor of an influential newspaper has been appointed to public office, with one exception, and in that case it was promptly declined. Whatever may have been the motive of this exclusion, the fact is eminently serviceable to the profession which it somewhat contemptuously ignores. We have never joined in the absurd and extravagant self-laudations of the power and purity of the press. But that the country must look mainly to the press for the reform of evils, the correction of abuses, and the preservation, in an endurable shape, of free institutions, we think is beyond dispute." * * * There is but one agency through which the people can be enlightened as to the real nature of the tyranny of politicians by which they are ruled, and that is the newspaper press. If that press becomes the mere tool of the politicians, it is, of course, the ally and accomplice of the tyranny from which the people suffer. It is only as it is independent of the ruling political hierachy—disinterested in its relations with the government, and devoted to the rights and interests of the people, that it renders service of the slightest value to the country. And the administrations cannot render the country a greater service than by excluding the controlling conductors of the newspaper press from public office, and thus relieving them from all temptation to betray or neglect the interests which are mainly committed to their care. Of the claims of editors to office, of which so much is said, we have nothing to say. It is doubtless true that they do create most of the "great men" of the country—they make most of the law-givers and executives of the nation—and in most cases they have much more reason to be ashamed than to be proud of their work. The country owes them no gratitude and no pay for that. The best service they can do the country is to watch the conduct, expose the faults, and denounce the crimes of the men they placed in power. They owe the reparation, at least, to the people for what they have already done. And they will find that service at once the most useful and the most honorable which they can perform.

IMPERSONAL JOURNALISM.—The editor of every paper is responsible to the public for the character of the paper; and his reputation for integrity, therefore, is important to the public and to the journal he edits. But the paper does not depend in any great degree upon the reputation of the men who write for it, for they are known only by what they write.

We are inclined to think it will be a sad day for journalism when the names and reputation of individual writers become a matter of more interest than the principles they espouse and the opinions they express.

Just in proportion as the profession becomes personal, does it become trashy, gossipy and worthless.

MISSION OF THE PRESS.—"I think it may be truly said the press, the free press, all over the world, has but one common mission—to elevate humanity. It takes the side of the humble, the lonely, and the poor,—always of necessity, a necessity of its own existence—as against those, who from mere position and power, hold in their hands the destinies of the lowly and the poor, for whom the press is instituted."—*Speech at Dickens Dinner*.

"The first lesson he gave his assistants was this: 'get all the news, never indulge in personalities; treat all men civily; put all your strength into your work, and remember that a daily newspaper should be an accurate reflection of the world as it is.'"

He used to say that years of assiduous iteration in a daily journal were necessary in order to create so much as a consciousness in the minds of its own readers of anything upon which they were not specially excited.

Mr. Raymond was in favor of having two classes of journals; one high-priced, and with superior typography and paper for the higher order of readers, and the other cheaply printed, for the diffusion of news among the masses. In the *Times* he sought to combine both of these features, and he made a journal which was at once enterprising, and contained the latest and fullest information, while it also contained writing up to the highest standard of quality.

A fitting conclusion to this exposition of Mr. Raymond's labors and traits as a journalist may be found in the following quotation from a late leading article, evidently by C. A. Dana, in the *Sun:*

"Near the crest of a heavily-wooded declivity in Greenwood Cemetery is a plain marble shaft bearing the name of Henry J. Raymond. The tomb, although perfectly isolated, is yet within six rods of the most frequented part of the grounds. The lot was chosen by Mr. Raymond, and the selection is characteristic of the man. In public life he sought a place near the front, but not at the actual front, as was best illustrated in the great work of his life, the founding of the *Times*. In that he aimed at a middle line between the mental eccentricity of the *Tribune* and the moral eccentricity of the *Herald*, at the time of those great newspapers' greatest greatness, marking out for the *Times* a mean between the two extremes.

HORACE WHITE,

FORMERLY OF THE "CHICAGO TRIBUNE."

QUESTION.—What do you consider the proper training for a journalist?

ANSWER.—I think that journalists must train themselves by practice in the several departments of the profession. It is the province of the superintending editor mainly to point out the errors of his subordinates. This is all the necessary or useful training which a young journalist can obtain from his superiors. The rest must be acquired through his own observation and experience. A superintending editor will, of course, give general, but seldom detailed or minute instructions to his subordinates. The chief editor should come up through the forecastle. It is not impossible that a successful chief editor should take his place from another walk in life, without previous training in subordinate places, but I should always think that his usefulness and success would have been much greater for such training.

Q. What are your views respecting Partisan *vs.* Independent Journalism?

A. The point of this interrogatory is not perceived. If it is an inquiry whether the readers and subscribers of newspapers prefer partisan or independent newspapers, that question does not seem appropriate to a discussion of journalism. As the owner depends upon the varying humors of the time, what may be true to-day may be false to-morrow. If partisan jounalism means that kind of journalism which looks to a political organization to furnish its opinions, it is to be reprobated as tending to repress the faculty of reason and subjugate the conscience. If it means that kind of journalism which exercises the utmost freedom of discussion between elections and there supports, as a matter of course, whomsoever may be nominated, this seems to be a compromise between independence and partisanship, which may possibly be excused on utilitarian grounds, but does not meet the approval of my judgment. I think the greatest service a public journal can render to its readers is to encourage them to form independent opinions. This can only be done by holding out to them an example of independence.

Q. Should all newspaper writing be impersonal?

A. All newspaper writing should not be impersonal. A newspaper article written by John Stuart Mill, or M. Thiers, or Henry Ward Beecher, would have more momentum if signed with the author's name than if published anonymously. The writings of John Smith would have much more influence if published anonymously on the editorial page of the London *Times* than if published on another page of the same paper with his signature. No inflexible rule can be applied.

Q. How about the relations of the Business and Editorial departments. Can they exist on an equality, or should one be paramount?

A. I think that in any case of disagreement the editorial department should be paramount to the business department. I have known cases where the two have existed on a footing of equality, without detriment either to the interests of the newspaper or its public interest. But this question is very much like asking whether a partnership for business purposes is better than a firm consisting of one. And the answer will depend altogether upon whom the partnership and firm compromise.

Q. Will you describe the features indispensable, in your judgment, to a complete newspaper, and mention what existing journal comes nearest to being a model?

A. A complete newspaper should be a chronicle of the news of the day, local, commercial, general, political, legal, literary and artistic (or so much thereof as is fit to be read by the old and young of both sexes), accompanied by editorial comments, discussion and criticism, with opportunity for the public to communicate their views through its reading columns, and their business wants and requirements through its advertising columns. Social and religious intelligence are proper subjects for journalism, if social privacy is not invaded, or the irreligious convictions of persons made light of.

Q, What is the basis of the power of the press?

A. I do not perhaps comprehend the drift of this question. I should say that the basis of all power is truth. The basis of the special power of the press is its power of repetition and multiplication.

Q. Is there a science of journalism?

A. There is no science of journalism as I understand the phrase. Journalism is an art.

Q. The organization of a newspaper;—Should a managing editor write himself?

A. The chief editor of a newspaper should be a good writer. To secure the greatest efficiency, he should be the best writer on the paper, for it will often happen that a subordinate, however excellent in committing his own thoughts to paper, will fail of catching the thoughts of another, especially in the haste of the late hours, which are the most valuable to a newspaper. I think, therefore, that the chief editor should write more or less, according to circumstances.

Q. What are the future tendencies of the press, toward the European type or one distinctively American?

A. I am not aware that there is any distinctively European or distinctively American type of journalism. Engglish journalism does not differ from American in type, but in detail.

Q. Shall we ever have another great *National* paper, such as the *N. Y. Weekly Tribune*, and is not the tendency of the press toward localization?

A. I think that the tendency of the American press is decidedly toward localization.

Q. How would you classify news, and which kind deserves the most space—local or general news?

A. Local news, including local market reports, should have more space and attention than general news.

Q. How about the use of the telegraph?

A. The use of the telegraph has become so universal among daily newspapers that its utility can no longer be deemed a debatable question.

Q. What are the qualifications of an editor—is versatility or special faculty most valuable?

A. The first qualification of an editor is knowledge, the next is the power of applying it to current events.

Q. Is a school of journalism possible?

A. I do not think that there is room for a distinctive school of journalism, though such a school is possible, just as a swimming school is possible. The ordinary curraculum of colleges might be better adapted to the requirement of journalism by adding to it the study of common and international law, and enlarging the course of political economy.

Q. What is the basis of a journalist's influence—his power of making and leading public opinion, or only of drawing and following it?

A. A journalist should, first of all, be a man. If the basis of a man's influence consists in following a crowd rather than leading it, then does the basis of a journalist's influence consist in following public opinion rather than leading or seeking to lead it. These are my answers to the questions propounded to me. I wish to add that an editor has no right to employ his columns for any personal end—either to advance himself in public position or to gratify personal revenge. He has no more right to do this than a judge on the bench has to employ his writs and bailiffs for similar ends. Nor has he the right to engage in any pursuit or enterprise outside of his profession which can bring his interests in antagonism to the public interests.

The following expressions of opinion upon newspaper management appeared in the *Chicago Tribune* while Mr. White was editor of that paper:

INDEPENDENT JOURNALISM.—The newspaper press of the country has grown up as part of the machinery of politics. It has never risen above the party standard. It, too, has received its inspiration and its guidance from the party convention. It has been compelled to accept as true, just and wise whatever has been so decreed by the party to which it belonged. There have been exceptional cases where journals have spurned this dictation; and, in every such case, such paper has been subjected to the denunciation and hatred of the party managers whose decrees it has disobeyed. It is, however, a remarkable fact that in proportion as these journals have rejected the absolute decree of party, and have incurred the hatred of party organizations, they have attained a higher and wider influence, not only in the party itself, but with the public generally. Business prosperity has increased with all papers in the proportion that they have maintained their independence and their freedom. The number of people in the United States who have long since become sick of mere party organs, and who desire newspapers which dare be independent, honest and truthful, has reached that point where it includes a great and increasing number of intelligent readers who do not live by or for politics. The time when men can be deceived by keeping from them everything but one side of a question has passed, and with its departure the party organ is falling into decay.

THE PROMISE OF THE HIGHER JOURNALISM.—Freed from the obligation to hold that whatever is proposed by one set of politicians is necessarily right, and that whatever is proposed by another set is necessarily wrong, a public journal can discuss questions from an intelligent and truthful standpoint. It will be under no obligation to paint the devil in robes of light, nor portray honest men in the garb of ruffians. It can hold the scales justly, and, appealing to popular intelligence, obtain better results than by appeals to their passions and prejudices. Journals of that class may dispense with the vulgarity, defamation and personalities which are the capital of the mere party organs, and we think the public will gladly welcome the relief. We know we are not mistaken in the demands of the people, who have been surfeited with the slang-whang of party politics. Slowly, perhaps, but surely, there will grow up an independent, but not neutral press, in which there shall be no advocacy of improper, of dishonest measures for men, and no avoidance of discussing them for fear it may hurt one party and benefit another. Other journals besides Mr. Greeley's, including many of the strongest in the country, are prepared to adopt the same course, and it is likely that, in a very brief period, the independent press of the United States will include the greater part of the heretofore larger and more influential papers. This is certainly true of the great cities, and the success of these will in time liberate the better portion of the country press. When the revolution shall be complete, and when newspapers shall depend solely upon their ability and enterprise, it will be found that both the press and the country will be benefited by the change.

DAVID G. CROLY,

OF THE "NEW YORK GRAPHIC."

AFTER some preliminary conversation, a question was asked calling for an opinion upon the general aims and objects subserved by the modern newspaper, and Mr. Croly replied:

Burke's definition of a public journal—as the history of the world for one day—is as good as any. Journals are realizing that idea more and more all the time. The conception of Herbert Spencer, that everything passes from the homogeneous to the heterogeneous, applies in a marked degree to journalism. The first newspaper was a simple matter. It undertook to give the latest news, endeavoring at first to cover the whole field with each paper But the history of journalism shows in a marked degree that process of differentiation by which one journal expresses opinions, another gives news, and a third is an advertising sheet. Journals are now started for the express purpose of giving special departments of news with greater thoroughness than is possible in the newspaper which attempts to cover the whole field. Hence we find that in London and New York, where journalism has its greatest development, every trade almost has its own organ.

Q. And do you think this division of interests will go on in journalism?

A. Yes. It is the doctrine of the division of labor as applied to the newspaper. I think the future progress of journalism in this country is somewhat in that direction. You will find that each party or phase of opinion thinks it necessary to have its own organ. In that sense all these classes of journals have a function, because there is an actual demand for thoroughness in some special departments.

Q. Then I am to understand that you think the journal which endeavors to represent all interests cannot effectually do so?

A. Newspapers that attempt to cover the whole ground are very likely to fail. Even papers that do attempt to give all the news are usually regarded as authorities more in one department than in all.

Q. What do you consider the most characteristic points of divergence in the best of our papers of to-day?

A. I think the most marked discrimination in journals is that between those which are organs of public opinion and those which are mere compilations of the news; hence we find that in London, for instance, the *Spectator* and *Saturday Review*, with the *Nation* in this city, do not attempt to give news, but simply comment upon public affairs and events, as recorded in the daily press.

Q. In reference to organs of opinion. The public are apt to suppose that newspapers create public opinion?

A. I think the correct theory should be, that public opinion influences the news of the newspaper. It is recorded, I think in "Carlyle's Life of Sterling" (whose father made the London *Times* what it is), that in order to find out what was the drift of public opinion, he used to send deputies and reporters into the public houses and marts of trade in London to hear what people said about certain public events; and his aim was to reproduce the opinions of the community around him on such matters. That has been the distinguishing feature of the London *Times* ever since. It has had the reputation of leading public opinion; whereas all it ever did was carefully to follow it. It has endeavored to "guess out" the drift of the governing class, what they want, and what their action would be on events as they come up. Sometimes it has missed. But generally, by rare tact and judgment, it has hit the mark. And it has had the reputation, therefore, of creating the public opinion of England; whereas it has simply followed, and by foreseeing the drift, has had the appearance of leading it. The point is just here: if a man should come from the moon and go to the city of London, what would interest him in the *Times?* It would not be the opinions of Mr. Delaine or Mr. Walters, or whoever happened to be its editor. But, after reading the events it relates in its news columns, after finding out what was going on in the world, then he would turn to the editorial columns to discern what the mass of people of London and England were thinking about. The value even of a party organ is that it gives expression to the best opinion of its party.

Q. With those views, what do you think of the future of New York journalism?

A. It is my opinion that in the next ten years some one of the four first-class morning papers of New York will take the lead of the three others in business and circulation. The tendency in all other large cities is to the concentration of business in some one or two hands. For instance, Mr. A. T. Stewart's establishment represents fifty or one hundred smaller establishments. When New York was one-third the size it is to-day, it had three times as many dry goods stores as it has now. The same law holds good in the newspaper business.

Q. This surprises me somewhat. Do the facts in the recent history of journalism here and abroad bear out the theory?

A. Undoubtedly. It is curious to note that notwithstanding the enormous growth of London the number of its daily papers is actually diminishing. Within the past few years the *Star* and the *Herald* have died, while the effort to establish the *Pall Mall Gazette* as a morning paper has failed. Hence there is no hope of any new paper starting that is likely to supplant the ones already in existence. The journal which has the advantage of the best theory and practice, and the wisest conception of what a journal should be, and which satisfies the popular demand with the most intelligence, is not only going to take the lead, but to practically monopolize the newspaper business.

Q. How do these views apply to our own sheets?

A. In my judgment, there is room for only three leading morning papers in New York: a great independent journal of public opinion, without reference to party, and one paper representing the best statemanship of each of the two great parties. If two organs exist for one party, with equal strength, it shows that one or the other is without the higher marks of journalistic ability. There is not room for more than one.

Q. Now, in regard to the business basis of such a journal?

A. I think that papers on the joint-stock principle are a mistake. A journal should be like an army, with one head, and with supreme authority and power vested in that head. You cannot put a newspaper into commission. Let four or five of the most brilliant journalists of this country be put in joint control and the result would be a very mediocre newspaper. It is an old saying, that a council of war never fights; and a council of editors will never do but the most obvious and commonplace things, no matter how high the ability of each one of the copartners. There must be a head. That head, of course, must avail himself of the varied talents of all his subordinates. He must receive, if you please, a great deal more than he gives. But there must be some centre of authority. It is a grave misfortune for any paper where it is so constituted that some one person is not the supreme authority. That person may have his adjutant, as King William has his, and the adjutant may be a much superior person to the head, as probably Von Moltke is to his head. But if Von Moltke were to be saddled with the joint responsibility of several other persons, there could be no grand strategy, nor any well-devised plans. Newspaper work is very much like the work of an army. There must be planned an active aggressive warfare, and occasionally startling *coups*, brilliant strokes of strategy and tactics, which are impossible for the looker-on to understand until the thing is worked out, which are difficult even for the projector to explain until the result justifies the completeness of the scheme. The trouble with joint-stock companies is that every incorporator is generally a financial man or a politician, and has his axe to grind. Whenever outside influences interfere with the work of a newspaper, it is always to its detriment. However, these joint-stock newspapers are, as a general thing, like all other corporations. The tendency with them is to individual ownership; the publisher in time becomes the proprietor. The publisher is the only person who knows exactly the financial condition of the paper; and if it is prosperous, he can afford to buy the shares of outsiders, when there are any for sale, because he knows what will be the exact return for his money.

Q. From this I should infer that you think a community of interest in a newspaper would be fatal to its success?

A. Not at all; while I do not believe in joint-stock newspaper companies, I do believe it would be wise if some of the large papers gave an interest in the profits to all who have anything to do with giving efficiency to any of their departments. There is no place where an industrial partnership would tell so well as in a great journal. When Mr. Greeley originally determined to make the *Tribune* a joint-stock company, it was on the theory that every person in the office should be interested in its success. This conception was a good one. But surrendering ownership was a mistake, because the stock once parted with, it became individual property, and could be transferred. If, in carrying out his theory, Mr. Greeley had retained his ownership, and had set apart say one-third or one-half the profits of the *Tribune*, to be divided among the editors and reporters, in fact through every department of the paper in a certain definite scale, it would have accomplished exactly what the co-operative scheme aims to effect. It would give every person a direct interest in the success of the paper. This interest, however, should never be transferable or marketable. It ought to be terminable at the option of the proprietor. While every person should be interested in the success of the paper, the property ought to be held by one man, or at most by two men. The wages system, as all employers of labor well know, does not work well in any class of employment where men have to labor, as it were, *con amore*. Once in the possession of the best salary they can get, most men will insensibly consider how they can earn the income in the easiest way. It is said that five years work uses up the enthusiasm of most of the employés of the London *Times*. This would certainly not be the case if the internal constitution of the paper were such that every person would be directly interested in its prosperity. But the wages system, in an employment that demands so much competition, energy, and exactingness as journalism does, cannot work well. And hence it has been found indispensable in all newspaper offices, in addition to the hired staff, to employ outside reporters and editors who are paid by the piece. Hence Bohemianism, penny-a-lining, etc.

Q. Has journalism any theory?

A. From time to time we are treated by gentlemen like Mr. Richard Grant White and others to articles giving their conception and theory of what a newspaper ought to be. A writer in a Boston paper wittily said, that if he had seventeen millions of dollars, he would like to publish such a paper as Mr. White planned in the *Galaxy*, but would hardly expect to get along with less money. But when we sketch an ideal of perfect dignity, decorum and elaborate culture in a journal, these are what we should call subjective conceptions, never realized in actual life. If the millenium would come, and all the readers of the newspapers were angels, it would do very well to publish these perfectly idealized newspapers. But the fact is, the great mass of readers are very imperfect human beings, and the editor who, without any *a priori* theories, understands just what the people want, and not what a few scholars call for, will make a very successful paper. He will find that dignity, fine writing, and elaborate arguments are all very well in their way—but that, after all, the motive which inspires the great bulk of the people to buy newspapers is curiosity. They want to know what is going on in the world. They like to have the news dressed up in a vivacious, lively and humorous manner, if the subject admits of it.

Q. Do you think that this public curiosity is in itself sufficient to keep alive a paper?

A. Certain recent successes in this city are due to the fact that people like wit, humor and vivacity. But I think that some of them have failed to comprehend that the public also demands truthfulness; that readers do not like to have their confidence abused. Now, a paper like the Paris *Figaro* will have a very large circulation in Paris, although it is a notably sensational and unreliable sheet. But after all, the newspapers of the greatest circulation are those that deal honestly by their subscribers. It is no harm for a paper to be sensational, provided the sensation has a real foundation in facts. The projector of the *Herald*, years ago, made it sensational. It had a very large circulation, notwithstanding its rough treatment of persons Mr. Bennett did not fancy. But it never deceived its readers in its news department.

Q. Personality seems to be a most important element of sensationalism in certain of our journals?

A. It seems to me inevitable that a certain class of papers will find it to their advantage to be personal. Human beings are very curious about one another. Nothing is more interesting to them in a newspaper than what their fellow-beings are doing. A newspaper that satisfies this desire will have a very great measure of success. The objectionable character of personal news is probably due to the fact that the first kind of personal intelligence which came before the public was the proceedings in courts. A great crime or scandal which found its way into the public courts was, when published, discovered by newspaper proprietors to be very attractive matter. Now, it is very unfortunate, of course, that the baser side of human nature should have been first presented in the journals; it has led to the impression that it was the coarseness that attracted the public, whereas it was the human interest which people have in each other's lives that made these domestic revelations attractive. A number of journals have come into existence, Police Gazettes and the like, to supply the supposed demand for impure reading. But it is remarkable that these journals have never reached a large circulation. Men may like to read these reports "on the sly," but they do not wish to take them home to their wives and children. And it is also notable that the papers having the largest circulation, like Bonner's *Ledger* and New York *Weekly*, for instance, are those which are least objectionable on the score of sexual morality. Now, it is curious that the very same passion to which the lewd paper appeals is also gratified by the *Ledger*. If there was no such thing as the passion of love, if there was no sexual appetite, there would be no *Ledgers*. But the *Ledger*, and corresponding papers, appeal to the sentiment and the romance of the sexual passion, and find hundreds of thousands of readers. The Police Gazettes appeal to the brute in men and women, and find their few readers.

Q. This would seem to indicate an approximation of the romance and the periodical press?

A. The London *Spectator* some time since referred to the curious fact, which it may be well to note, that the modern novel and the newspaper are beginning to assimilate, and are becoming very much alike. The popular novel of two hundred years ago dealt with the ideal world, with fairies, ghosts, etc. Mrs. Radcliff's and Monk Lewis' romances were among that list. The popular novels, in their characters and plots, were remote from human interests. But the progress of fiction-writing has brought the novelist down to the affairs of everyday life. The popular novels of the day, like the cotemporary plays, are intensely realistic. Anthony Trollope deals with the love affairs and business interests which might occur to any respectable New York or London family. Had Trollope lived in the time of Mrs. Radcliffe he would have composed romances in the mysteries of Udolpho vein. Dickens and Thackeray drew their characters from everyday life. On the other hand, the newspaper in times past thought it beneath its dignity to discuss anything of a domestic or social character. The topics treated were abstract, and remote from men's daily lives. But now journalism is taking greater hold of social questions. It is this feature which gives so much interest to our story papers and magazines. If people could find in their newspapers the same mental pabulum that they look for in their magazines, they would not read the magazines or novels so much as they do, for truth is really stranger than fiction. But, unfortunately, the newspaper has heretofore been compelled to deal with topics furnished by the police station and the divorce court.

Q. How about society news?

A. Society news is, I think, legitimate. Take, for instance, the vexed question of noticing ladies at balls. A lady who goes to a ball dresses with an eye to be commented upon by all her friends, male and female. A woman who has been seen by two or three hundred persons in an evening can have no real objection to have her costume described in a newspaper, if it is not done unkindly, or in a manner to injure her self-respect. This is a common occurrence in the court circles of Europe, and is not deemed objectionable by the most cultured people abroad. I instance this as one of the ways in which certain weekly papers succeed—by giving fashionable and personal intelligence. It shows that people are interested in that kind of news.

Q. Do you think we follow the French or English newspapers in our development?

A. I am inclined to believe that American journalism will grow more like the French than the English. Heretofore we have followed English models in our impersonal journalism—in withholding the names of contributors. But the active political life of the American people and the personal character of their contests make them identify every paper with an individual; and the curiosity to know who does certain things is so great that it will be gratified somehow. Now, while the editorial opinion of the paper should be impersonal, because it represents not an individual, but the public, there is no reason why, in the local sketches of the paper, in its correspondence, its art reviews, book notices, and the like, the names of the contributors should not be given. Our experience in the last war in that matter was very remarkable. To protect itself, the Government insisted that the names of the correspondents should be given with their letters from the seat of war. The result was a class of writers who were a real credit to American journalism—men like Whitelaw Reid, Shanks, George Alfred Townsend, Thomas W. Knox, A. D. Richardson, William Swinton, J. B. Stillson, and a great many others who could be mentioned. At the close of the war many of these men were remanded to private life. The London *Times* attempts to be anonymous, but still its leading contributors, such as Dr. Russell, are known. And it is thus greatly to the interest of the paper when such is the case. For causes which it is needless to mention, correspondents of our leading American journals, so far as they are anonymous, have no weight or effect on the public opinion.

If a name is attached that is known to the public it is vastly more valuable. The anonymous correspondent does not care beyond making a readable letter to please his employer. With the name appended, the person wants to satisfy himself and the public.

Q. What is your opinion about the relative advantages to a paper of original and selected foreign articles?

A. I feel satisfied American journals are making a mistake in supposing they save anything by copying from English publications. It is a very remarkable fact, that although the English journalists and essayists have cultivated letters in a way we have not on this side the Atlantic, and although, on the whole, their articles are very much better written than articles are in this country, the American reader prefers the mediocre American to the English writers. Osgood & Co. failed to make a success of *Every Saturday*. The sale for the *Eclectics* and *Living Ages* is limited. They are not written by Americans for Americans. There is no end to the sale of the New York *Weekly* and *Ledger;* but the peculiarity of these papers is, that although many of the articles are commonplace as compositions, yet still the sale is enormous. It may be set down as a rule that no journal which depends upon reprint matter can ever hope for a great sale. There are some few English novelists, like Charles Reade, Wilkie Collins, or George Eliot, who are a real attraction. This interest does not attach to the essay writers.

Q. But the leading journals here employ the best pens abroad for special work continually?

A. Yes, and with success. I think that one of the directions which journalism is likely to take is in employing the very best pens, like Motley's, Bancroft's, Kirke's, and the like, to write up contemporary history. In these days of telegraphs and cables the news comes to us in so scrappy a form, that very few persons have a conception of the *ensemble* of events as they occur. We are all very much interested, for instance, in Cuban affairs. But how few intelligent men could give a connected story of events in Cuba for the last two years. And yet all the news has been published. What the ideal newspaper requires is the employment of historians, week by week, or whenever occasion offers, to take up the threads of current history and reproduce it intelligently, and write it with as much vigor and brilliancy as the history of the past has been written.

Q. What, in your opinion, is the best form for a newspaper?

A. I think the newspapers of the future are to be in the shape of the *Pall Mall Gazette* and the London *Spectator*. The quarto sheet will not do, because you cannot get all the news into it. The eight-page paper is objectionable, because people do not like to look at the inside. But the sixteen pages, more or less, can be increased or diminished with the requirements of the news and business. That, I think, will be the shape of the journal of the future. The only specimen of it in contemporary journalism is the *Pall Mall Gazette*.

Q. But would this improvement in the shape of the daily journal have the effect of changing its price; and would not the other improvements aid in the change?

A. Yes; New York papers have, I think, erred in times past in the matter of excessive cheapness. When the *Herald* was published at two cents to compete with the six cent papers, the reason of its success was not its cheapness so much as because it was a better newspaper. I think the four leading papers should charge five cents.

Q. Is there not room for a cheap morning newspaper?

A. Yes; one class, and a very large one, wants the

cheapest paper. There ought to be a penny morning paper. These people want something like the Philadelphia *Ledger*, that would just give the outlines of the news, and plain common sense comments thereupon. And I also think it possible that New York might well sustain a ten cent daily paper. The mistake of the *Pall Mall Gazette* in London was in trying to furnish a paper for the same price as the *Telegraph* or the *Times*. It aimed to become as cheap as its rivals, but it did not have the advertising; this comes only after long years of publication. A paper may have an immense circulation and very little advertising; or it may have a small circulation, and abundant advertising; people take their business to the paper which is long established. Advertising is a matter of routine, rather than of judgment. The newspaper projectors who start with the expectations that immediately they have a large circulation their advertising business will be proportionate, will find themselves mistaken. This is the main reason why it is almost impossible to start a rival journal to the great dailies now in existence. The enormous expense of running a paper at the same price as its rivals, without any prospect of getting the advertising business until long years are past, is too great.

Q. How could a high-priced paper be made to succeed?

A. As I said, I think a ten-cent paper, if the proprietor understood his business and had the money to spend, would pay in time, if not after the first month. A very large class of the American people do not care for price, if they can get the best article. We have the costliest hotels, the most expensive horses, dry goods and liquors, of any people on earth. Americans are not stingy, and would not begrudge the price for a paper they really wanted, even if it cost them as much as a segar or a "drink." Of course a paper of that kind could not expect a very large circulation. The class of readers it would command would be limited, but could afford to pay for it.

Q. What should be the characteristics of such a paper?

A. In the first place, it should be a model of typographical excellence, and superior in many of its features to any of the journals published. It would start with this advantage, that what circulation it gained would pay, which would not be the case with a paper published for four cents, and with no advertising patronage. The low priced papers that were printed before the war labored under the serious disadvantage of requiring the advertisements to pay the editorial expenses of the paper. Many journals depend upon their advertisers for support, rather than upon their readers; yet I think papers should be published, not so much for business people as for the reading community. I think that all the New York papers before the war could have afforded to raise their price to three or four cents, and I believe the leading papers to-day would give better satisfaction at five cents, which is their price, by the way, in the rural districts.

Q. Do you think that journalism pays its employés as much as it should? That is, are not journalists, as a rule, poorly paid?

A. Journalism has not paid as it ought, owing to the competition for positions. This is greatest in those departments which involve merely writing. There must be a sharp discrimination made between writers and editors. There are a few positions which pay fairly, but many young men are willing to accept a low price because of the *eclat* of being connected with a leading paper.

Q. Is not this a discouraging view of the subject to a young man ambitious of becoming a journalist, as many young men are?

A. I would never advise a young man to make newspaper work a permanent life-business, unless he had unusual fitness for it. A few years on a newspaper might be an advantage by giving him a knowledge of the world he could get in no other way.

Q. But what would you advise men of special talents, such as stenographers, to do?

A. It is different with short-hand reporters. For every good short-hand reporter there are a hundred persons who have tried to become such and failed. To be a good short-hand reporter requires peculiar physical and mental abilities. If one has not special faculties for it, his time in studying it is wasted. Short-hand reporters are paid very high rates for occasional work.

Q. What other classes may find permanent employment on newspapers?

A. Well, leading editorial writers, men of great brilliancy and force, make a fair living. Good correspondents generally command their price. In the present arrangement of newspapers there are only five or six persons in an office who make fair salaries. Some of the rich papers do not pay so well as the poor ones.

Q. What is your idea of the future improvements in the local news department of a paper?

A. Your question is a very broad one. The larger a city grows the less value is its purely local news. When New York had a hundred thousand inhabitants, every one was interested in every target company that passed through the streets. Every fire, concert, ball and dog fight had its local value. But when New York becomes a real metropolis, the person who lives in the First Ward will take very little interest in what occurs in the Twelfth, except it be of human interest. An inhabitant of the Ninth Ward has scarcely more concern in a murder in Mackerelville than in one in Kansas. The tendency in very large cities is to give the go-by to purely local news, and to direct their attention to the general news of the world. The London *Times*, for instance, has no city department like that of the New York papers. The news is sent to it by an outside agency, and the editor select what he wants. If any matter of special interest occurs, as for instance a murder of peculiar atrocity, he is notified, when he sends one of his special correspondents to write it up. But the news that is merely local is taken care of by the Clerkenwell *News* and Marylebone *Gazette*, and the like smaller papers. When I lived in Orange, I was interested in church affairs, concerts and lectures, because in a small place you know everybody. In New York I do not know my next-door neighbor. Hence the newspapers instinctively give items from the suburbs that they would not give from their own city. An effort was made by an enthusiastic reporter some time since to establish a journal to give the local occurrences of all the suburbs. The paper did not take, because residents of Elizabeth do not care about the local affairs of Westchester County, and the people of Westchester had no interest in the affairs of Brooklyn. Hence the smaller a place the more value has its local news; the larger, the more interest in the general news. The time will probably come when the New York papers will be like those of London, and surrender the publication of merely local news to papers devoted to that subject.

In conclusion, Mr. Croly remarked, I converse thus freely because I have already written on the subject in *Putnam's*, and because I had on my mind for some time the idea of a work on *Journalism, its Theory and Practice*, which I wish I could find leisure to write. It is quite time that people began to learn the business. There is no profession so exacting and which requires so much training. The very fact that the men who are good critics and literary writers are poor editors, and that good news-gatherers often cannot pen a paragraph with an opinion in it, shows that a great variety of special talent is required in a newspaper office.

J. C. GOLDSMITH.

LATE EDITOR OF "FRANK LESLIE'S ILLUSTRATED."

QUESTION.—Do you anticipate any new morning papers, or any readjustments of daily journalism in New York?

ANSWER.—No. None of the editors appear to be ruining their journals; and the journals are stronger to-day than they were five years ago. It is folly to measure the young men of the press by the reputations with which their predecessors died. Bennett, Greeley and Raymond, at the age of say 35, were not more powerful and were no better known than their successors are at the same age. The *Herald* is twice the paper it was ten years ago. All it ever lost was the elder Bennett's paragraphs; for, though every journalist can write a paragraph, I know only three men in New York who can write a really good one. The *Tribune*, if you will think, is to-day what Greeley, in his card resuming control in 1872, hoped to make it. I once saw a note in which Greeley said that a certain copy of the *Tribune*, edited in his absence by Reid, was the best issue of an eight-page paper he had ever seen. If Reid could please so stern a critic as Greeley, he ought to please many people. So, I think the *Times* is just as cool, practical and utilitarian as it was under Raymond, and it has greater strength and less evasiveness. The *Sun*, like its namesake, stands alone. It covers an undisputed field and a fat dividend. Its field has not been disputed for a share of its profits, because Dana's peculiar strength as a writer and a fighter makes capitalists and politicians afraid of him. No competitor could have Associated Press news. But Dana's personal strength is the *Sun's* safeguard against a rival in two-cent journalism.

Q. What about weekly journals?

A. The time for weekly journals devoted to miscellany has passed away. I saw that while with the *Leader*, of which I edited all, excepting, of course, its politics, with which I had nothing to do. At the same time weekly and monthly journals devoted to special trades are increasing in numbers and wealth. They are gradually forcing the daily press to find strength in the telegraph.

Q. You must, as editor of *Frank Leslie's*, have an insight of illustrated journalism?

A. Two years experience, which I finish this week for a rest. The fault of the business is that it is made narrow in its scope and unjournalistic, lacking all reasonable system such as we journalists were trained under. " Art is long, and time is fleeting," is true practically and poetically. Artists will not seize the journalistic idea, and they frequently spoil a subject by leaving out the idea and presenting what they call "technique."

Q. What then is the secret of *Harpers'* success?

A. Mainly money, which its owners judiciously pay for a strong man at the head of each department. Each man is absolute in his own department. The editor writes nothing but brevier, and therefore writes well. The manager, Mr. Conant, obtains literary matter, descriptions and miscellany, and selects news subjects for illustration. Mr. Parsons, who is an able artist, chooses the size and treatment of a subject. Nast chooses his own subjects and works at home. Leslie tries one "editor," who attends to all these things. The Harpers have command of fine stories, which retain the interest of the reader. Thoughtful men like to read Curtis' calm and elegant English. Then the paper publishes pictures of sentiment, which *last* in the mind of the purchaser for years. Many of these pictures are from Europe; but if *Harper's* sell over one hundred thousand papers with European sentiment predominating, showing that people want that more than news, how great an influence the paper would wield if one-half the sentiment were American. Winslow Homer has done some fine work in this line; you remember his "Dad's Coming." Tom Worth has done some excellent sketches. He is great in his line. So is Shepherd. Joe Becker would be, with much chastening. Such men have ideas, and don't see merely with their eyes. They want coaxing and encouraging, and few men can draw them out. Even *Harper's* has not got out of our artists half that is in them. It should do for America what the London *Graphic* does for Europe, though *Harper's* far surpasses the *Graphic* in its letter-press. *Harper's*, however, should have more news illustrations. It could add thirty thousand to its circulation. *Leslie's*, on the other hand, runs all to "events of the day," something that happened recently. Leslie won't have romance, sentiment, illustration of human life in its many phases; he calls it "allegory." Now, Rowell's Directory proves that the number of people who prefer "allegory" is greater by two or three to one than the number of those who care only for transient and precarious news. Illustrated events make circulation; studies of character and life keep it. Do you remember one picture called "Blind :" a poor blind fiddler playing before an unoccupied house? It kept a greater number of readers than a dozen murders could make. Yet I think *Harper's* errs in not following the London *Graphic* by giving a greater quantity of news for family eyes, and adding illustrations of

American life by American artists. I would always balance a picture by Berghaus with a picture by Shepherd or Homer. It has seemed strange to me that *Harper's* does not more elaborately illustrate its fine stories as the London *Graphic* does.

Q. Why is there no great correspondent writing from New York to a Chicago or San Francisco journal as Smalley writes from London?

A. First, all the high-priced talent finds occupation and money on New York papers. Second, no Chicago paper offers to take a Smalley from a New York journal by paying him twice as much money as he gets. Provincial journals want correspondents at ten dollars a week, and get them. Then, they may quote the salient paragraphs of our good writers. Our journals, even in New York, under-estimate the value of the scissors. It is one thing to reprint, and another thing to use care in reprinting. I remember cutting down a column article from the Sacramento *Union* into a half-stick editorial note in the *Illustrated*, and within three weeks the *Union* innocently reprinted the note, and gave a column of comment on it. Watterson's *Courier-Journal* shows a style of reprinting that makes one envious. The San Francisco *Chronicle* excels in this way. Dana is an adept with the scissors as well as with the pen. There is as much good news wasted in the exchange and foreign files every day as comes over the wires. Bowle's wholly-written paper has its peer in the *Courier-Journal*, which is original only in spots. The Chicago *Tribune* makes admirable use of the scissors, especially in its foreign news.

Q. What is the main strength of a journal?

A. The man who runs it. The journal is a complete index of the manager's mind. A wretched manager may permit a subordinate to do good work, but the general character of the paper will be wretched. Every one of our good papers has a man of character at its head, and the power of the paper is a measure and an illustration of his strength. I don't believe in the absurd notion that our present editors had journals ready made for them. No paper can carry an idiot, nor can an idiot save a paper. Gossips said that Raymond made the *Times* for Jennings. If Jennings had not been equal to the *Times* of to-day, either the paper would have fallen or Jennings would have fallen. I tell you, nothing succeeds like success. Reid's enemies said he could not succeed Greeley. Why, man, he merely went on as he had been going on for three years—managing. He did not try to be an advocate like Greeley. He is constantly becoming more of a journalist than a writer. No successful manager can afford to write much. Men like Bennett and Reid plan their battles and find their Murats and Messenas for executing them. They are satisfied to ride along the line, inspiring the cowards and praising the brave men. The victory is none the less theirs. Greeley was merely a great writer, but the *Tribune* developed a larger number of good journalists than all other institutions combined. Reid is more practical than Greeley was, has tact, treats his men so that they are loyal from mere liking, and is a skillful manager. Jennings, I think, runs more to writing, and he writes with the precision of a judge, always seeming to be charging a jury. Every sentence is a decision, and his last words read like a law report, as if he were summing his views all up in "motion denied," or, "judgment affirmed." The *Times*, however, is so practical that its treatment of social and sentimental subjects is cold, hard and utilitarian. Men do not live by bread alone, and we should not feed canary birds with syllogisms. Men trust the *Times;* they have an affection for the *Tribune*. Bennett?—well Bennett minds his own business, and the *Herald* is just what it appears to be on the outside.

Q. How do you value provincial journalism?

A. It is the most charming of vocations. Fancy a man going home to a noon dinner and taking a walk across a goose-pasture after "tea!" Watterson, with the brain of a Frenchman, the head of a mocking bird, and the stomach of a hoodlum, ought to be happy in Louisville. He need have no dreams of circling the world; he brings what is nice to Louisville breakfast tables. His paper is small enough to feel all his power, and big enough to escape cord-wood subscriptions. I fancy that Watterson is just Bohemian enough to like beer as well as champagne. His journalism shows both; and though Dr. Johnson says he who drinks beer thinks beer, Watterson makes the cheeriest journal in the land. As a thorough, everyday, *full* provincial newspaper, the Chicago *Tribune* surpasses all others. Technically it is a model, and is representative. It is sensible, after the manner of the New York *Times*, and though always instructive, is sometimes commonplace. For gruff genius, Halstead makes the best showing. He writes like a publicist, and sometimes calls names like a bantering boy. I ought to have included Halstead among those who know how to quote and reprint.

Q. What is your idea of country papers?

A. You must ask my friend William Walter Phelps, who has defined them. There are many of what might be called country papers, that, by reason of good editorship, rise into wide importance, showing that a journalist who wishes to do good work, and even great work, need not resort to a very large city. There is Ellis H. Roberts' Utica *Herald*, the power and value of which give him strength as a national statesman. He will yet be Governor. John M. Francis, of the Troy *Times*, and recently Minister to Greece, has risen above countrified journalism. So have Locke of the Toledo *Blade*, Bailey of the Danbury *News*, Pomeroy of the La Crosse *Democrat*, Wurts of the Paterson *Press*, Brownlow of the Knoxville *Whig*.

Q. What do you mean by a real countrified paper?

A. One that has no importance outside its county; for example: the Pontiac *Bill-Poster*, the Bergen County *Democrat*, or the Philadelphia *Ledger*.

Q. In speaking of Reid, you distinguished between journalists and editorial writers: have you ever made a classification?

A. No; but, though there are a few men who are both journalists and writers, one quality always predominates according as the possessor is a moralizing recluse or a man of the world. Among writers I should place Greeley, Bryant, Dana, White, Jennings, Godwin, Congden, Carey, Godkin, Chamberlain, Marble, Bromley, Roberts, Francis, Bowles, Townshend, Bundy, Nordhoff. Among journalists, Bennett, Reid, Hudson, Young, Raymond, Cummings, (the Massena of journalism), Dr. Wood, Connery, Hassard, Halstead, Watterson, Hardy, Croly, Charles De Young, Gibson, Zebulon White. Of course you will not understand me as meaning that the journalists cannot write, or the writers manage an enterprise. There are Cobbetts for writing and Shermans for fighting; yet Cobbett was something of a soldier, and Sherman is far from being a dull writer. Not every good writer can write for a newspaper, as you may see in letters sent by authors, lawyers and divines to the daily press, wherein they love to repeat, "I do not know that I have anything more to say." Dr. Wood always treated such men mercilessly. If I wanted a really available journalistic *column* article on the Public Lands or the United States Senate, I would much rather let John McCabe, the foreman of our composing room, do it, than to put it into the hands of a Bancroft, a Kinglake, or a Sumner. Even Phillips, who is terse, loses everything by compression of space.

Q. How would you educate the young journalist?

A. I believe our printers and pressmen correctly call me "the boy;" so I suppose any scheme of education that I should lay down would be one of dreamy ambition rather than of experience. The books I read, or am always "going to read," are not many. Reid and Croly think of a school of journalism. I don't. Give the boy a good academical education, not omitting Latin and the modern languages, put him to writing wrappers on a large daily journal, and let him work up to the city department. That would make a Cummings of him, if it were possible to make another naughty but immense Cummings. Cummings was a great journalist, worthy of study, and he wrote fine *descriptive* articles in first-rate reporter's English; but his mind did not moralize, and he couldn't write an article, full of intense convictions, on the Lord's Prayer. For style of writing, for form, strength and compression, study the broad-axe English of such men as Greeley, Cobbett, Dana, Congden, Halstead, Godkin, Gibson, Swift, and White. If you would add something of personality, of "true inwardness," study John Henry Newman, Robert Browning's prose, if you can get hold of it, Thoreau, Carlyle, Tennyson, Shelley and Thackeray, not forgetting Light Horse Harry Watterson, who is a compound of Shelley, Steele, and Dick Swiveller. These writers have more or less *song* in them, and show you how to be personal without being an ass. If you are commonplace read Hugo and Phillips. The wants of your subjects will tell you what information you need. My idea is that successful men read a few books much. The best-used books in Phillip's library seem to be Bacon's Essays and the English Constitution. Buckle, on the other hand, reads everything. Some one told me that Hugo can't read English books. I consider the State histories and books of travel in America as of great importance. In order to compete with men of older experience, read not only political history, but also political gossip as you find it in Greeley's " Recollections," in Parton's books, in biographies of men mainly. There is a class of books which suggest topics for writing—give suggestions of how to treat live subjects. DeTocqueville is at the head of these, and I should add Guizot, Voltaire, Carlyle's biographies, Machiavelli, Benthamy and Hume's essays. I do not think a man can read too much on subjects that affect the economies of life—Greeley's forte. You remember the anecdote of Daniel Webster winning a suit by knowing all about a mustard seed. Well, Greeley and Franklin won men's hearts by telling them something new about old work. They studied the science of common life. I would say, go further, and study, as the *Times* sometimes studies, the little domestic economies. The editor who will pleasantly convince a thousand women to throw away frying-pans and get gridirons will do as much good as he who advises a thousand men to vote for Paddy Teufelsdroch for Alderman. I'll warrant that on the first of May you shall see twenty brevier articles on the humorous side of moving, and that you will not see on about the 25th of April a single article in any type whatever advising women about kinds, colors, values and prices of carpets. N. C. Meeker, with a hatful of such subjects, is worth a half dozen cynical geniuses like N. Crinkle Wheeler, prettily talking about *sea-green Mirabeaus* and *poudrette and point-lace*. If you would put your practical wisdom into cheery paragraphs, study the elder Bennett, who knew how to write paragraphs better than any man of his day, unless we except Weed and Prentice. It is a great art, that of paragraph writing. Dana and Bromley excel at it. A paragraph of two sentences is the model paragraph; but long or short, it should first tell a fact, and then point a moral as quick as a flash. Greeley couldn't write a paragraph; nor could Young. The very qualities which made them good leader-writers prevented them from writing a paragraph. There lenses were convex. Bennett's and Prentice's were concave. Hugo is a great paragraph writer, and he furnishes you with a naughty model. The first part should be like the demand of the English Colonel at Waterloo; the conclusion should be like Cambronne's reply.

Q. What are specimens of good reportorial style?

A. Oh! "Robinson Crusoe," Reid's Gettysburgh, Young's Commune, Scott's novels, Cumming's Manhattan Club Conclave, Pickwick Papers, and Walpole's Letters.

Q. Do you believe in leading or in following public opinion?

A. Both. In quiet, twilight times, when peace reigns, interpret to people their own half-distinct opinions. Have you never heard a man say, as he read a revelation of good sense, "I have often thought of that?" The truth was in him, and the article had brought it out. On the other hand, in times of turbulency and consternation, let men's minds be *led* from chaos to clear truth. It is only in such times that civilization takes a step higher, makes one of those upward spiral movements which Goethe calls historical. Then the true journalist is a John the Baptist, the voice of one crying in the wilderness. Then men become great. Witness Demosthenes as an orator, and Patrick Henry, and Sam Adams, and Chatham, and Sumner. Phillips, I remember, compared the anti-slavery agitation to the ever-restless ocean, which is pure because never still. There are hot times when men's feet turn towards truth, and when he is the leader who, at the right moment, gives the command to march.

MURAT HALSTEAD.

"CINCINNATI COMMERCIAL."

[Part of an address before the Kentucky State Press Association, May 20, 1874.]

IF we of the press should ask our best friends, not of our occupation, to tell us faithfully in what estimation the world holds us, and they should kindly consent, for our sake, to enable us to see ourselves as others see us, we might be surprised to find it the opinion of the judicious that we have not reached the perfection of public usefulness; and that the press, viewed from the highest points, and weighed in the largest balance, would be found seriously wanting.

The newspaper sings the song of the poet, who has the merit of candor, if not the gift of melody—"I celebrate myself." The virtues of advertising have been much commended, and certainly the press partakes freely of its favorite prescription—taking, indeed, the lion's share of the medicine that is—the opposite of an "oblivious antidote." Whatever then it may lack, our business has the amplest conspicuity. Our lights shine like the lamps of the cities on the hills.

The printed paper sheet is one of the elements of the atmosphere of the age. The balm and spices, political and personal, that give the familiar flavor, enter peculiarly into the airs that lap this Continent. One-half of the world's fourteen thousand periodicals are issued in North America, and one-half of these in the Valley of the Mississippi, so that we may be sure the people who are sinful in this quarter of the globe—measured by the newspaper census—are sinners against the light and knowledge that the "able editor" radiates.

If there is one thing that troubles us more than another, it is not obscurity—nor is it lack of influence. The press has affluence of power, but it appears rather in stimulating than in directing the forces of popular movements. One cannot be confident that it does not sometimes augment the tenacity of original sin and strengthen the vigor of total depravity. Its capacity in exciting revolutions and enkindling wars has imposing examples, and has readier recognition than any ability it may possess to guide with wisdom the fiery storms it has fanned; but there is an impression abroad that sometimes after sowing the winds the press reaps with singular advantage the harvest of the whirlwind.

It may be that we wield among the implements of our industry the trumpet of Fame and the thunders of Jove, and that we possess the goose that lays the golden eggs of the day; but it is to be remarked that the cheap facilities of publicity lead us into the temptation to magnify our office. Now, shall we not, under a sense of responsibility inconsistent with ostentation, correct the besetting tendency to exaggerate our prerogatives—if indeed we have any—and considerately define the limitations of our duties and labors.

There is an illustrious sentence written by George Mason, of Virginia, that is apt here:

"No man or set of men is entitled to exclusive or separate emoluments or privileges from the community, but in consideration of public services."

These are words of wisdom, and there are no persons to whom they may be more useful than those described as "members of the press." We must not consent to be reckoned as a caste—to be classified as a tribe—a peculiar people set apart for stated service and special censure or reward. We must resist the presumptions of ignorance not in our midst, and the affectations of the vain among ourselves, that our rights are not precisely those of our fellow-citizens.

There are no privileges of the press that are not the privileges of the people. Any citizen has the right to tell the truth—speak it or write it—for his own advantage and the general welfare. No editor can properly claim in court or on the street more than that. Our equality in rights with our neighbors is positive. If we have the means of addressing a larger audience than others have, there is an increase of responsibility, not an enlargement of right. If we strike with the longest pole we may " knock the persimmons " from the tree-tops out of the reach of other sticks, but the fruit is not ours until we gather it; and as for the grapes that are sour, we must learn to look upon them with, if possible, more than the fox's philosophy, for they will glitter on the inaccessible arbors forever.

It is implied in the severe and luminous words we quote from George Mason, that in consideration of public services men become entitled to emoluments and privileges from the community. We enumerate among those emoluments wages in proportion to works—the good will of honest men—the reputation for helpful deeds that asserts title to public respect and confidence; and among those privileges, the enjoyment of the enmity of the vicious, the malice of the robbers of the people and the hatred of the swindlers of the poor. No set of men—not even those who have charge of the administration of the laws—are in a more commanding position to render themselves worthy of grateful remembrance than that in which it is practicable for us to place ourselves. Competency for the public service can come only from dutiful preparation for it. If we accept no favors, we may exact justice. If we claim for ourselves only what we earn, we can deny to others that which they do not deserve.

The thing needful first in establishing a base of operations for the help of the people, against those who are mighty in cunning to devour their substance, is integrity; and with it belong the courage of convictions and the consciousness of independence. With these we are equipped for the field, and the field is the world.* * *

We come, then, to assert the considerations of keeping faith with our subscribers, and of honorable dealing with the public at large, as well as of our own moral attitude, urge that in our columns the reading matter and the advertisements should always be kept apart and distinct; and that there should be between the press and the State a separation as clearly defined as between the State and the Church.

This means, in regard to the distinction of advertisements and reading matter, that we have space to sell, not opinions of which we make merchandise; and in respect to the separation of the press and the State, it does not mean absence from affairs, but identity with the people— activity with productive industry, not partnership with consuming officials and their co-operative contractors.

If we print, as matter selected for the public information, or as prepared by ourselves for the benefit of the general reader, that which represents an individual interest, and are paid for it, how can we escape the imputation that we have sold our influence with those who repose confidence in us?

An article appears in editorial position and type in a respectable journal—or to be exact, in a journal that to confiding readers seems to be responsible—recommending as a safe and remunerative investment the bonds of a railroad or canal, in course of construction from Greenland to Siberia. A flattering tale is told of the genial climate and fertile soil of the happy land between Hudson's Bay and Alaska—of the early apple blossoms and the grasses and wild flowers of the long summer-time, and the fruits, the corn, and sweet fodder, and all the ripeness of lingering autumn—in the superb region, watered by the abounding rivers that run to the Polar Sea and tempered by the soft winds from Northern Asia rich with the musk of the roses of Spitzbergen. Among those who read this glowing fiction (which is made to bristle with certificates and statistics), and who, as they understand it, take the word of the editor they believe in for its truth, are men and women who have little hoards of money, the net product of many years' hard work and hard saving; and they want to place it where it will be safe and yield a moderate income. So they invest their capital, made precious by their hopes and prayers, and sacred by the purity of the devotion it represents, in the "gold-bearing bonds" that have no other security than the production of tropical fruits in the Arctic Sahara!

Has not the editor assisted in the robbery of those poor people, and is not the money paid him, for his indorsement of a rascally romance, in the nature of a bribe? Is it sufficient that he disclaims responsibility for an advertisement? Certainly the advertisement should be classified so that there could be no mistake as to its character as matter paid for, and representing not the editorial judgment, but the enterprise of an irrational adventurer, or an unconscionable scoundrel. It would seem that the subscriber for a newspaper should have a reasonable assurance in its principles and methods of business, that it is not to be used by sharpers to cheat him.

The advertiser is, however, the difficult person to deal with. He is often in need of admonition and instruction for his edification and building up in the knowledge of that which belongs to him when he purchases admission to our columns. We must fix the point in the public understanding that the newspaper is not the product of the favoritism of advertisers—that the editor does not exist solely by the grace of the Being who puts an advertisement in his paper, but has in his daily labor, if in nothing else, visible and rightful means of support—that newspaper property is, like other property, fairly productive if carefully managed—that the subscriber, decently dealt with, gets the worth of his money—that the advertiser does not bestow a benefaction and confer a solemn and everlasting obligation, but engages in a transaction of a purely business character for his own benefit—that he does not patronize the press, but that the press furnishes him the indispensable means of reaching the public, and when he has paid the bill is on equal footing with him. Now, if he proposes to purchase anything more than space, the advantage of good position and the most attractive style that can be offered for the display of his matter, he mistakes his relations with the press, or they are not of a sort that should have our approbation.

Perhaps some advertisers may hesitate to come down from the pedestal they have occupied for a long time as the patrons and benefactors of the press. It may be, if they cannot occupy our columns as they please, that they will withdraw their inestimable boons and permit the press to languish and the people to mourn; and it is evident that we should proceed so as to guard against the peril of misfortune so sore.

Still, the press we think strong enough to determine the law of its business, and to "relegate" the advertiser to his own proper part of the paper; and there can be no doubt that the managers of newspapers who have the nerve to lay down the law and live up to it, will find themselves sustained on all sides, keeping the good things they have got, and reaching out with strengthened hands for the golden promises of the future. In the make-up of the newspaper we must "draw the line somewhere" between the matter that is for the general entertainment, information and instruction, and that which is for the advancement of individual purposes; and we should draw the right line once for all—that paid matter shall be published so that the fact will not be concealed. If this could be declared and established by the press as an invariable rule, an immense and perplexing embarrassment would be removed. We should gain much, and nobody could lose anything that ought not to be lost. The advertisers who are fond of editing our papers for us would not, perhaps, give up the habit of dictating, and the vanity of advertising editorially, without protesting a good deal, but presently there would be among them the dawn of a brighter intelligence and the clearness of the better way. Unquestionably they would have advantages in accepting fully the responsibility for the publicity of their own enterprises. When it becomes known that the editorial article is purchasable, its force has passed away.

Advertising agents are vigorous in their opinions, and it seems to be their finest stroke of business to thrust an advertisement into a place where they are told it cannot go, and to get rates which they are assured it is impossible to obtain; but in spite of the theory of those agents it often occurs that a simple advertisement has strength that a local paragraph or an editorial notice cannot have. The advertiser has familiar knowledge of the transactions in which he is engaged, and knows how to express himself about them in the most telling terms; and when he goes before the public fairly, giving his own clear-cut expression to his announcement, identifying it with firm-name and location of business, it comes out with the ring of reality, genuine, stamped with authenticity and commanding confidence. It has the official tone, for it is by authority on the subject treated, and has the value of obvious verity. Many business men thoroughly understand this. Their experience teaches that the efficiency of an advertisement that appears as the thing it is, exceeds that of any false pretense, local or editorial, or of any article smuggled into the "reading matter" that is so dear to the hearts of the negotiators whose schemes demand the deception of the customer. This is the lesson it is important to teach the others.

The art of the accommodation of the advertiser, and the ways of pleasing him, we should cultivate and employ. When he has been taught the principles upon which he can proceed with us, we may count upon him as amenable to reason. Then we must take him into the sanctum and impart some of that intelligence about the details of our relations with the world which, though evolved long ago from our experience, has not passed into the common fund of information and taken the common form of precepts.

All should know that an advertisement is not conspicuous in proportion as it is displayed—that there is great prominence of type without attractiveness to the eye—that excessive solicitation is repulsive—that if the classification of advertisements is careful and complete, and the make-up of the paper according to a system that is plain, the reader knows where to look for what he wants, and turns there without regard to the size of the type, the oddity of arrangement, or the location of the classification head—whether it is inside or outside, first page or last.

We can illustrate this by a familiar instance. It would be preposterous, in Philadelphia, to hold a public meeting, for a religious or political, social or benevolent purpose, without advertising it in the *Ledger*. When the Philadelphian wants to know what meetings are to be held, he looks, not to the local column, but to the advertised notices. If he should see a "local" reference to a meeting he would not know whether it was authorized or or not; but the regular advertised notice, according to the custom of the city, give the names and date, hour and place, and is exactly to the point. There is no nonsense about it, and it means business. Here is a public policy worthy to be studied and imitated; and if the Philadelphia system were generally adopted it would save us from many amiable but presumptuous demands —from unprofitable repetitions of wearisome commonplace, and confusion that is irritating.

The English style of newspaper advertising has much to commend it. In posters flaming on the walls, in sign-boards, in utilizing famous scenery with glaring announcements, England surpasses us. The Young Men's Christian Association competes, in placarding landscapes, with the jocund proprietors of patent medicines, and with the London *Telegraph*, which proclaims throughout the land and along the sea the joyful tidings of the "largest circulation in the world." The beauties of nature are of course enhanced by the gigantic lettering of the most notable spots with the most famous texts of Scripture. But the advertising in the journals of England is neat, not gaudy. It is high-priced, and the prices are unchangeable. It is the boast of the London *Times* counting-room that the price of advertising has not varied a penny a page for a quarter of a century. The advertisements in the first-rate English newspapers are rigorously classified. The people seek their "wants" under the appropriate heads. Among the advantages of this system is the promotion of the beauty of typography. The heavy rates charged for advertisements, and firmly maintained, yield a large revenue from a small space, and this gives room for the use of plain type in the reading matter. If we could rid ourselves at once of the grotesque displays, and of the fraudulent advertising as reading matter, the appearance as well as the character of the American newspaper would be improved; and without reducing our profits we might enlarge our type and spare the eyesight of the students of current history.

We pass from the discussion of business management to our larger relations with the people. Rings—and there is a whole history in the word—are combinations to control public affairs in private interest.

Rings rule in the Court Houses, the State Houses, the City Halls, and the National Capitol. The ring is the reality of power. Congressmen, Legislators, Councilmen—these are the puppets that leap, and mouth, and dance as the master touches the wires. The boast of the Bourbon, "I am the State," was folly. Our sovereign may speak to the same effect as a matter of business. It is from this State—from the sovereignty of rings—that we should separate the press. The condition of the country under ring rule—which is nothing new indeed, but constantly taking under exposure shapes that augment its odium—excites indignation, disgust and alarm.

In Lowell's poem, written in Florence on the death of Agassiz, are these terrible lines, whose fitness, we may fear, will make them stick for some time:

> "I scanned the festering news we half despise,
>   Yet scramble for no less,
> And read of public scandal, private fraud,
> Crime flaunting scot-free while the mob applaud,
> Office made vile to bribe unworthiness,
>   And all the unwholesome mess.
> The Land of Broken Promise serves of late
> To teach the Old World how to wait."

Now, however the news may fester, it is not unwholesome. The news is the truth, and the truth is profitable to all men. It is not the editorial duty to prepare a proper article of intelligence, or to tamper with its coloring, but to hold the mirror up to nature. Our citizens have no guardians. They are responsible for themselves to themselves. There is neither priest, nor soldier, nor editor ordained to administer the truth as the people can bear it. It is information, rather than instruction, that they demand. The whole truth is their requirement and right, and it is at our hands they should receive it. We must presume them capable always of the application of the facts for their own enlightenment; and we want the winds stormy as need be and the sunlight fiery as may be, in all the places of public business, without sensitiveness for the feelings of the great poets abroad or of the small politicians at home.

We do not assume too much, and perhaps will not be contradicted in asserting that the main dependence of the people for the degree of relief that it is rational to hope for from the desolating evil of the times, is upon the press. If the press should prove untrue to the people, and the burdens of wrongs—under which there is, thus far, greater fatigue than resentment—accumulate, there are deeper and darker troubles for us in the future than in the past. There is no exemption here from the curses that have blighted other lands. We must live uprightly and deal justly with our neighbors if we would have peace; and we should remember the universal law that uncleanliness means pestilence, and that the inheritance of profligacy is famine.

How shall the press be purified and made strong for the work of reformation? That which is above all required is the unfaltering faithfulness of the press to the people. Our proposition is to disassociate the editors and the rings, to enlighten public sentiment on this topic, and trust to the creation of public opinion against the patronage of the press by officials—to make the submission of the press to the base uses of the rings, State, municipal, or national, an intolerable disgrace. Official advertising is a baleful delusion. It don't pay in any sense. It gives the agent of the ring having the patronage to bestow a grip upon the editor who accepts it; and the plain rule that one good turn deserves another is not in operation, for the editor is expected to give ten favors where he gets one—and if he does not repay his self-styled patrons in that proportion at least, he is accused of ingratitude. The editor who is not in jobs is not out for lack of opportunity, for the press is appealed to incessantly to participate in some of the enterprises planned to divide the spoil gathered by taxation or yielded by unwarranted monopolies, and newspaper influence is equivalent to cash; but the editor who pays for a share in a job with his "influence," not only participates in the swindle, he sells himself into servitude and becomes a slave of the ring.

Of course, we need not talk about the abolishment of official advertising. That is impracticable. And yet the great mass of advertisements of an official character are frauds—they are manufactured as a part of some scheme to take money from the pockets of those who have earned it, and without giving an equivalent, to place it in the pockets of those who have not earned it. There is contamination in that money; and when the press participates in the profits of plunder, it is not only impossible that its influence should be in behalf of the right, but it must inevitably become the chosen weapon of the wrong. The freedom of the press from legal restrictions prepared in the interest of dynasties, or other forms of despotism, to harass and intimidate those who are against their perpetuation, is important, but the freedom of the press from official favor is to us of greater pertinence. We should guard against the loss of the liberty of the press by insisting that it shall have no favoritism from the authorities.

There have been times when, and places where, editors found it troublesome to pay for their share of the beverages consumed in a social way. Occasionally even yet it occurs that hats, fruit, poultry, bottles of sparkling drink, suits of clothing, boxes of segars, even jugs of oily, old, copper-distilled Kentucky whisky (the very blandishments of bribery), are bestowed upon us as testimonials of affection or of the gratitude that is a lively sense of benefactions to come. This is a mild phase of patronage, but in all its forms, though it may be sweet to the mouth, it is bitter in the belly. Perhaps it is the true way to acknowledge these attentions in those graceful paragraphs that you all know so well how to turn, saying at once—Thank you, and pray do not do so any more.

Now do not let us be alarmed by the phrase "Independent Journalism." It is overworked, and to many it has not a soothing sound, but it is descriptive of a considerable fact. The independent journalist is one who is qualified to exclaim with Junius:

"Whenever Junius appears he must encounter a host of enemies. But is there no honorable way to serve the public without engaging in personal quarrels with insignificant individuals, or submitting to the drudgery of canvassing votes for an election? Is there no merit in dedicating my life to the information of my fellow-subjects? What public question have I declined? What villain have I spared?"

If Junius had been the editor of a newspaper we presume he would have found it in his temper to accept personal quarrels rather than permit public infamies, for it is at times difficult to strike a blow that harms a villain without hurting somebody, and we are not always able to be impersonal, or to enjoy the advantage he had of being anonymous.

How far the press has failed in the complete performance of its duty, we see in the fact, that while there is a "Boss" in every city in the country, there is but one in the penitentiary. It should appear to the people—and we must make it appear—that there are most honorable careers not associated with office holding; that there are better places than official positions; that the information of our fellow-citizens is of greater consequence than to win their suffrage for individual aggrandisement; that the drudgery of canvassing votes does not become the best manhood, and is harmful to the people; that the public service most advantageous is not through flatteries; that there are surer measurements of popular confidence than by counting ballots; that it is excellent to have a giant's strength and to use it like a giant in facing all public questions with perfect candor and sparing no villains.

Twenty-five years ago there were two journals issued on this continent that could be called independent, viz., the *Herald* and the *Tribune*, of New York. They were conducted by the men of genius who founded them. Each expressed the character of the man who made it. James Gordon Bennett was a news man. Horace Greeley was a man of opinions—ideas, if you please. Bennett's paper had the larger circulation—Greeley's the greater influence. Bennett was not of any political party, and despised them all, and their leaders with them, and laughed over his own defeats. Greeley was always on higher ground than his party occupied, was hopeful of its statesmen, and grieved with a personal sorrow over its discomfitures. In one sense he was a party man, and believed in other men, but he never spared the rod among his partisans when he believed they betrayed the cause of the people. If the qualities of the two great journals—the *Herald* and *Tribune*—could have been combined, the product would have been almost the ideal newspaper. Distinct, hostile, but associated in their location and by their strong contrast, they were the only American journals to be counted out of party calculations—known to be alike fearless and unpurchasable. Now there is no considerable city in the country that is without a newspaper, and often there is more than one, either absolutely independent, or approximating that condition; and the more independent journals are, as a rule, those highest in public favor.

A great share of the work appointed for the press, it is clear, can not be done by the journals of the cities alone. To the thousands of weekly newspapers in the United States another thousand has been added since the close of the war. The weekly press increases in numbers faster than the daily press in circulation, and the host of editors of the town and county papers are thoroughly aware that they are a power in the land. Let us avoid, if we can, the hasty expression of an unsound hope, but we may trust that they will some time take up independent journalism for themselves, and give it breadth and volume and triumphant illustration. With their comprehensive aid in the promotion of the general welfare, by earnestly and constantly telling the truth of public concern, irrespective of inferior considerations, the service of the people by the press will be well done and glorious. Then the rule of the rings will be overcome, and the republican form of government approved as the thriftiest and most honorable, as well as the strongest known among men; there will be no more sneering across the seas, at "the land of broken promise;"—and if the people of the Old World have been taught to wait for us to brighten the paths of the progress of mankind, they need be no longer detained by the dimness of our example.

In a letter to the editor of the Port Huron (Mich.) *Times*, Mr. Halstead gave a condensed statement of his views about journalism, as follows:

"My notion of the duty of a public journalist is that he should print, first of all, the news, and next that he should speak of facts without favor; and that he should regard himself as conducting a private business, never seek office, or place himself in the position of a tool of politicians and the instrument of rings.

"Cincinnati, March 1, 1870."

In a letter written on the occasion of the dedication of the *Public Ledger* building, Philadelphia, June 5th, 1867, Mr. Halstead said:

"I have an especial admiration for a truly and thoroughly independent newspaper; a paper that is conducted for the express purpose of placing before the public intelligence of general interest, without any partisan or sectarian bias or coloring ; the publication of facts, irrespective of whom they may help or hurt.

"But the feature of the *Ledger* that commends itself to me most decidedly is that of making a rigorous distinction between advertisements and reading-matter. I read with especial pleasure recently, in the proceedings of the District Court of your city, the testimony that in the *Ledger* ' no paid matter was allowed to appear in the local or editorial columns.' I can say to you that, after a long struggle, we have definitely established that rule in the management of the *Commercial;* that no paid matter, under any circumstances, appears in the paper, except under the regular classification heads of the advertising departments. I consider that an essential feature of an independent journal, and one the general establishment of which is necessary to insure the self-respect of journalists, and to make the newspaper business legitimate and honorable."

FREDERIC HUDSON,

FORMERLY MANAGING EDITOR OF "THE NEW YORK HERALD."

QUESTION.—Have you heard of the proposed training school for journalists?

ANSWER.—Only casually, in connection with General Lee's college, and I cannot see how it could be made very serviceable. Who are to be the teachers? The only place where one can learn to be a journalist is in a great newspaper office. General Lee would have made a great failure if he had attempted to found a course for journalists in his university. College training is good in its way, but something more is needed for journalism.

Q. What did the old style of journalism of the time of the *Argus* and *Washington Intelligencer* amount to?

A. They were thought to be very grand affairs in those days, and did possess great influence in their peculiar way. They were edited by politicians, like Croswell, Ritchie, Hill, Weed and Blair, who were in close communion with the party leaders of the time. These last decided what policy to pursue, and the organs then gave the cue to the smaller papers throughout the country, who had simply to follow suit to their lead, as there was no such thing as an independent paper in those days. The editors of that period were simply party hacks, and not journalists. The Washington *Globe*, the Richmond *Enquirer*, the Albany *Argus*, were the "thunderers," but the Richmond Junta, the Ritchie Cabinet and the Albany Regency furnished the lightning which was to strike the public. I remember Mr. Blair once called on Mr. Bennett, and was shown through the *Herald* establishment. He was amazed, and seemed to have no idea how such a concern could be managed. The editors of thirty years ago, with their ponderous discussions of politics and political intrigues, had no conception of our notions about journalism, yet some of them exercised great influence on public opinion in the way I have described.

Q. What is newspaper enterprise?

A. That expression is a very comprehensive one. If I were now in charge of a great metropolitan daily I would make use of the telegraph instead of resorting to the mails. Enterprise in getting news is the thing of prime importance in journalism, and by it the New York journals will always maintain their supremacy, as they can afford to give better reports than any other journals. Of course I keep in view the new modes of transmitting newspapers to distant points. Newspaper enterprise, in the days of the old stage-coaches, consisted of pony expresses. In the days of steam, horses, of course, became useless, but carrier pigeons were available. Now, electricity does the work, and it should do all the work. The pneumatic despatch lines or tubes are yet to do their part.

Q. How was it the *Herald* obtained its high reputation for liberality in paying for news?

A. We never had any fixed rate, but paid what each piece of news was worth. We never paid too high a price. I saw, lately, a printed anecdote about some one bringing a piece of news to the *Herald*, after taking it to the other papers, who had refused to pay more than a small price for it, if they took it at all, while we were glad to get it, and paid handsomely for it. I don't recall the exact case in point, but it is an illustration of the style we practised, and doubtless is substantially correct. There was a difference of opinion in the different offices as to the value of a piece of news. There were very few journalists in the United States twenty or thirty years ago. The country is now full of them. In judging of news, only a few knew how to estimate its real value. Our modern journalists are alive to everything, and know the importance of every item as clearly as the tea-tasters in China know the quality of the different kind of teas placed before them. Attention should be given to the relative value of news in regard to the space allotted thereto; and the details of an event should not be given beyond the power of those interested to read. Thus labor reports should not be very long, because mechanics have very little leisure for reading. All they need, with exceptions of course, are the salient points, clearly and comprehensively given. But tact and experience will always regulate this matter.

Q. What do you think of the "one-man power" in the management of newspapers?

A. I am in favor of the "one-man power." Each nation has a head. Armies have their generals-in-chief. Ships have their captains. Shareholders are sometimes necessary to furnish money, but they should not have interference with the management of the paper. They are thinking of dividends, and nothing else. All the power and responsibility should be vested in one man; that man must be an able one. This singleness of character should distinguish every newspaper, which should bear the impress, on every line, of one presiding mind. To do this properly an editor must be a man of commanding intellect and originality. To do this would be no child's play, but it is work which is as fascinating as it is laborious, and of which one might never tire.

Q. Have you any special theory about newspaper organization?

A. I think a newspaper should be thoroughly systematized and divided into departments. Newspaper establishments, those on a large scale, I mean, are like nations. They have their home government and their foreign agents. They must, therefore, be thorough and efficient in organization, and there should be promotion from the ranks for services rendered.

Q. Do you think it possible ever to reach anything like a science of journalism, when its leading professors differ so radically on most of the leading points relative to the management of a newspaper? May it not be that each successful journal supplies a want, and that no one can be made to suit everybody?

A. If you could combine the views of all the leading editors, I think it might be possible to perfect a science of journalism. The *Herald*, to my mind, approaches the ideal paper as near as any that I know. It is always progressive, and is scientific to that extent. Journalism, however, is not a science, but an art, and the success of an editor depends greatly upon the news at his command, and the way he handles the subjects as they come up. In taking the daily events of the world and presenting them clearly on his sheet before the public, the journalist is an artist—a Vandyke, a Murillo, a Raphael, a Michael Angelo. But in journalism, as in painting, you will find a great many daubs. A great metropolitan journal should contain the latest literary, artistic and scientific news, equally with other intelligence, with comments, if need be, by the ablest specialists in each of these departments. An account of a new painting, a new mowing machine, or a new printing press, superior to those in existence, is news, and is to be treated as such.

Q. How about the price of our great dailies—could it be any less than at present?

A. I think Mr. Greeley was wrong in his desire to cheapen the price of daily newspapers. He was originally opposed to one cent newspapers. He subsequently changed his mind. The people will pay for a good article. The war put up the prices too high, but they will ultimately come down. It is not judicious to rely too much on advertisements for revenue. Circulation should bear its proper proportion. Newspapers cost too little already, and are too expensive to be sold for any less than two and three cents. But, after all, these things are controlled and regulated by surrounding circumstances.

Q. Is it likely that evening papers will ever rival their morning contemporaries? Since the telegraph has been so widely extended, they get nearly all the news by daylight, which gives them a great advantage?

A. Yes, that is partly true, but I doubt if they can make much headway, owing to the short time they have for getting their news in type. Besides, people haven't much time to read in the afternoon, and prefer to have something light and lively. Yet there has been great improvement in the afternoon press of late, and it will, no doubt, develop a good deal more in the future.

Q. Is not the present system, of giving precedence to the publishing department of a newspaper over its editorial department, a mistake?

A. Yes, and it was never allowed in the *Herald*, where the business management was always secondary to the editorial policy. Corporation advertising is too small an inducement to buy up or influence a great journal like the *Herald*, or *Times*, or *Tribune*, or *Sun*. All public advertisements should be treated alike. The chambermaid is as important, as an advertiser, as an alderman or a president; indeed, more important to a housekeeper.

Q. What is your view in regards to party politics and newspapers?

A. No great journal can be a party organ. This was the cause of the inferiority of the *Tribune* and *Times* in New York to the *Herald.* The latter takes sides, but it is not restricted to one side. The London *Times* is an illustration of how independent a great journal should be. The charge that Walter was corrupt, and sold out the *Times*, is untrue. He is credited with having influenced the English Government, by the weight of his paper, to side with Spain when that country was invaded by Napoleon. Yet, afterwards, when the Spanish Government sent Walter a service of plate in recognition of his services, he was quite indignant, and sent it back without even letting his family see it. That is true journalism.

Q. Are there not too many newspapers being published?

A. No, not in New York, and there is room for more. When the *News-Letter* was the only paper published on the Continent it printed only three hundred copies. They help each other, and make newspaper readers. With a good supply of readers everything else follows to make up journalism. I do not overvalue editorial writing, but rather take the view of Parton in rating it as less influential than the mode in which the news is collected and presented. It is the *tout ensemble* of the newspaper every day that makes or mars its power as a public organ. A journal must not be good in spurts, but good every day. It is like raising hot-house plants,—one night's error in allowing frost to get at them may spoil a season's labor. Yet editorials may be made very influential. A journalist should not anticipate events, but should keep just in advance of them. If I state to-day what will take place three months ahead, the public do not care, but if I can announce what will happen this very noon, the information carries all the force of omniscience. It matters little about a journalist's consistency, as it is called, if he keeps pace with public opinion. Frequently inconsistency is only apparent. Think of the Spanish proverb : *Il sabio muda conscio, il nescio no.* New light which an editor receives changes his opinion, as was strikingly shown by the action of the *Herald* regarding the Mason and Slidell seizure, and the course of the London *Times* on the Burlingame mission. But there are certain principles which must always guide a journalist.

Q. What about anonymous writing then ?

A. I believe in that. The newspaper should be supreme, and the writer secondary. During the war our war correspondence was all signed, but that was because the War Department wished that it should be done, and not because we wanted it done. Anonymous writing helps a paper also, as it gets all the credit of each contributor's talent. Many public men have dabbled in journalism in the intervals of other occupations. Caleb Cushing was a good journalist, and has written much for the press. Lincoln would have been very valuable in a newspaper office, as his fund of humorous anecdotes would often have come into play. Daniel Webster tried to write editorials, but only made essays, which were good in their way, but not the thing for a daily newspaper. More and better work can be got out of a second-rate man, who is allowed ample freedom, than from one of superior merit who is hampered by petty restrictions. It is a great art to write well for a daily journal, and requires the highest and most practical talent. I would prefer a Messonnier or Leach or Cruikshank as my illustrators, to a Church or a Bierstadt.

Q. Do you think the *Herald* will continue to be as great a paper under the younger as under the elder Bennett?

A. Yes, I believe Mr. Bennet, Jr., inherits his father's journalistic genius. His yachting inclination is no more than Bonner's or Vanderbilt's love of horses, which certainly does not interfere with their business activity. He has inherited too much money to go through the drudgery of editing, but he will develope talent and enterprise everywhere. The *Herald* itself shows his journalistic talent. The 12th of July issue, and that of the day following, was a stroke of editorial genius, and I have no doubt was his work; the Livingstone enterprise was a great success; and he has kept the *Herald* up to its old standard, and up to the times, in spite of the talk to the contrary, and I guess he has only just commenced work. Let us see what he will do.

EDITORIAL PERSONALITY.

The " war of papers " did not have its origin on this continent. Although it has been more violent here than in any other country, leading to duels and street-fights It began in England as far back as 1642. Previously the wits of the theatres and coffee-houses made butts of the newspapers. The war was the first sign of intellectual vitality in the press. It was a conflict of brains. Those editors who accuse others of being villains, liars, forgers, blasphemers, in our day, are not originals. Such epithets were applied to the *Mercurius Aulicus* and *Mercurius Aquaticus* by the *Mercurius Britannicus* in 1642, when the editor of the latter said, " I have discovered the lies, forgeries, insolencies, impieties, profanities, blasphemies of the two sheets." Our modern pen-warriors use no stronger expressions. They are a little more sententiously thrown at each other. They use one epithet at a time. That is all the difference. There is more force and point in the modern mode. When a political friend of Govenor Marcy told him of his mistake in the expression of "to the victor belongs the spoil," in the heated campaign of Jackson's time, he replied that all politicians held the same opinion. "Yes, yes," said his friend, "but they are not so silly as to put it in half a dozen words that every body can remember." When Horace Greeley applied to William Cullen Bryant or John Bigelow the epithet "you lie, villain, you know you lie," he merely condensed the expression of the *Mercurius Britannicus* of 1643.

Such a warfare was not an evil. It was needed two centuries ago. It vitalized the press. Abuse, like everything else, can be overdone, but it will always correct itself. All difference of opinion is healthy. All elements need disturbance. If a newspaper goes too far in its criticisms, that journal suffers. Other newspapers do not. All trades and professions differ in views and in opinion of each other. There is no more *esprit du corps* among clergymen, lawyers, physicians, or merchants, than among editors. Journalists parade their jealousies and differences on the public clothes-line, where everybody can see them. They wash their "dirty linen" before the people, and in the most exposed places. Other professions simply use their own premises for this purpose.—HUDSON'S *History of Journalism, p.* 63.

GEORGE W. CURTIS,

EDITOR OF "HARPER'S WEEKLY."

[The following statement of the relations of newspaper and reader, taken from the Editor's Easy Chair, in *Harper's Monthly*.]

"ALTHOUGH it is an age of newspapers, it is not yet certainly decided that whatever is new shall therefore be considered news, or fit for the public eye. An inquisitive child, poring over the advertisements in many papers, would grievously perplex his father if he should insist upon an explanation of much that he reads; and the perplexity would become profound if his mother should join in his request. And there are reports and descriptions of many aspects of life which are undoubtedly very new to many readers, but which are like the advertisements, very difficult to explain. When a man calls upon an editor to state why he admits to his columns certain notices or advertisements, the usual reply is that the editor is not a moral censor. He offers to the public a vehicle of communication, and he does not, and can not, guarantee the truth or the propriety of the thing communicated. This is a general plea, which is not true in detail. For, in the first place, the editor does regard propriety of form. If a man should send to a reputable neswspaper an announcement that a cock-fight would take place in his house upon a certain day, or that he had a dog-pit for which he solicited public favor, or should offer still more questionable advertistments yet of things not forbidden by statute, the reputable newspaper would decline. Yet if many of the same objects were sought under phrases not obnoxious to instant censure, although well understood by the editor, they would often be admitted; while some he would reject under every pretense; and often, but not always, not so much for the reason of immorality itself as that certain immorality is hurtful to trade. So he is a moral censor in such matters, after all; and the question is upon what principle his censure shall proceed. Clearly the principle of the newspaper must be that it will not directly nor indirectly consciously connive at immorality. By assuming the responsibility of publication its conductor has not divested himself of his individual accountability. The rhetoric of advertising is universally understood. But the case is essentially different when the editor really does know that the enterprise to which the public is exorted to give money is a cheat, and he can no more honorably advertise it than he could pick pockets.

"If, then, the editor must discriminate, upon what compulsion must he? how far and in what way may he plainly expose the vices that lie hidden like man-traps and spring-guns all around the path of the great journey? What is the press but a detective's lantern? How can it be more advantageously used than by being turned on skulking villainy. * * * There is indeed danger that in exposing a peril you advertise it, as in deprecating a policy you may suggest it. * * * But it is a great mistake to suppose that newspapers cannot deal with certain universal vices, because to speak of them is to advertise them, and really multiply vice. It is in this, as elsewhere, a question of method. A preacher may so set forth Christianity as to disgust every sensible hearer, and to repel those whom another should persuade as the south wind persuades birds in spring. There is no difficulty, however apparently unmanageable, that a newspaper may not deal with successfully if it deals skillfully, but the timidity and pruriency that are sometimes observable in the press, are due mainly to the public itself—to the reader.

"The excuse of a single reader—of that one, for instance, who is at this moment reading these lines—is that one man does not count; that his influence is nothing. And it is remarkable that an age which preaches so loudly the gospel of individual action, which asserts the very unit of society to be the individual, should be the time also in which every man is so likely to depreciate his individual influence and weight, and so apt to forbear the attempt to exercise it.

"If the public—if any number of persons—wish the press to grapple with great evils, to expose evil-doers of every kind, and not only to rebuke vice in the slums, but dishonesty and corruption in high position, it must sturdily sustain it, while it holds it to the strictest responsibility. It was Cain who asked, "Am I my brother's keeper?" and there are many and many who still excuse themselves under the same plea. While, therefore, the honorable editor, whatever he may say, does not make his paper—as he ought not to make it—a mere dead wall upon which every quack and criminal may paste his placard at pleasure, but aims to make the honest, not the dishonest, convenience of the public his private profit, the individual reader has the same interest with the editor in the general well-being. He must do his part. It is not, indeed, entirely true either that the press makes the public, or the public the press. But there is an immense reciprocal influence."

THE LIBERTINE PRESS.—"If shrewd and honorable editors make an interesting paper, without pandering to the blackguard taste of the public, they detach from the support of the blackguard papers those who buy them, because they find them more entertaining than the other; and thus the line will be drawn. But honorable men who become journalists will prefer to make money honorably, and will decline the other kind of service. In this way the real dignity and worth of the press may be advanced, while just in the degree that the libertinism increases, the character and civilizing power of the press will decline. * * *

"It is in this way that the encroachments of the libertine press in this country are to be opposed. The active work must be done by the editors. If they denounce and then embrace, they must not be surprised that the public embraces without denouncing. They must show that libertinism is not essential to the liveliest and the most attractive of newspapers, and then the blackguard journals will go to their own place and patrons."—*Harper's Weekly.*

POWER AND RESPONSIBILITY OF THE PRESS.

From a letter read at the banquet given at the opening of the Public *Ledger* Building in Philadelphia, July 4, 1867, we quote:

"ALBANY, N. Y., July 3, 1867.

"MY DEAR MR. CHILDS: I was very sorry that my duties at the Constitutional Convention here prevented my accepting your kind invitation to the great newspaper jubilee. Yet I might perhaps have wisely run away to you, for it is the newspapers, rather than conventions, which make governments and constitutions. They, more than any other influence, mould public opinion, which is, in this country, and at last in all countries, really the government: and it is to them that the legislators look for the encouragement or censure of their work.

"In this country we are all politicians, and the newspaper is the great political school. How gladly, therefore, should I have met so illustrious a body of teachers as that you assembled at your feast! How profound, also, is my sense of their power and responsibility! Louis Napoleon's summer guests, emperors, sultans, and kings though they are, are not truly so significant a company as yours. And as this feeling of the essential dignity and influence of the editorial profession increases, may we not hope that the sense of its responsibility will deepen? If the newspaper is the school of the people, and if upon popular education and intelligence the success and prosperity of popular government depend, there is no function in American society which requires more conscience as well as ability."

In a speech at the dinner given by the New York press to Chas. Dickens, April, 1868, Mr. Curtis spoke of the press as follows:

"The paramount duty of the literary press is purity; of the political press, honesty. Our copyright law, as you are aware, Mr. Chairman, inflicts a fine for every repetition of the offence, so that the fine is multiplied as many times as there are copies of the book printed. So the man who, as a writer for the press, *says what he does not believe, or defends a policy that he does not approve, or panders to a base passion or a mean prejudice for a party purpose, is so many times a traitor to the craft represented at this table* as there are copies of his newspaper printed. And as honest or even dishonest difference of opinion is entirely compatible with courtesy, as even *denunciation is a thousand-fold more stinging and effective when it is not vituperation, decency of manner becomes the press no less than decency of matter.* When the manners of the press becomes those of Tombs pettifoggers, or Old Bailey shysters, or the Eatanswill Gazette, its influence upon society will be revealed by a coarse and brutal public opinion. While we boast of the tremendous power of the press, let us remember that the foundations of its power as a truly civilizing influence are, first, purity, then honesty, then sagacity and industry. It may sometimes seem otherwise; but it is an illusion. A man may build up a great journal as he may amass any other great fortune, and seem to be a shining miracle of prosperity. But if he have neither love, nor honor, nor troops of friends, his prosperity is a fair orchard bearing only apples of Sodom."

INDEPENDENT JOURNALISM.—" Hitherto the newspapers calling themselves independent have been too often merely the meanest trimmers and panders. They have apparently thought independence consisted in abusing one party to-day and another party to-morrow. But we do not know one truly independent journal in the country whose sympathies are not with one of the two great parties. The man who thinks that both are equally bad, and who does not care which prevails, is a man without opinions, or without principle, or without perception, and in either case is wholly unfit to be an editor. But the more deeply an independent journal sympathizes with the principle and purpose of a party, the more strenuously will it censure its follies and errors, the more bravely will it criticise its candidates and leaders, for the purpose of keeping the principle pure, and of making the success of the party a real blessing. The public will gradually learn that only in such papers can they find true statements of events, with comments that aim at the public welfare, and not merely at a party success. In such, also, and only in such, will public men be considered impartially, and the plain tendency of an independent press will thus be to elevate the national life and character, and to keep party spirit within its due bounds.

"But only as really able men enter the profession of journalism is such independence possible. Hypercriticism, cynicism, captiousness, persiflage, are not its characteristics; but profound conviction, tact, knowledge, humor and good temper. Fifty such journals, from Maine to California, prosperous, sparkling, vigorous and rigorous, would rattle the dry bones of party hacks, and instill a most wholesome terror in charlatans of every kind."—*Harper's Weekly.*

A CONDENSED STATEMENT.—In a note lately written to the editor of the present work, Mr. Curtis briefly summed up his views of the functions of the press as follows: "What our press most needs is conscience and courtesy. It has plenty of wit and ability. I feel of the press what Carlyle evidently feels of the world—'What a world it might be! but what a world we make of it!' A journal should be neither an echo nor a pander, but I know several of both kinds."

Mrs. JENNIE C. CROLY.

(JENNIE JUNE.)

QUESTION.—I know that you were one of the first women connected with daily and weekly journalism, may I ask how long since you began this career, and what has been your connection with journalism during that time?

ANSWER.—It is nearly twenty years since I applied to a daily paper in this city for a place on its regular staff, and was refused on the ground of simple impracticability. It had struck me as strange that amid the multiplicity of papers and periodicals no one of them represented women, or the subjects that had special interest for women, and still believing that there was a place for them somewhere, I wrote an article addressed specially to women, took it to a weekly paper, and boldly (it really required some courage), asked the editor to make a "women's department," and give me charge of it. The editor was a good and enterprising man; it struck him favorably—he offered me three dollars per week for a department to be called "Gossip With and For Ladies." Subsequently another paper offered five for a column of "Parlor and Side-walk Gossip." This was the beginning of departments for ladies—editors did not like "women"—in weekly journals, and it was not two years before every paper of any pretensions in the large cities had them.

Q. What range of topics was selected by women for their first efforts in journalism?

A. The experience of the earlier experimentalists was

probably very much like my own—a "range" of topics was not permitted—discussion of new books it was said would interfere with the regular book "reviewer," the same in regard to pictures and the drama, and when I, for example, very naturally asked: "but, Mr. H., what then can I write about?" he said, "Why, there is always dress and fashion," and that, I presume, gave me the bias which made me a fashion writer.

Q. How did these beginnings in journalism affect women generally?

A. Well, they opened a new field of employment for them: some of them, like myself, found them only stepping-stones to editorial work, and admission to the regular profession of journalism.

Q. How is it that so many women seek journalism as a means of livelihood, and what is the accepted idea of qualification among them for such a career?

A. Within the past ten or fifteen years an immense number have been thrown upon their own resources from among a class who had never previously been called upon to contribute actively to their own support—probably not more have attempted journalism than have become milliners and boarding-house keepers, but we are in a position to estimate the number of the former, though not the latter. Qualification, I fancy, has little to do with the matter—it is taste, and the necessity of doing something for a livelihood. Then the most absurd stories have been told as to the amount of money earned by women employed as editors and correspondents, and this has excited the imaginations of girls and women, and led them to suppose that fame and fortune waited for them at the threshold of every newspaper office.

Q. What proper place has women in journalism?

A. It is difficult to define it until women have been

trained with a view to a professional career. At present the only training women have received has been in the newspaper office itself. And though this is valuable for general routine work, yet it does not qualify them for the special work which pays. Women in newspaper offices, therefore, as elsewhere, are drudges, obliged to do a large amount of work for small pay, because their general and special culture has not fitted them for the best places; when the education which a large number are now receiving has developed and trained their faculties, my opinion is, that the brightest journalists will be found among women. And, as politics loses the absurd importance which is attached to it in this country, and social and educational questions come to the front, the place for women in journalism will become enlarged, and their experience necessary to the discussion and solution of the most interesting problems.

Q. Why are women not more employed in daily journalism, and what have you found to be the principal obstacles to women obtaining a regular place on the staff of a daily paper?

A. Sex alone, not at all capacity. There are plenty of women who would be preferred as workers to men, if they were not women. But men are not accustomed to act with women from a business point of view, and their presence oppresses them. They will stand carelessness, negligence, even drunkenness from a man, because that is in the regular order of things, but a woman, without trial, is generally understood to be a "nuisance" in a newspaper office. Then, it is true that they cannot as yet be put upon subordinate routine work. A large part of the work of a daily paper has to be done at night, and editors say, with truth, that a sense of impropriety attaches to the idea of a woman going unattended to night meetings for the purpose of reporting them, returning late to the office, writing her report and travelling home alone after midnight. Still, there are many things that a woman can do upon a daily journal, and women could be used upon them much more than they are, with benefit to the journals themselves. There are many events constantly taking place which can be properly described by women, and of which indeed an intelligent woman can alone take true cognizance. Many social and educational questions also are best treated from the woman's stand-point, or, at any rate, made more interesting and valuable by giving her side of them.

Q. Could women, in your opinion, conduct a daily paper successfully?

A. Not a first-class morning paper, at least not at present. That needs force and nerve, such as few women possess, in conjunction with trained faculties, and an impartial judgment, such as few men possess; but I think women could conduct a daily afternoon paper successfully, and I think New York needs just such an one. A paper that would pay special attention to the meetings, the interests, the movements, the ideas, and the needs of women; that would make itself a sort of bureau of exchange, and be at the same time bright, newsy and impartial.

Q. What do you consider the natural place of women in journalism; is it not as correspondents that they are most successful?

A. Certainly, their successes so far have been mainly won as correspondents, and undoubtedly their vivacious style fits them for this kind of writing; but is not this evidence of their fitness due to the fact that correspondence is the department in which they have been principally employed? But this may not be so in the future. At present there are sixty papers in the United States edited by women, and as editors, editorial writers, and the like, they are fully as successful as the average of men. I think the periodical representative of social and domestic life will naturally, in the future, fall into the hands of women, and that they will also find a large place in the field of regular journalism.

Q. In what can women best fit. themselves for work in journalism?

A. There are no schools of journalism, even for men, outside of the newspaper office itself; and it is only by proving a natural fitness for the work that women can be admitted to a place which exists, but does not wait for them, and can only be reached by slow and persistent effort. Boys are put in newspaper offices, as they are put in lawyers offices, and bullied and shoved into acquiring respectable proficiency in the profession; but as yet, only the women can obtain a permanent place whose acquirements and natural fitness render them valuable acquisitions: there is no opportunity for them as apprentices. While, therefore, general education does much in disciplining and training their faculties, the knowledge of technical routine is acquired only by slow experience and the rare chance for observation. These circumstances will be modified as women obtain larger and firmer footing, and as the necessity is felt for the early admission and training of girls into professions as well as boys. At present, the principal requisite for women, after as thoroughly good and practical an education as they can receive, is action on business principles. Journalism must want something they can give, it must not be altogether they who want the money and fame, which they fancy journalism can give them. Newspapers are not charity hospitals, they are very hard workshops, and no woman should venture into the field who is not prepared to accept this fact.

HORACE GREELEY.

FOUNDER OF "THE NEW YORK TRIBUNE."

Mr. Greeley was intended by nature to be an editor. In his boyhood he says he had "no other ambition than that of attaining usefulness and position as an editor, and to this end all the studies and efforts of his life have tended"—while in his autobiography he gives as the dearest wish of his mature years, "I cherish the hope that the journal I projected and established will live and flourish long after I shall have moldered into forgotten dust, being guided by a larger wisdom, a more unerring sagacity to discern the right, though not by a more unfaltering readiness to embrace and defend it at whatever personal cost; and that the stone which covers my ashes may bear to future eyes the still intelligible inscription,—

"FOUNDER OF THE NEW YORK TRIBUNE."

Mr. Greeley thus describes, in his "Recollections of a Busy Life," the beginning of his literary labor: "Beyond a few boyish letters to relatives and intimate friends, I began my efforts at composition as an apprentice in a newspaper office, by condensing the news, more especially the foreign, which I was directed to put into type from the city journals received at our office; endeavoring to give in fewer words the gist of the information, in so far, at least, as it would be likely to interest our rural readers. Our editor, during the latter part of our stay in Poultney, was a Baptist clergyman, whose pastoral charge was at some distance, and who was therefore absent from us much of his time, and allowed me a wide discretion in preparing matter for the paper. This I improved, not only in the selection, but in the condensation of news. The rudimentary knowledge of the art of composition thus acquired was gradually improved during my brief experience as a journeyman in various newspaper establishments, and afterward as a printer of sundry experimental journals in this city ; so that I began my distinctive, avowed editorial career in *The New Yorker* with a considerable experience as a writer of articles and paragraphs.

Mr. H. J. Raymond, in an autobiographical fragment written a few years since, thus referred to Mr. Greeley's editorship of the *New Yorker:* " The calm, dispassionate character of its (*the New Yorker's*) articles, their strength of argument, all the more conspicuous by reason of the absence of passion,—the accuracy of its statements won for Mr. Greeley * * * public confidence." The *New Yorker* failed after seven years existence, owing to peculiar circumstances, including a financial crisis, and Mr. Greeley, after successively editing the *Jeffersonian* and the *Log Cabin*, two campaign papers, started, on the 10th of April, 1841, the New York *Tribune*. The times was not propitious, nor were the affairs of its founder in a hopeful condition, " with no partner or business associate " (to quote his own words), " with inconsiderable pecuniary resources, and only a promise from political friends of aid," he had to contend against the risks incident to every new enterprise of the kind, which were increased by the National gloom due to the sudden death of President Harrison and the doubtful prospects of the Whig party. Yet Mr. Greeley was hopeful and earnest. In referring back to this period in his " Recollections," he says : " I had been ten years in New York, was thirty years old, in full health and vigor, and worth, I presume, about $2,000;

half of it in printer's materials." Mr. Greeley has thus described in characteristic language what his object was in founding the *Tribune*. " My leading idea was the establishment of a journal removed alike from servile partizanship on the one hand, and from gagged, wincing neutrality on the other * * * * I believed there was a happy medium between these extremes,—a position from which a journalist might openly and heartily advocate the principles and commend the measures of that party to which his convictions allied him, yet dissent frankly from its course on a particular question, and even denounce its candidates if they were shown to be deficient in capacity or (far worse) in integrity." Such was his design; how it has been carried out every one is aware.

In a speech at a press dinner given by the Sorosis, Nov. 28th, 1869, Mr. Greeley, in replying to the toast " Country Farming and City editing, " said, " I have been at work on the press for forty years; and this seems to be the hardship: You work for days, and months and years, and what have you to show? Something, I hope, in mental growth; something in firmness of purpose; something in clearness of intention, but outwardly, nothing. Thirty years have passed away, and where is the fruit of all that labor? How can your labors compare with those of the man who has produced a book? "

On the 10th of April, 1871, the *Tribune* being thirty years old, the founder of the paper gave a succinct and edifying history of his labors and achievements as follows:

"The *Daily Tribune* was first issued on the 10th of April, 1841; it has therefore completed its thirtieth, and to-day enters upon its thirty-first year. It was originally a small folio sheet, employing, perhaps, twenty persons in its production; it is now one of the largest journals issued in any part of the world, containing ten to fifteen times as much as at first, and embodying in each issue the labor of four to five hundred persons as writers, printers, etc., etc. Its daily contents, apart from advertisements, would make a fair 12mo. volume, such as sells from the bookstores for $1 25 to 1 50; and when we are compelled to issue a supplement, its editorials, correspondence, dispatches, and reports (which seldom leave room for any but a mere shred of selections) equal in quantity an average octavo. The total cost of its production for the first week was $525; it is now nearly $20,000 per week, with a constant, irresistible tendency to increase.

"Other journals have been established by a large outlay of capital, and many years of patient, faithful effort; the *Tribune* started on a very small capital, to which little has ever been added except through the abundance and liberality of its patrons. They enabled it to pay its way almost from the outset; and, though years have intervened, especially during our great Civil War, when, through a sudden and rapid advance in the cost of paper and other materials, our expenses somwhat exceeded our income, yet, taking the average of these thirty years, our efforts have been amply, generously rewarded, and the means incessantly required to purchase expensive machinery, and make improvements on every hand, have been derived exclusively from the regular receipts of the establishment. Rendering an earnest and zealous, though by no means an indiscriminate support, for the former half of its existence to the Whig, and through the latter half to the Republican party, the *Tribune* has asked no favor of either, and no odds of any man but that he should pay for whatever he choose to order, whether in the shape of subscriptions or advertisements. Holding that a journal can help no party while it requires to be helped itself, we hope so to deserve and retain the good will of the general public that we may be as independent in the future as we have been in the past."

In May, 1851, during a visit to London, Mr. Greeley appeared, by invitation, before a Parliamentary committee, of which Mr. Cobden was a member, and gave some valuable testimony in regard to the state of the American press at that date, part of which is condensed herewith from Parton's " Life of Horace Greeley : "

MR. COBDEN.—" At what amount of population does a town in the United States begin to have a daily paper? They first of all begin with a weekly paper, do they not?"

MR. GREELEY.—" Yes. The general rnle is, that each county will have one weekly newspaper. In all the free States, if a county have a population of twenty thousand, it has two papers, one for each party. The general average in the agricultural counties is one local journal to every ten thousand inhabitants. When a town grows to have fifteen thousand inhabitants in and about it, then it has a daily paper; but sometimes that is the case when it has as few as ten thousand; it depends more on the business of a place than its population. But fifteen thousand may be stated as the average at which a daily paper commences; at twenty thousand they have two, and so on. In central towns, like Buffalo, Rochester, Troy, they have from three to five daily journals, each of which prints a semi-weekly or a weekly journal."

CHAIRMAN.—" When a person proposes to publish a paper in New York, he is not required to go to any office to register himself, or to give security that he will not insert libels or seditious matter? A newspaper publisher is not subject to any liability more than other persons?"

Mr. Greeley.—"No; no more than a man that starts a blacksmith's shop."

Chairman.—"They do not presume in the United States that, because a man is going to print news in a paper, he is going to libel?"

Mr. Greeley.—"No; nor do they presume that his libeling would be worth much, unless he is a responsible character."

Mr. Cobden.—"From what you have stated with regard to the circulation of the daily papers in New York, it appears that a very large proportion of the adult population must be customers for them?"

Mr. Greeley.—"Yes; I think three-fourths of all the families take a daily paper of some kind."

Mr. Cobden.—"The working people in New York are not in the habit of resorting to public houses to read the newspapers, are they?"

Mr. Greeley.—"They go to public houses, but not to read the papers. It is not the general practice; but still we have quite a class who do so."

Mr. Cobden.—"The newspaper, then, is not the attraction to the public house?"

Mr. Greeley.—"No; I think a very small proportion of our reading class go there at all; those that I have seen there are mainly the foreign population; those who do not read."

Chairman.—"Are there any papers published in New York, or in other parts, which may be said to be of an obscene or immoral character?"

Mr. Greeley.—"We call the New York *Herald* a very bad paper—those who do not like it; but that is not the cheapest. There are weekly papers got up from time to time called the 'Scorpion,' the 'Flash,' and so on, whose purpose is to extort money from parties who can be threatened with exposure of immoral practices, or for visiting infamous houses. I do not know of any one being continued for any considerable time. If one dies, another is got up, and that goes down. Our cheap daily papers, the very cheapest, are, as a class, quite as discreet in their conduct and conversation as other journals. They do not embody the same amount of talent; they devote themselves mainly to news. They are not party journals; they are nominally independent; they are not given to harsh language with regard to public men; they are very moderate."

Mr. Ewart.—"Is scurillity or personality common in the publications of the United States?"

Mr. Greeley.—"It is not common; it is much less frequent than it was; but it is not absolutely unknown."

Mr. Cobden.—"What is the circulation of the New York *Herald?*"

Mr. Greeley.—"Twenty-five thousand, I believe."

Mr. Cobden.—"Is that an influential paper in America?"

Mr. Greeley.—"I think not; a certain class of journals in this country find it their interest or pleasure to quote it a good deal."

Chairman.—"As the demand is extensive, is the remuneration for the services of the literary men who are employed on the press, good?"

Mr. Greeley.—"The prices of literary labor are more moderate than in this country. The highest salary, I think, that would be commanded by any one connected with the press would be five thousand dollars—the highest that could be thought of. I have not heard of higher than three thousand. In our own concern the ordinary remuneration is, besides the principal editor, from fifteen hundred dollars down to five hundred. I think that is the usual range."

CHAIRMAN.—"Are your leading men in America, in point of literary ability, employed from time to time upon the press as an occupation?"

MR. GREELEY.—"It is beginning to be so, but it has not been the custom. There have been leading men connected with the press; but the press has not been usually conducted by the most powerful men. With a few exceptions, the leading political journals are conducted ably, and they are becoming more so; and, with a wider diffusion of the circulation, the press is more able to pay for it."

MR. RICH.—"Is it a profession apart?"

MR. GREELEY.—"No; usually the men have been brought up to the bar, to the pulpit, and so on; they are literary men."

CHAIRMAN.—"Do not you consider that newspaper reading is calculated to keep up a habit of reading?"

MR. GREELEY.—"I think it is worth all the schools in the country. I think it creates a taste for reading in every child's mind, and it increases his interest in his lessons; he is attracted from always seeing a newspaper and hearing it read, I think."

CHAIRMAN.—"Supposing that you had your schools as now, but that your newspaper press were reduced within the limits of the press in England, do you not think that the habit of reading acquired at school would be frequently laid aside?"

MR. GREELEY.—"I think that the habit would not be acquired, and that paper reading would fall into disuse."

MR. EWART.—"Having observed both countries, can you state whether the press has greater influence on public opinion in the United States than in England, or the reverse?"

Mr. Greeley.—"I think it has more influence with us. I do not know that any class is despotically governed by the press, but its influence is more universal; every one reads and talks about it with us, and more weight is laid upon intelligence than on editorials; the paper which brings the quickest news is the thing looked for."

Mr. Ewart.—"The leading article has not so much influence as in England?"

Mr. Greeley.—"No; the telegraphic dispatch is the great point."

Mr. Cobden.—"Observing our newspapers, and comparing them with the American papers, do you find that we make much less use of the electric telegraph for transmitting news than in America."

Mr. Greeley.—"Not a hundredth part as much as we do. The advertisements are one main source of the income of daily papers, and thousands of business men take them mainly for those advertisments. For instance, at the time when our auctioneers were appointed by law (they were, of course, party politicians), one journal, which was high in the confidence of the party in power, obtained not a law, but an *understanding*, that all the auctioneers appointed should advertise in that journal. Now, though the journal referred to has ceased to be of that party, and the auctioneers are no longer appointed by the State, yet that journal has almost the monopoly of the auctioneer's business to this day. Auctioneers *must* advertise in it, because they know that purchasers are looking there; and purchasers must take the paper, because they know that it contains just the advertisements they want to see; and this, without regard to the goodness or the principles of the paper. The greater number of small advertisements in papers, the greater the advantage to their proprietors."

Mr. Greeley belongs to that class of minds who do not care to theorize about their work, and he has said but little publicly upon the subject of journalism. We understand, however, that his views were substantially the same as those set forth in Whitelaw Reid's lecture on journalism, excepting those on the relations between the editorial to the publishing department of a newspaper, which he thought need not be at all antagonistic. He believed in enterprise, in collecting, information, and the large outlay made of late years by Messrs. Young and Reid with this object had his entire sanction. He upheld also the final importance of a newspaper furnishing local news, and he frequently criticised country editors for their neglect of this truth. In a letter to the Port Hudson (Mich.) *Times*, dated March 2d, 1870, Mr. Greeley gave the following condensed statement of his ideas of journalism:

"In my conception, the best use of a journal is to print the largest practical amount of important truth—truth which tends to make mankind wiser, and thus happier. Other matters must also be printed in order to obtain access to minds that would otherwise be closed to the truths thus commended; but the aim should be that first indicated."

Mr. Greeley did not entertain much faith in any method of journalistic training beyond that afforded in a newspaper office; when Oliver Johnson once asked him how an editor should be made, he answered humorously, " I guess you'll have to feed him on printers' ink."

The following letter was written by Mr. Greeley to a newspaper man, who asked his advice about leaving a country town for the city : " My own course uniformly has been to stick to anything I could find to do, and never leave a place so long as any work remained to be done there. I think you will find that the wise course. It may seem that larger wages may be earned elsewhere ; but expenses are usually proportionate to earnings, and removal exposes one to the loss of all the position or reputation he may have gained. Character is the basis of business and prosperity, and character is more easily established or developed in the country than in any city. Men seldom bound to fortune or position ; they must grow. After a few years you will be wanted to conduct a journal in your own region ; look carefully into the inducements, and be not too hasty in accepting, for your time will come. Be careful of debt ; he who owes nothing, and has a chance to earn his daily bread, is happier than he is aware of. Make friends and gain knowledge; a few years will render them useful to you."

When " John Paul " (Chas. Webb) applied to him for advice about becoming a journalist, he advised him to go home and study hard in the intervals of work, to read the newspapers carefully, and to endeavor to acquire a good prose style of writing.

Mr. Greeley's occasional use of violent personalities seems to have been condemned by his better judgment, and the following sentence, from a long article written in 1869, would evidently imply that he was unconscious of this bad habit. He said : " The *Tribune* is very often impelled to controvert the views set forth by one or another of its cotemporaries ; we are not aware that any of them has had reason to complain either of the spirit or the terms in which this duty has been performed. None of them can truly say that we have chosen to degrade such controversy from a discussion of principles into an exchange of personalities. No journalist can truthfully say that we have dragged him before the public, unless in palpable self-defence."

In addition to these statements of opinion we append the following extracts from Mr. Greeley's published writings :

"THE COUNTRY PRESS."

"We are to recognize the worth and the usefulness of the country press. It is probable that no class of men in the community do so much honest and advantageous work for so little pay as the editors and publishers of the newspapers of the interior. They deserve all the support and aid which can honestly be given them. The good ones among them are among the most valuable sources of true progress and enlightenment, and even the inferior ones have a use and merit of their own."

OFFICE HOLDING EDITORS.

In an editorial in the *Tribune* of April 19th, 1869, Mr. Greeley said, in reference to the subject of editors excepting office:—" He (the editor of the *Tribune*) does not regard with admiration the practical monopoly of all important civil trusts by men bred to the law, nor does he hold that Ben. Franklin degraded or disparaged the editorial profession by serving his country successively as embassador and Postmaster-General."

NEWSPAPERS SHOULD BE INDEPENDENT OF PATRONAGE.

"It seems to us that it would be better for a newspaper to die than to live dependent upon official patronage. If there is public advertising to be done, it is reasonable to expect, from the fairness and the common sense of the authorities, that it will be sent to the papers which can give it the widest and the best publicity. A journal receiving work in this manner, and charging for it an honest price, is thereby laid under no obligation whatever to any man or to any party. No paper can afford to accept what is ordinarily called official patronage on any other terms."

" Still more impossible is it for a journalist to reconcile independence in his profession with office-holding. If there is a man in the United States better fitted than any other, by nature, by temperament, by long experience and standing in the Republican party, to harmonize effectually the positions of an independent journalist and an office-holder under the administration, that person is John W. Forney. But a year's experience convinced him that the work was too heavy even for him. A journalist who holds an office writes in a straight jacket."

" These evils could to a certain extent be modified by a proper civil service reform, such as we have frequently demanded, and the President has promised us. If this were once established, an editor might accept an office, if he had time and inclination, without any sacrifice of self-respect. But for another class of papers, which seem led by innate servility of character to flatter power and palliate its errors, no reform can ever accomplish anything. Not only the men in authority can do no wrong in their eyes, but even the lesser rogues in the ranks of its own faction must be defended at all hazards * * * the moment a wrong or an outrage is traced home to one of its own color, it feels that its whole duty lies in abusing the prosecutor and shielding the criminal. We are glad to believe this old fashioned partisan journalism is passing away."

AN EARLY VIEW OF INDEPENDENT JOURNALISM.— "That what styles itself an 'independent' journal is inevitably a fraud, we have long felt and known. The essence of its profession is an assumption of indifference to the ascendancy of this or the opposite party, which does not exist. In a free State, whereof the people are intelligent, no journalist is or can be indifferent; and an affectation of impartiality necessarily cloaks some selfish and sinister designs."

"What! is no one indifferent to the rise or fall of parties in our country?"

"O, yes! There are many so imbecile, or so profoundly ignorant, that they do not even know who is President, or which party triumphed in the last Federal election. There are ecclesiastics whose days and thoughts are so intently fixed on heaven or Rome that they know nothing of political parties. There may be men so music-mad, or so absorbed in scientific study and investigation, that they heed not the surges of political contention. But none of these edit journals devoted to news and public affairs; and we are speaking of journalists. One of these may devote his columns to religion, or music, or chemistry, or agriculture, and maintain a rigorous silence with reference to politics. He does not affect indifference; he simply practices reticence. But the editor who devotes his thoughts, his pen, his columns, to the discussion of transpiring events and the men who influence and figure in them, is led, by the exigencies of his daily vocation, to pass judgments thereon; and these judgments necessarily incline him to regard one party with more favor than its antagonist. If a knave, he may be suborned to write adversely to his convictions; but even this will not wholly efface them, and cannot render his profession of indifference other than a lure and a cheat.

"If a journal professing indifference to party success, and extensively read by men of diverse views, *could* have an editor-in-chief who really felt such indifference, he must have assistants in his work; and these would share neither his impartiality nor his responsibility. They would evidently give a coloring to their narratives or their criticisms ,favorable to the party with which they respectively affiliated; and they would be bribed by unscrupulous party managers to do this if their scruples or their attachment to their positions restrained them from so doing without prompting or pay. Of this truth, the history of our city press of the 'independent' variety affords notable confirmation.

"The New York *Herald* was founded, and has throughout been edited, by one whose mental constitution forbade his being a Whig in the past or a Republican in the present. Profoundly imbued with the conviction that politics is a mere game—that every man has his price—that a virtuous woman is one who has not yet been found out, and an honest bank officer one who has not yet found his opportunity to make a satisfactory grab—he could not be other than a hard-money, free-trade Democrat of the 'Loco-Foco' stamp. Hence you may read in his columns, throughout the summer of 1837, the most confident and positive assertions that the banks (which had just suspended specie payment) would *never* resume—that their notes would steadily and rapidly depreciate in value until they became as worthless as the old 'Continental' shinplasters. So the first suggestions of a railroad to the Pacific were ridiculed by him as on a par with proposals to build a bridge across the Atlantic or a tramway to the moon. A cynic, a sceptic, and at heart a monarchist, the editor of the *Herald* could take no other view of our current politics than such as identified him with our sham Democracy; yet he has, for this very reason, been to the Republicans a fairer, more manly antagonist, than any other professedly 'independent' journalist. He has not concealed his elemental convictions; but he has often set forth facts calculated to incite adverse conclusions in minds differently constituted from his own."

Mr. Greeley's views on independent journalism changed very decidedly toward the close of his life, and almost his latest utterance was a declaration of his allegiance to this principle. In his card of November 6, 1872, resuming the editorship of the *Tribune*, he announced his honest purpose to make his paper "a thoroughly independent journal, treating all parties and political movements with judicial fairness and candor."

No account of Mr. Greeley would be at all complete without some reference to the manner in which he was bored by applicants for aid and advice. The following lively sketch of his trials from these pests is composed in his happiest vein.

MENTAL PACK-HORSES: "There appears to be a class of young men and women in the present generation who, either from sheer laziness or indigence of brains, beg ideas and decisions for the regulation of their daily life from other people, precisely as they take their shoes to be cobbled, or their garments to be patched. These people are generally full of lofty imaginings and unrest; like Antony, they have immortal longings in them; whereupon they perch themselves complacently with folded hands on the pillar of their discontent, and despise men who have the will and common sense to work heartily at whatever is set before them, whether it be to their liking or not. The editor of a newspaper is usually selected by this feeble-minded generation to bear the burden of their incapacity. There is not a day, probably, when he has not the private affairs of some helpless innocent placed in his hands, with requests for aid, from assistance in matrimony to the loan of a five-dollar note. The office of a newspaper, we had fondly imagined, was clearly outlined —first to give the history of its time, and afterward to deduce such theories or truths from it as should be of universal application. * * * A man who collects news and eliminates general principles from it, is not thereby constituted a mental pack-horse for the inabilities of his readers; neither is he a butcher or wet-nurse for the public. He is not bound to furnish either strong meat for men or milk for babies. What he may do individually concerns himself alone; editorially he is bound to urge upon these helpless aspirants the truth of the old saw, that he is best served who serves himself. The man who stood calling for the ferry-man never crossed the river, while he who plunged boldly in reached the other side and went on his way."

"There are work and wages waiting for every man in this country, but they who cry loudest for help are usually the least likely to obtain either. We confess we do not see the pathos in tales of want and helplessness told with folded hands. The ants are a people not strong, the prophet tells us significantly, yet they prepare their meat in the summer."

Mr. Greeley did not possess great executive talent, but he knew how to employ others to attend to the work of the *Tribune* without hampering them by needless restrictions. He was a severe critic and a stern disciplinarian, and required that his directions should be followed to the letter. All the triumphs of the *Tribune* shone with a reflected light on Mr. Greeley, yet he was always willing to give the credit for any striking article or stroke of enterprise to its rightful owner. He was proud of every success of the *Tribune*, and though seldom given to personal praise, he frequently indulged in high compliments to others about the brilliant work of his staff.

The following letter, addressed to Mr. Reid when managing editor of the *Tribune*, is highly characteristic:

SWITZERLAND, MASS., July 26, 1870.
REID:

Please accept my congratulations on the contents of yesterday's (Monday) paper. I consider it the very best issue of an eight page daily ever made in New York, considering that *my* poor little paragraph about Adm. Porter did not get in, though I sent it from Bethlehem in season. I think this a hearty acknowledgment. I hope Meeken's letter is in this week's Weekly; if not, be sure it gets into next week's. I want to get home on Saturday, but may not; I mean to start for Saratoga on Tuesday, to attend the meeting of the Rep. St. Committee.

Yours,
HORACE GREELEY.

WHITELAW REID, Esq.,
   Tribune Office, N. York.

(P. S.) What *does* your paragraph about Conkling and Fenton to-day mean? I can't guess.

Mr. Greeley so infused his individuality into the *Tribune*, that it is hard to separate him from the paper; yet he had a just conception of the distinction between the personality of an editor and the journal which he edits. Usually, in replying to direct personal references to himself, he signed the articles with his initials or full name. In his view, a newspaper should not be limited to fighting the battles or advancing the interests of its managers or owners, but it ought to be an organ of opinion, and be responsible to the public more than to persons or parties. He once quarrelled with a near friend because a notice of some kind was asked in the *Tribune*, and he said then, with much energy, that he wished it distinctly understood by his friends that the *Tribune* was not run in their interest, but in that of the public.

Mr. Greeley preferred to do his writing with his own hand instead of employing an amanuensis, as is the common practice with most persons who have much correspondence to perform. Though an admirable extempore speaker, as shown by his speeches during the last presidential campaign, he lacked the faculty of dictation, while he had no talent for suggesting topics for others to write upon, which the elder Bennett possessed in a remarkable degree. When his mind was filled with an idea, he was so eager to put it on paper, that he could not wait to dictate it to another. The pen steadied his thoughts. He several times tried to dictate to an amanuensis, but he never had the patience to continue, and always ended by taking the pen in his own vigorous hand. He was such an active writer that he performed almost as much work alone as most persons would do with an assistant. Sidney Smith's advice to Lord Brougham, "not to attempt more work than three strong men could accomplish." might well have been repeated to him. His splendid physique and perfectly temperate habits, stood him in good stead. He could toil terribly, and he was never idle. Probably no other person of his age in the Union accomplished as much work as he did on an average. His usual quota in the *Tribune* was one and a-half columns of editorial, besides answering a dozen letters; but he frequently wrote much more. During the presidential campaign of 1842 he averaged four columns daily, while, at the time of the Fenimore Cooper trial, he wrote a report of the proceedings comprising six columns in one day, in addition to his other work. He has been known to come down to the *Tribune* office at eleven in the morning, when there was an extra amount of work on hand, and remain in his chair without ceasing to write until nearly midnight; yet this is only a single example of his power of endurance. Nor was it his habit to take any respite after these periods of extra exertion, as Henry J. Raymond, another great worker, did; but he kept steadily on

in the traces, as if work was pleasure as well as duty.
All the relaxation he had was obtained on lecture tours
or travelling, and the word "rest" was not in his vocabulary. His various books, agricultural and other addresses,
and innumerable contributions to different periodicals,
have all been written in the intervals of his labors in the
Tribune. Mr. Parton is considered an industrious book
maker, and yet he has hardly exceeded Mr. Greeley in
the bulk or number of volumes written during the past
few years; while, if all that Mr. Greeley has written in
the *Tribune*, and elsewhere, was collected, it would rival in
quantity the voluminous works of Voltaire or Walter
Scott.

Mr. Greeley introduced the now general practice of always printing the exact language of an opponent whom he
wished to controvert, as a matter of fairness to the latter.
He also tried to avoid making statements or charges
without sufficient basis of fact. The few successful
libel suits against the *Tribune* show how careful was his
practice in this respect.

He was a good critic of what others had written, and
considered it calmly and in a judicial spirit. Once, after
reading a violent attack on himself in the *Round Table*, he
calmly proceeded to criticise the article on account of its
needless length.

Mr. Greeley latterly visited the editorial rooms of the
Tribune but seldom, and one might be a constant frequenter there without ever seeing him. Yet he kept a
keen eye upon the paper, and if anything went wrong,
the offender was likely to hear from him, promptly.
Many stories are told illustrative of his lynx-eyed vigilance in this respect, but a single one will do as a specimen: One day a speech of several columns length, by
Schuyler Colfax, appeared in the *Tribune.* The same

morning the gentleman who had charge of all such documents in the paper was sent for by Mr. Greeley, and entered the *sanctum* in some trepidation. Mr. Greeley, on seeing him, stopped his writing for a moment, and taking up Colfax's speech, he ran the point of his pen down the column until about the centre, when he stopped and said: " That period ought to be a comma," and then dismissed the astonished sub-editor without further remark, and resumed work on his leader.

He once stated to Don Piatt that he believed the reason of his success in the *Tribune* was that in the beginning he had at once re-invested all the money made by the paper, and thus was able to keep on improving its quality continually.

On one subject connected with the business management of a newspaper Mr. Greeley's views were very positive, namely: that every publisher of a newspaper should be required by law to publish an exact statement of the circulation of his paper, as a simple act of justice to his advertisers, and as being in the nature of the law against fraudulent weights and measures.

Mr. Greeley desired above all things to give the *Tribune* the widest circulation of any paper, consistent with keeping up its standard of quality, rather than to make it merely the richest, most powerful, or best edited jorunal. Hence he insisted on keeping the price, except for the daily edition, at the lowest possible figure, in order to attract readers. He objected very strenuously to display advertisements, and wanted to abolish them. He also proposed doing away with titles to leading articles, after the English plan, but neither change was ever carried out, in the *Tribune* during his lifetime.

Though Mr. Greeley seldom wrote except on certain special subjects, yet he took a deep interest in every department of the paper, and watched its course critically One of the last editorial suggestions which he made before his nomination to the presidency, was about arranging for a new Italian correspondence, and he always had a keen eye for improvements in the *Tribune*. He took a deep interest in European affairs, and had very decided views about them, though he seldom gave expression to them publicly. He did not consider it within the province of an editor to foretell events, and he once warned one of the young men on the *Tribune* editorial staff against attempting to predict what was about to take place. "It is quite enough," he said, " to tell what has already happened without trying to do any more."

Though his will was absolute in the management of the *Tribune*, Mr. Greeley did not care to direct every feature of its policy, but allowed his lieutenants liberty to decide many things without consulting him. When the *Tribune* was once committed to a line of action, in his absence or otherwise, he simply followed suit and adopted its tone in writing on the same subject, unless it should happen to be a matter of great moment, on which he held entirely opposite views. Sometimes, when a controversy had been begun in this way, he would say to his second in command, "This is your fight, and you must take care of it yourself."

Mr. Greeley always catered to the good taste of his readers by printing specimens of the best literature of the day. In a speech at the press dinner given in New York to Dickens, he mentioned the fact that in the first number of the first periodical with which his name was connected, appeared one of the earliest "Sketches by Boz." In the early numbers of the *Tribune*, specimens of the writings of Emerson, Carlyle, Fourier, and other thinkers of the time, were also printed; and the same appreciation of what is best in literature, science and art has ever since been exhibited in the *Tribune*.

As a means to form an estimate of the value of Mr. Greeley's labor as a journalist, we quote the following judgments by some of the most discriminating of his cotemporaries:

Mr. I. B. Chamberlain, of the *World*, a political opponent, yet personal friend, says: "Mr. Greeley's remarkable power, when traced back to its main source, will be found to have consisted chiefly in that vigorous earnestness of belief which held him to the strenuous advocacy of measures which he thought conducive to the public welfare, whether they were temporarily popular or not. Journalism may perhaps gain more success as a mercantile speculation by other methods; but it can be respected as a great moral and political force only in the hands of men who have the talents, foresight, and moral earnestness which fit them to guide public opinion. It is in this sense that Mr. Greeley was our first journalist, and nobody can successfully dispute his rank * * * Journalism, as he looked upon it, was not an end, but a means to higher ends. He may have had many mistaken, and some erratic opinions, on particular subjects; but the moral earnestness with which he pursued his vocation, and his constant subordination of private interests to public objects, nobly atone for his occasional errors. He has been an alert observer for forty years, and whatever may be thought of his powers of logic and coordination, he has few equals, and no superiors, in divining the drift of public sentiment."

Frank B. Sanborn wrote of Mr. Greeley that: "As a journalist he was prodigious. None but journalists know exactly how surprising his powers and performance were, but the great fact of the *Tribune* is satisfactory evidence to the world that he was no common man. His weaknesses were very palpable ones, and it suited the purpose of his opponents always to magnify them; but he had many great qualities—among which must be reckoned a masterly style of writing. The puny, piddling critics who pitch upon his abusive epithets, his occasional vagaries of thought and expression, and speak of these as the chief traits of his style, only display their own narrowness and malice. He wrote English as effectively as Cobbett or Franklin,—not so elegantly as the latter, but still with a fine sensibility to that which is permanent in a style. Like Abraham Lincoln, whom he greatly resembled in many of his qualities, he had condensed and purified and strengthened his mode of expression until in its latest and best examples it was almost perfect. His newspaper was like and unlike himself. It grew out of his central and permanent purpose to leave the world better than he found it; it represented his aspirations and ideas, and the admiration he felt for men and methods that he did not fully comprehend; and so it often seemed on a higher level than the editor himself occupied. But, again, it shared all his jealousies, and crudities, and spites, and cutaneous eruptions of meanness and ill-temper; it was wise and unwise, lofty and creeping, humble and conceited, right and wrong, at the same moment and in every number. Above all things, he adhered to the political party in which he found himself, and could hardly look at facts or opinions, save through the party medium.

Mr. Frederic Hudson says he used to ride home quite often in the cars with Mr. Greeley after their respective papers had gone to press, and had many talks with him about newspapers. The impression he gained was that if

Mr. Greeley would devote himself to the *Tribune* alone, and ignore politics and farming, he would be one of the greatest journalists.

John Russel Young, who had abundant opportunities for learning the character of his former editorial chief, credits him with large benevolence for classes and ideas; good judgment in advising as to the business management of a newspaper; (and this opinion is confirmed by other authorities) kind in his personal dealings, yet a strict disciplinarian. He says Mr. Greeley would have been the greatest journalist in the world if he had not a mind to be a leading politician. He raised his courage, independence and application, and says that no editor so thoroughly separated the animosities of his paper from his personal animosities.

Charles A. Dana has given the annexed estimate of Mr. Greeley: "Those who have examined the history of this remarkable man, and who know how to estimate the friendlessness, the disabilities, and the disadvantages which surrounded his childhood and youth; the scanty opportunities, or rather the absence of all opportunity, of education; the destitution and loneliness amid which he struggled for the possession of knowledge; and the unflinching zeal and pertinacity with which he provided for himself the materials for intellectual growth, will heartily echo the popular judgment that he was indeed a man of genius, marked out from his cradle to inspire, animate, and instruct others. From the first, when a child in his father's log cabin, lying upon the hearth, that he might read by the flickering fire-light, his attention was given almost exclusively to public and political affairs. This determined his vocation as a journalist; and he seems never to have felt any attraction towards any other of the intellectual professions. He never had a thought of being a physician, a clergyman, an engineer, or a lawyer. Private questions, individual controversies, had little concern for him except as they were connected with public interests. Politics and newspapers were his delight, and he learned to be a printer in order that he might become a newspaper maker. And after he was the editor of a newspaper, what chiefly engaged him was the discussion of political and social questions. His whole greatness as a journalist was in this sphere. For the collection and digestion of news, with the exception of election statistics, he had no great fondness and no special ability. He valued talent in that department only because he knew it was essential to the success of the newspaper he loved. His own thoughts were always elsewhere."

"Accordingly there have been journalists who, as such, strictly speaking, have surpassed him. Minds not devoted to particular doctrines, not absorbed in the advocacy of cherished ideas—in a word, minds that believe little and aim only at the passing success of a day—may easily excel one like him in the preparation of a mere newspaper. Mr. Greeley was the antipodes of all such persons. He was always absolutely in earnest. His convictions were intense; he had the peculiar courage, most precious in a great man, which enables him to adhere to his own line of action, despite the excited appeals of friends and the menaces of variable public opinion; and his constant purpose was to assert his principles, to fight for them, and present them to the public in the way most likely to give them the same hold upon other minds which they had upon his own."

Mr. George Ripley, whose long association with the *Tribune* entitles his judgment of Mr. Greeley to great weight, has made the following admirable estimate of the latter's capacity and performance as a journalist:

"Mr. Greeley had remarkable qualifications for the profession which he adopted. A quick perception of the significance of events, a keen scent for intelligence, an accurate judgment of the mutual relations of occurrences, a ready appreciation of the drift of popular currents, and a sympathetic comprehension of the public temper of the hour, were among the gifts and acquirements which he brought to his task. His fund of information was vast and varied. His memory was a marvel. His ingenuity in argument and illustration was inexhaustible. A clear, direct, forcible style, of almost painful conciseness, but illuminated at times by flashes of wit, by touches of tenderness, and by the happiest of homely metaphors, set forth his clear and earnest thought; while a singularly magnetic temperament infused a great deal of his own fervor into the men who worked with him. Thus equipped, Horace Greeley could hardly fail to make a great newspaper; but he did not make it to sell. The *Tribune* never was a commercial speculation; and if it prospered under his management, and grew to be a far grander and richer thing than in his early days he had dreamed of making it, this was not because he ever sacrificed the utterance of a single conviction for the sake of pecuniary profit, but because truth will force its way, and honesty in the long run will compel the respect of mankind.

"The success of Horace Greeley is the best encouragement for the journalism of the future. It teaches our profession that a nobler career is open to us than that of the thoughtless gatherer of news and gossip, or the huckster of literature who deals in anything that people want to buy, and the blackguard whose abusive tongue wags at the command of whoever will pay for its service. 'He who by voice or pen,' said Mr. Greeley, 'strikes his best blow at the impostures and vices whereby our race is debased and paralyzed, may close his eyes in death, consoled and cheered by the reflection that he has done what he could for the emancipation and elevation of his kind.' But this shall not be his only recompense. The story of Horace Greeley teaches us that it is the journalist of strong convictions, unselfish purposes, and unflinching courage, who wins at the last the honors and prizes of his calling, the respect of his fellow laborers, and the affection of his countrymen.

"He was a journalist to whom intrigue and management were utterly unknown; and well will it be for the *Tribune*, and for all other newspapers, if his example shall be followed and his singleness of purpose scrupulously imitated.

"The *New-Yorker* shows the fastidious accuracy of Mr. Greeley's literary judgment. Almost all the selections are from first-rate sources, and are worthy of their respectable origin. This critical skill Mr. Greeley never lost. If he found a young man writing well in the *Tribune*, he usually took occasion to let that writer know his opinion of him; if he found a man, young or old, writing badly, he had a very decisive way of hinting either at reformation or resignation. He knew good work when he saw it; he was what some editors are not—a careful reader of his own newspaper; and if he discovered in it clumsiness, negligence, bad taste or inaccuracy, the offender might depend upon being brought to account. So, his staff of writers knew what to expect in those days when he was almost always at the office; and this knowledge restrained the ambitious, chastened the imaginative, incited the indolent and warned the careless. Men who were quite his equals, and perhaps his superiors in mere scholarship, recognized the accuracy of his judgment, and were sure that if they pleased him they would not displease that great *Tribune* constituency which he understood so well.

"As a writer of pure, simple, and direct English, Mr. Greeley is entitled to a high rank. His knowledge of the laws of the language was excellent, and in all the haste and heat of newspaper composition he rarely violated them. Generally, his leading articles were models of their kind. They were arranged with a sort of mathematical precision, and both in their facts and their argumentation they were apt to be troublesome to his antagonists. If the subject were one which excited the writer so that he became thoroughly earnest, his fine powers of sarcasm, of irony, and sometimes of wholesome vituperation, were exhibited at their best. There is an account of his trial for libel upon Mr. Fenimore Cooper, originally printed in the *Tribune*, and reprinted in Mr. Parton's 'Life,' which, in its wit, humor and incisive irony, has hardly been surpassed by any English writer. In some respects Mr. Greeley reminds us of Cobbett, but with all the vigor and directness of that celebrated journalist, he had none of the coarseness which continually disfigures the pages of 'Peter Porcupine.' Of the work of his profession he never had enough. When he was at the height of his health and strength there seemed no limit to his powers of application and endurance. For one who wrote so rapidly, he was singularly accurate, and even as a work of reference, his 'History of the Rebellion' has great value now, and will be still more valuable as time goes by. In certain parts, his 'Recollections of a Busy Life' seems to us one of the most charming of autobiographies, charming as books of that kind almost always are. It is full of graceful narrative, engaging confidences, and reminiscences of men and things which interest everybody.

"The model newspaper, in his view, was not merely the

organ of pet theories, but an instrument of practical good, teaching the ignorant, leading the blind, succoring the poor, fighting for the oppressed, developing national wealth, stimulating industry, and inculcating virtue. To make the *Tribune* this, he put away from him all thirst for renown, all appetite for wealth, all desire for personal advantage. He never counted the cost of his words. He never inquired what course would pay or what would please his subscribers. He held in magnificent disdain the meaner sort of editor 'who sidles dexterously between somewhere and nowhere,' accumulates riches by the daily utterance of silken sayings, and goes to his rest at last 'with the non-achievements of his life blazoned on the whitest marble.' The journalist who strives only to print what will sell, seemed to him as bad as the parson who preaches only to fill his pews. Mr. Greeley never hesitated to go counter to a base and selfish public sentiment. Those who have watched his career will recall scores of instances in which he has deliberately offended political friends and sacrificed pecuniary interests to espouse an unpopular cause. In defending what he believed to be the right, his courage was magnificent. He was deaf to popular clamor, insensible to the jangling of the dollars. The stern and thorny path by which an editor must climb to greatness demanded, according to him, 'an ear ever open to the plaints of the wronged and suffering, though they can never repay advocacy, and those who mainly support newspapers will be annoyed and often exposed by it.'

"All who have been other than careless readers of the *Tribune* know that, in the conduct of this newspaper, he never suffered himself to be betrayed by any considerations of party expediency into any politic sophistications of the truth. He was quite as sharp a censor of those with whom he was allied as of those to whom he was usually opposed. He was never for a moment blind to the mistakes and misdeeds of those with whom he was politically associated. As he was in the beginning so he continued to the end, for accusations of inconsistency did not in the least frighten him from unremittingly saying that which he believed to be true. How little he was merely a party man is evident from the fact that scores of public characters who were nominally with him were constantly and noisily accusing him of treason, and were just as constantly laughed at for their pains. No member of the party was so often read out of it, no newspapers jibed and snarled so bitterly at the *Tribune* as those which called themselves Republican. When poor, struggling, and almost without any save political friends, he said in the advertisement of the first number of this journal that he should give to the Whig Administration 'a frank and cordial, but manly and independent support, judging it always by its acts, and commending those only so far as they shall seem calculated to subserve the great end of all government—the welfare of the People.'

* * * * We ask of thousands upon thousands, still living, who for more than a quarter of a century have been daily observers of the *Tribune*, if, under the immediate direction or under the inspiration of Mr. Greeley, it has ever, making due allowance for human infirmity, fallen below the standard which from the first he determined upon. It was a Whig journal, but was it ever the unquestioning slave of the Whig party or of the Whig leaders? It was a Republican journal, but did it ever seek to hide the faults or to extenuate the errors of the Republican leaders? When was it the custom of Mr. Greeley to take measures upon trust? When did he fear, while favoring the candidates of a Convention, to cast contempt upon so much of its platform as failed to commend itself to his head or to his heart? • So well was this understood in all political circles, that his support of any party measure years ago ceased to be counted on as a matter of course, so that when he did heartily acquiesce in any policy, his countenance had a value indeed!"

R. R. BOWKER.

(RECENTLY LITERARY EDITOR OF THE "MAIL.")

Mr. R. R. Bowker, though one of the junior journalists of New York, has had a valuable experience in certain fields, especially college and evening journalism, and the department of literary criticism. He became associated with Charles S. Sweetser in the early days of the New York *Evening Mail*, and remained with that paper nearly seven years, under both administrations. His statements relating to certain matters within his experience, especially the training of journalistic students, will therefore be found worthy of attention.

Question.—What do you believe is the true education for the journalist?

Answer.—There are two kinds of education for the journalist: the practical training of the composing-room and Knock-about College, and the development that comes of a regular college course, or its equivalent. The first gives him "the knack," and fits him capitally for routine editorial work, especially in news editing. Some of the best men in this field have come direct from the case. The composing-room abounds in common sense, and produces capital criticism of the editorial room. But the man who is to help conduct, to have a share in moulding public opinion through a great paper, needs the best and broadest education he can get. He needs the world's experience as well as experience of the world, and to assimilate that means study. After all, your self-made man is a great deal more conceited than a college graduate of any common sense, for it puts modesty into a man to find that his new ideas, and half the new ideas of his day, were old two thousand years ago, as Plato will tell him, and to learn how much he can't learn. Journalism needs this wide view. There isn't any danger, on the other side, of a journalist forgetting that he lives in his own times. The college-educated man is the more pliable of the two, and you can better add the practical education to that of the college than expect a self-made man to stop midway and get rid of his narrowness by study. The Harpers' is the best organized publishing house in the country, and they work on this idea. The younger members of the family are first sent to college; they then go straight to case, and must work their way up through the technicalities.

Q. How about college journalism?

A. College journalism, as a practical school for the profession, should not be overlooked. On these little papers each man has a chance to do everything, or to see everything done, and he gets his intellectual development and his technical training side by side. During Junior year at college I started the *Collegian,* an eight-page fortnightly, and the few months' work there, with nobody else to edit, publish, report, read proof, make up, and what not, gave me a year or two's advantage in journalism. For I found, when I was given the chance, the day after Commencement, to try the city editorship of the *Mail,* that I knew a good many simple things older editors, who hadn't been through the composing-room, had never learned, and this gave me some degree of usefulness at once.

Q. Do you believe in "professional training" for editors?

A. Yes and no! Not very much in "schools of journalism," because journalism isn't a specialty of knowledge. It hasn't, and can't have, a literature of its own, like law, theology or medicine; nor can its training be compared with that of the school of science. The college itself is the school of journalism, for the breadth of its *curriculum*, and that alone, corresponds to the breadth of training, principle and information a journalist requires. If he can spare the time, the course of a law school is very useful to him, especially if it be supplemented with special study of history, political and statistical geography, social science and economics, and this is as near a special school, perhaps, as you can wisely come. Major Bundy, after he graduated from Beloit, went through Harvard law school, and afterwards read a year or so in his father's library on constitutional and economic subjects, and this splendid start enabled him to write the newspaper letters that saved Wisconsin from setting the precedent of an attempt at secession in the North, and, when now he does put forth his strength, to print some of the most vital and telling leaders in current journalism, as in the reform campaign of '71.

Q. Tell me about the system of training you put in practice?

A. It seems that when a man gets on the first round up of the professional ladder he ought to set about helping somebody else up. Besides, a man should be working, as far as possible, at the best class of work he knows how to do. It is bad organization and waste of force to let a $50 man, for instance, do any part of the work a $20 man can do about as well. So I thought, after I got to be literary editor of the *Mail*, and had a good deal else inside and outside on my hands, that I could do more for the paper, help train another man, and do better for myself, by paying a personal assistant, who should answer letters, keep accounts, and do minor and routine work at the start and gradually get into higher and higher journalistic work. One of the brightest men of our college, two classes after mine, was glad to come at a salary sufficient to live on and which should be raised a dollar a week every three months if he did well—a rising scale since adhered to. The plan was that he should stay a year or two, and by that time we hoped he would be trained to take a regular position, wherever it might offer, and make room for a new "student in journalism." You know how well McAdam turned out; he became while there literary editor of the *Christian Leader*, and left to become its chief, and he made an admirable paper until it was sold away from him to proprietors out of the city. Two such have so far served what may almost be called regular apprenticeships in journalism, and have become practiced journalists, and others have had some little training; at one time, indeed, I found it paid to employ a phonographer also. A small office is the best place for such apprenticeship, and the editorial staff of the *Mail*, under both administrations, had been on such thoroughly good terms with each other, and with our chief, that every one was willing to give the new comer every chance. His desk was right alongside of mine, so that I could turn at any moment to make suggestions or point out anything of journalistic significance that came up in the course of my own day's work, and could revise with him anything that he did. At the very first he was taken over the composing room, and made acquainted, as far as possible, with its details, and those of the press-room, and the methods of collecting news, the divisions of editorial work, and to some extent the methods of the publication office were directly explained. When one of the staff was temporarily away, he took his place under supervision, so that he became a "floating editor," much to every one's convenience, and by summer he could be relied upon to supply the several desks during vacations. Thus he got a practical knowledge of each department, the exchanges, news, editing, etc., besides the work immediately connected with our room, and was of real service to the paper, though he cost it nothing. As soon as possible, I set apart a minor department which should practically be his and of which he might get the credit, although of course having to look over the work, as the person responsible to the *Mail* for it. Altogether the plan worked excellently—to the equal satisfaction of both.

Q. But don't you think a large office possesses many advantages for training?

A. Certainly! many positive advantages, and the small office has many defects. The evening newspaper would be the better for more organization than it is apt to have, but it does not require the thoroughness in that way which is a necessity to the "great daily." You could scarcely change a man around on a morning journal as you can on the small evening paper. But it would train him to thoroughness in any one line of work,—a most important lesson,—while the latter gives him adaptability and quickness. Versatility, without training in thoroughness, is apt to betray a man into poor work. The well-trained journalist needs both experiences—perhaps the evening paper first, as the morning journalist is apt to get into ruts. Morning journalists, when they come on an evening paper, are apt to seem slow, for, remember, the body of the work on an evening paper must be done, to keep it fresh, within about four hours— 8.30 to 12.30—while the morning journalist has from afternoon to midnight. And the "beats," in mere news, are now confined chiefly to evening paper rivalry,—and these are themselves an education in quickness. Once, under favorable circumstances, the newsboys had the *Mail* on the street in nine minutes, if memory serves me, from the time the boy appeared at the editorial rooms with the news.

Q. What is the scope of afternoon journalism, according to your ideas?

A. Afternoon journalism has not had its fair share of the development of the last few years. For one thing, it doesn't often pay the salaries to get and keep the best men in staff positions. Most of the evening papers, it is true, can't afford it, but some of them might have two or three times their present circulation if well pushed,—with sufficient money spent editorially,—and, therefore, two or three times their present advertising rates and income. Advertising is of two kinds, that which the reader seeks and that which seeks the reader. The one paper in a place, as the *Herald* in New York and the *Eagle* in Brooklyn, that holds the first kind, just because it " has always had it," is a gold mine. That doesn't depend on circulation, and no amount of enterprise can get it away. Mrs. Smith, who keeps boarders, or Bridget O'Flaherty, who wants a place, pays forty cents a line, not because 70,000 people take the *Herald*, but because the few who want such rooms, or such service, go out and buy it. In the other kind of advertising, which commonly pays one half to one cent a line per thousand circulation, the evening paper has the advantage; it is read at home and at leisure, and being usually smaller, the " ad." has more relative prominence. There is nothing in the nature of things why the respectable evening dailies should be so very far behind the circulation of the morning ones; but the publishers don't seem to have learned how to spend money as well as where to save it—the great point of business success in journalism. The *Graphic* has shown most enterprise in pushing its circulation, and is seen everywhere, although it costs more than the "blanket sheets."

There are some fields in which the evening paper promises to be the journal of the future. But to hold these, it can't essay too much. For a long time to come, and perhaps always, the morning paper must be the only one to attempt completeness. Journalism is just now confronting the same difficulty the colleges are perplexed with—the new fields and the enormous increase of news in the one case and knowledge in the other. The solution is to be found only in the most thorough organization and the most careful observance of "perspective,"—relative importance. There isn't a more absurd superstition in journalism that the habit of the evening papers of re-dishing the morning paper news and giving it not so well—so as to make the "history of a day" complete. "Do you know if you read this," says Ruskin, " you cannot read that "—and none of us have time for news that isn't news. The morning paper posts us as to what we ought to know to keep ourselves in line with the world, as we go to work in the morning; its business is to be approximately complete. The afternoon journal is a going-home paper, is read at home, and should be a rest and recreation after the day's hard work. It needs a peculiar quality of its own; not less earnest, purposeful, true to the high calling of journalism, than the " great dailies ;" it should have especial snap and sparkle, like a bright woman's talk—and, by the way, it is strange there are not more women editors on the afternoon dailies. E. E. Hale would be a man to make an evening paper. The early *Mail* had this brisk and piquant quality, and not much else—for it had no telegraphic facilities to speak of, and its early issues look most like a chatty "bill of the play." But this proved enough to make it a pecuniary success from the start, if the business weaknesses of the inventive temperament in its founder hadn't tied it all up. Chas. H. Sweetser was a remarkable journalistic inventor; he started six papers in four years, and all of them had ideas. Sometimes he would have the freak of giving the paper a different stamp every day; once, in the rage for itemizing, in '68, he told me to fill up the first page with items, and then, to "crowd the mourners," he put the whole four columns in nonpareil! Journalism seemed to be in the family blood. Henry E. Sweetser, who died soon after the sad and lonely death of his cousin, became famous as "the arithmetic man" of the *World*.

The evening paper has two great opportunities. On this continent it gets the day's news of Europe about noon, and the better part of the salient home news is fish for its net. Of the important news of the year, eight out of ten plums, nowadays, fall to the afternoon journal. And it should seize its second opportunity to become the critical journal. People want to read criticism at leisure, that is, after work, and moreover criticism is the one thing on the evening paper that can be written at leisure. The musical or dramatic critic of the afternoon paper can take his night's rest, and be fresh for leisurely work in the morning. It is absolutely surpriing how such strong and artistically finished work as Hassard's in music, and Winter's in drama, on the *Tribune*, can be dashed off in the midnighth our left to the morning critic; and these men, on an evening paper, would have far better opportunities and more receptive readers. The last is true also of art and literary criticism.

Q. What are your ideas about the latter?

A. In ideal journalism, the literary editor should be a sort of managing editor in his department—calling on the best outside scholars in each division of knowledge to review the important books. But this is not only costly, but has many drawbacks; you can't get promptness, which is important here as everywhere, and you may get too special a view of the book for the public at large. So if a literary critic is catholic, conscientious and modest, having a wide range of culture and knowledge of books, knowing his own limitations and regarding them, filling out his own knowledge as regards a work under review from other books and other men, he may safely depend upon himself for most of his book-noticing. He has also a certain advantage in being himself a representative of the general public, and prophesying its own view. The literary department of the *Tribune* has been a " one-man-power "—and the greatest power in the country—though Dr. Ripley is an encyclopedist and excep-ceptional. The leading literary papers receive nearly a thousand books a year; some of these demand a careful study for days, to others a practical worker can give all the notice that is desirable after five minutes at title-page and preface; others it is waste to speak of at all. As regards the two divisions of criticism, the appreciative or "Mr. Gently" school—as Mr. Curtis happily named it from its present head, Dr. Ripley—and what may be called the incisive or "Mr. Snarley" school, it would seem that the first is most just, and can do most good. To tell what is in a book is the first step toward telling what kind of a book it is, and after you have given the good points, if it is mainly a good book, then is the time to point out its faults. That is more interesting to the public and more likely to do good to the author. The other school seeks faults first, as the staple diet of criticism. The *Nation* heads this class, and perhaps exerts less influence than its ability earns, because it is so distinctively critical and ignores the fact that the best way to get rid of evil is to encourage good. The chief current criticism upon the *Tribune* is that its editorial page lacks something of the virile positiveness that made Mr. Greeley, right or wrong, so tremendous a power; but then, in these *ad interim* sort of times, perhaps we must tear down before we can build up. But contrast the literature and criticism of New York in Poe's day and Dr. Ripley's, and the facts tell their own story. Of course criticism hasn't made all the difference, but it has done a great deal.

Q. How about new papers in New York?

A. There is always room for new papers—as has been often said of new men—in a great city, if they can do something of importance that needs to be done, sufficiently better than others are already doing it. But this means a great deal. Not only must there be brains, and the money and skill to buy brains, but any quantity more money to give the new paper time to prove its right to live. And this means scarcely less than half a million capital for a new morning, and a hundred thousand for an evening daily. The best paper can't gain a constituency in a day—or a month. It is admitted that the *Times* lost money till its fourth year. Moreover, nobody should attempt a new daily without throwing away the first issue. In every one of the twenty false starts within ten years, the first number was behind time and crude, and a blow in the face of success. That ought to have been edited and printed—and then thrown in the waste-basket, as a proof-sheet, without the public's catching sight of it. The machinery having thus been started, No. 2 could safely make the bow to the public. The growth of the opposition telegraphic network, and the promise of the American Press Association are a great help to new papers.

Q. Do you think journalism as promising in the future it holds out to young men as law?

A. Scarcely in money, unless the great dailies, by combining to gather the body of their news reports as they now combine to get most of the telegraphic and some of the city work, can save money in one place to spend it on editorial salaries. It pays more at the start, but seems to average less. Adam Smith's law, that equal talent must be equally rewarded in whatever calling, nevertheless holds good. The money salary is less, and the supply great, because the glamour about journalism makes a host of people willing to take the " honor " or " privileges " of journalism, or more nobly, its great influence, as part of the wages. And as to one who wants to do real good in the world, and can reach a responsible post in journalism, his influence is vastly broader and greater than that of his peer in the law. Of course, there is "always room at the top." If a man can make himself " necessary " to a successful paper, he may win a share in its proprietorship, and thus make money, or he may save money in his early years and wait his chance to buy in. But a man soon begins to doubt whether any one person is necessary in journalism, or anywhere else; no man was ever so identified with a paper as Horace Greeley with the *Tribune,* and it has been proved that even he was not necessary to it. A newspaper is, of course, a "grinding corporation," yet most journalists who try to do good work and refuse to lift a finger for notoriety are apt to win all the reputation they earn, and no more is good for them. How few men in any profession are really known!

Q. What of the future of journalism in general?

A. Ah, he would be bold who should attempt answer to that. Progress nowadays distances Prophecy. The burlesque extravagance of the writer in *Harper's Monthly*, who prophesied that the newspaper of A. D. 2000 would be a continuous sheet printed in each of our homes before our eyes, is already made fact in the paper ribbon of the gold and stock quotation company. What with such improvements in telegraphy as Mr. Gray's method of transmission by musical vibrations, now being adopted by the Western Union, there seem no physical obstacles in the way of a reporter sitting before a speaker in New York and himself telegraphing the words into type in Chicago through the typesetting machine there—although this would need a phonetic alphabet, like that of Prof. Bell's "Visible Speech." Its intellectual development is as problematic, but we may be sure that the journal of the future will answer to the need of that better public of the future which present journalism is doing so much to train.

WILLIAM HYDE,

EDITOR OF THE "MISSOURI REPUBLICAN."

QUESTION.—Mr. Hyde, what is your journalistic record?

ANSWER.—I edited weekly papers in Belleville and Sterling, Illinois, from 1854 to 1857. Have been continuously employed on the *Missouri Republican* since January, 1857, as legislative reporter, local reporter, city editor, news editor, telegraph editor, political writer, &c.

Q. From your experience of nineteen years, do you regard editing as a science?

A. No; it cannot be learned from rules.

Q. What is your idea of editorial training and qualification?

A. I have little faith in a premeditated, or perhaps I should say, long-meditated espousal of journalism as a profession. I don't know a first-class editor who, in early youth, had any well-defined idea of being such. A good common school education, a fair familiarity with ancient and modern history, a knowledge of the fundamental principles of law and political economy, and the acquisition of a perspicuous, forcible and pleasant style, form the basis of the training necessary. To this add the natural qualities of quick, impartial, discriminating judgment, and an intuitive perception of the popular taste, together with the tact of ready and versatile application of resources, and you have the principal materials for the making of a successful editor. I will say that one of the best schools of journalism is at the printer's case. Though not a printer myself, I have found it highly advantageous to acquire a tolerably thorough acquaintance with every practical feature of that branch of labor. But, above every other qualification, is a characteristic known as the "nose for news," by which is meant unwearying alertness and insatiable hunger for something "ahead of the other papers."

Q. What are the best modes of enterprise, and how about the telegraph?

A. The best modes of exhibiting enterprise are in the judicious expenditure of money and employment of talent in the collection of important and interesting news. An illustration is at hand in a fresh number of the New York *Herald*. A dispatch of three lines stated that Brigham Young had resigned as trustee of the Mormon church, and was going to remove from Salt Lake to Arizona. The editor of the *Herald* forthwith dispatched Brigham, asking him to telegraph to that paper his reasons at length, and the next morning the *Herald* presented a very interesting and elaborate message on the subject, signed by the Mormon President in person, and one that everybody would read. This is the kind of enterprise that tells, and almost any editor knows scores of such instances.

A large corps of intelligent and ready writers, who can be relied on to report with promptness any scene of excitement or unusual interest, is a necessary adjunct of enterprise in the newspaper business. A great public event, which calls large masses of people together—a terrible calamity involving loss of life and property—any casualty of extraordinary proportions—affords a field for newspaper enterprise in the collection of all the facts and details of interest, and in the preparation of the same in a graphic and picturesque manner.

Q. What is the province of journalism?

A. To inform, to teach; to disseminate general knowledge; to liberalize human thought; to promote loyalty to law; to uproot radicalism and one-ideaism; to make the world conservative and pacific; to "render unto Cæsar the things that are Cæsar's;" to infuse the spirit of a practical common-sense morality for its uses to mankind on earth.

History, theology, science, the arts, are fields too extensive for the journalist, and the attempt to popularize abstruse subjects must always fail. Hence, there is no danger that newspapers will displace books and magazines. Authorship and journalism are essentially different in our day, and there is no probability they will ever assimilate. There is as much likelihood that the press will displace colleges as that it will do away with books and magazines.

Q. May I ask your views in reference to journalism, independent of party trammels?

A. There is a greater tendency towards independence now than at any previous period in its history. The examples set of late year by the New York *Tribune*, Cincinnati *Commercial*, Chicago *Tribune*, and some other Republican newspapers, together with that of leading papers on the Democratic side, has worked a considerable revolution in the press of America. It used to be that both Republican and Democratic journals prided themselves on being "organs," and even advertised themselves as such in their prospectuses; but organship is fast getting into disrepute, and we see a freer, bolder spirit. The ancient servility to party is confined chiefly to impecunious sheets "thinly" supported by ambitious politicians, or depending largely for sustenance upon sheriffs', executors' and other legal advertising, together with the jobwork dispensed by county officials. Journals like the leading ones of our principal cities rely for support upon their facilities for disseminating news, and upon the legitimate advertising patronage that is sure to follow the attainment of a large circulation. When once a paper reaches the point where people buy its edition for the information contained, its income will depend very little upon the editorial opinions it expresses, if they are given honestly and without the purpose to offend. Some editors have lately discovered this fact who have been long groping in ignorance of it.

Q. Is impersonality essential in a journal?

A. That is a difficult question to solve. If you had asked: Is impersonality necessary to the permanent success and character of a journal? I should say, *yes*. Few editors who are known to the people are not better known, that is, more favorably, than they deserve to be, on their merits. Not only does journalism not require brilliant geniuses, but brilliant geniuses about a newspaper office are generally very much of a nuisance. The business needs practical, thoughtful, active, plodding, enterprising men, and such men are rarely brilliant. Your poets and scholars, your profound philosophers, and men with great humanitarian schemes and missions, are unfit for editors. Their range of vision is too circumscribed. But a man who possesses the ability to manage a paper successfully, and who becomes famous as an editor, sails under false colors before the public, for the public give him credit for qualities he doesn't possess, and are ignorant of the very traits whereon his success is founded. The personality is, in some sense, therefore, a fraud. There is scarcly a day wherein I, for instance, do not among those who know my position on the *Republican*, receive credit for originating articles contributed by Mr. Grissom, Mr. Dimmock, Mr. Garrett, Mr. Williams, Mr. Buell, or some other gentleman who habitually writes for our editorial columns, whereas in many cases my only share in the articles is the having approved them. This is true with all editors-in-chief or managing editors; so that where there is an announced or commonly known editor, he receives from the popular judgment either more than his due, or a meed different from his due. But there is another view of this question of personality in journalism. There are very few instances where the editor in charge of a first-class paper represents a full proprietary interest. It is the firm or the corporation who speak, and, therefore, it should be the care of all editorial writers to divest their articles of any features of self. The concern is far more powerful than can any member of it, or any representative be. It is not well to bias the mind of the reader by considerations merely personal to the editor, for the expressions of a newspaper must stand by what is said, and not upon the man who said or wrote them. Hence, introduction of the names of editors into their own columns, besides being in bad taste, and usually the offspring of egotism, is hurtful to the paper's influence. Scarcely so bad, and yet detrimental to the interests of the press, are the frequent reciprocal references we see in some journals, whose managers evidently belong to a "mutual admiration society," and who seem determined not to allow the fact to be forgotton that they are on terms of more than mere acquaintanceship with distinguished gentlemen of the profession.

Q. What sympathy have you with the "Bohemian" notion, that firmly established convictions are obstacles to perfect success in journalism?

A. None. No man is fit to lead in any walk of life whose conduct and. teachings are not governed by fixed principles. I know it is said only fools are consistent;

that times change, and men change with them; that circumstances alter cases, etc. But consistency is the mark of sincerity, and is a jewel whose pure ray shines amidst all changes. If the end sought is an honorable and just one, the means of attaining it vary, and arguments may shift, but the purpose will be seen through all, and, when reached, the track behind will not be crooked. Convictions are to the conscientious editor as the pilot's constant thought of his destination.

Q. Cheap or dear papers—which are we tending toward?

A. I see no signs that cheap papers—I mean one cent and two cent papers—will ever attain influence and power like their contemporaries, which, costing vastly more money, must be sold at a higher rate. The stingy, brittle, illegible little sheets hardly *profess* to reach the classes that control the avenues of popular thought and action. Their news is in a condensed and skeleton form; their editorials made up from the encyclopædias and patent office specifications, and their existence makes no appreciable ripple upon the course of events. On the other hand, the high-priced journals will be always looked to as the models and patterns of the newspaper press. So far as cost of production is concerned, they are far cheaper to the reader than the low-priced sheets, and the profit bears a ridiculously small proportion to the expenditure—much too small, indeed.

Q. Is the field of your circulation contracting or expanding, and do you trench on the local country press, or *vice versa?*

A. Instead of trenching on the local country press, or the local press upon us, I think our interests, properly viewed, are reciprocal and harmonious. The newspapers of Missouri and Illinois are conducted generally by an exceptionally talented and enterprising set of men. We derive great help from their labors in making up the *Republican*. In those rural districts where our paper has the largest circulation the local press is most flourishing. We make it a point to "club" with all country papers desiring it, and hence it is generally found that the country people take their local papers for country and neighborhood news and local politics, and some good metropolitan journal for general news, telegraphic dispatches, commercial matters, &c. There ought to be no rivalry between the city and country press.

Q. Do you class the new generation of journalists as better than the old, and if so, in what respect?

A. A great revolution has been wrought in journalism within the past ten or twelve years. I think the last war and its incidents aroused our newspapers to a degree of energy and enterprise unknown before. There was developed by that conflict a wonderful greed for news, and the circulation of such papers as kept pace with the times grew immensely. With prosperity came improvement, and the vigor that was then infused into the business has vastly increased. The scope of editorial labors has been largely broadened, until now the character, ability and excellence of American newspapers are admitted everywhere. It cannot perhaps be said that the old generation of journalists were not as good as the present with respect to capacity; but they were never under such pressure as there is now. And look where you will, the brunt of editorial work is done by young men; indeed only young men could stand up under such tests of physical endurance as the business now exacts.

Q. Do the New York papers still take the lead as organs of opinion?

A. We, in this part of the country, are almost wholly indifferent as to the editorial opinions of the New York press, and of course do not concede leadership to that quarter. In my judgment (stated modestly, I hope), there is not a newspaper in New York that shows more ability in its editorial colums than any of our first-class Western journals of Chicago, Cincinnati or St. Louis. The centre of political influence is being transferred to the West, and it will not be many years before the whole country will acknowledge leadership in journalism to one of the three cities just mentioned.

Q. How should a paper be managed? Do you believe in the one-man power plan?

A. The direction of a newspaper should be lodged in the hands of one man only, full and complete authority being given him over all the leading departments, he to be answerable by discharge or otherwise to the proprietors. There must be a homogenity about the editorial departments. The editor should, of course, consult the proprietors or stockholders, and be governed by the controlling voice as to the general policy, but the details should be left entirely to him as long as he holds the position. Mr. Lincoln used to say that one bad general was better than two good ones, if the two were at cross purposes; and the remark will apply to editors.

Q. Shall we ever have another great national journal like the *Weekly Tribune*?

A. I hope not. I never regarded the *Tribune* as a national newspaper. Most of the time I have been reading it it has seemed to be more sectional than otherwise. Its late course—I mean its course since the war—has been pacific, conservative, and highly commendable; but not more so, and not more deserving a national reputation, than that of half a dozen others I might name.

Q. Is a school of journalism possible?

A. For any practical good, no.

THEODORE TILTON.

LATE EDITOR OF THE "GOLDEN AGE."

THEODORE TILTON thinks that the path of success for a young journalist lies in "sticking to his profession, working like a beaver, believing all he says, and keeping out of the legislature and other temptations." At another time he told the writer that the first essential of an editor is an intuitive perception of what is interesting. Again, in an obituary sketch of Dr. Josiah Leavitt, in referring to the latter's qualifications for editorial work, he said: "To be a journalist, a man must be more versatile and magnetic. He must be both a Bohemian and a statesman."

Mr. Tilton's position as a journalist is rather an anomalous one, and resembles that held by Horace Greeley. He has no affinity with the type of editor to which Bennett, Raymond, Dana and Marble belong, whose aim is first to give the news about current events, and who make a secondary thing of discussion. Mr. Tilton, like Mr. Greeley, is purely a didactic teacher, who is indifferent to the mere gathering and presentation of facts, and cares only for the combating of wrong, whether in institutions or opinions, and the diffusion of what he deems right principles in politics, religion, and in other fields of investigation. He therefore places more value on convictions than on knowledge, and cares nothing about newspaper editing as ordinarily conducted. In his view, all the great questions of the day should be treated by journalists. The anti-slavery question was the great topic when he began to write for the press, and in his opinion it has now been replaced by the woman question, which, with labor reform, education, and like subjects, he believes are absorbing equal interest with politics in the public mind, and he has therefore given them the largest share of his attention.

Theodore Tilton says the journalist is like a musician, or artist. His first duty is to master the technical part of his profession—or, as Bulwer recommended to a young painter, to practice brush-work without stint. Having mastered the general principles of writing, and gained some experience in newspaper editing, the journalist can make up his mind what branch of his profession he will devote himself to; and as an artist selects landscape or portrait painting, or the musician religious, sentimental or classical music for his specialty, so the journalist will confine himself to political writing, literary or dramatic criticism, correspondence, or some other branch of his profession.

The effect of the growth of the American press, in Mr. Tilton's opinion, has been to enlarge the field of criticism and improve its quality. Private judgment has been strengthened by the merciless sifting of everything, and the truth is now oftener got at than formerly. There is less of *ex cathedra* statements in print and speech, while both writers and orators are more guarded in their utterance.

The following extracts from an article in the *Golden Age* contain Mr. Tilton's latest views on his calling:

"We know what journalism was—a puny, inefficient, scant chronicler of events which were too great for its grasp. We know what journalism is—an immense power that threatens to supersede sermons, lectures, books; and aims to give an epitome of the world's progress. But the journalism of the future is the only journalism that we contemplate with unalloyed satisfaction.

"The journalism of the past (shall we call it the iron age of newspaperdom?) certainly had its advantages over the journalism of the present, which we will venture to call the age of brass; and Mr. Froude, if he had looked for easy illustrations of his main position, might have detailed them with telling effect. The journalism of the past was not a waste-basket or a rag-bag; it was not a bundle of hay with a needle in it; it was not a cosmogony or treatise on the universe and incidentals. It was not characterized by that vast 'enterprise' that maintains a staff of foreign correspondents in the back office; that 'interprets' news when there is any, and fabricates news when there is none; that has its spies in every corner. If its motive was more lenient towards private infirmities, and more considerate of private delicacies than the present heroic standard of morals requires; if it shrunk prudishly from withdrawing the veil from the secrecies, then fondly deemed sacred, of domestic life, and timidly avoided the now-applauded custom of butchering men and women for the entertainment of the populace; these defects, happily supplied to-day, were due to its want of power. It may be pleaded in mitigation of them that it occasionally eulogized virtue and sacrificed vice whenever it discovered them in their usual garb. The journalism of the past was certainly deficient in many cardinal respects. It had no 'interviewers,' no reporters who graduated the length and quality of their reports according to the price which the lecturer or preacher paid the scribe; no scandal-mongers; no purveyors to those natural appetites for the horrible or the obscene, which are so strong in the vulgar crowd, and which, being natural, should be fed. But there is an advantage in having some things—a good many things—left to the imagination. There are questions that should not be prematurely asked, and other questions that should not be prematurely answered. The claim to omniscience is a positive one; and the claim to sanctity is not without its objections. There are some things it is not important to know; and it is a fair question whether in saying too little the journalism of the iron age did not commit a more venial fault than the journalism of the brazen age does in saying too much.

"Better than either is it to say on important matters what is true—be it much or little—to say nothing what is not *felt* to be true; nothing in passion, nothing from prejudice, nothing for effect; to search and sift till the nearest possible approach to the truth is reached; to search and sift everything till the heart of truth or error in it, the soul of good or evil in it, is found.

"Journalism once told little or nothing. Journalism now tells all there is, and a good deal beside. The journalism of the past contained old things. The journalism of the present contains new things. The journalism of the future will contain true things. True things are hard to come at, but a disposition to find true things is unfortunately harder. But if there is to be a golden age of improvement for journalism, this disposition, and this alone, will discover it.

"The press is forfeiting its influence by its falsity. At bottom, men and women love the truth. And if they have no intellectual instinct to tell them what is truth, they have a moral instinct that tells them whether or no there is a purpose to give the truth. They cannot decide on what is true or otherwise in fact. They can decide on what is true or otherwise in feeling. They cannot detect ignorance. They can detect insincerity. **An insincere** press will be discredited. Even great ability will not sustain it long. The press, with half the wealth it now has, and twice the sincerity, would more than double its influence. We mean to add, if we can, something of this element as our contribution to the improved journalism of the future."

E. L. GODKIN,

EDITOR OF "THE NATION."

FUNCTIONS OF THE PRESS.—The principal functions of the press under a popular government are two in number—the supply of news and criticism of the government—not the " he-has-made-mistakes-as-who-has-not" style of criticism, but the incessant, vigilant, remorseless turning over, day by day, of the acts of men in power, with a view to calling the attention of the public to all sins of negligence, or ignorance, or intention, which anybody entrusted with authority may have committed or may be proposing to commit, and the commendation to the public favor of such measures, passed or suggested, as the editor may deem commendable. This is not altogether agreeable work, and it is work which may be made to cover a great deal of prejudice and passion and resulting injustice, but it is unavoidable work. It is one of the various imperfect instruments by which the affairs of men in this democratic age have to be conducted. Newspaper critics are often unfair, just as ministers are often dull, and treasurers dishonest, and judges corrupt, and as trains run off the track, and steamboats blow up. The check on their unfairness, and the only check, is the condition of public sentiment. As the readers are, so will the newspapers be. The defence of public men against carping critics, who never have any facts to support their judgments, and never have anything to propose in place of what they condemn, lies in the fact that the public speedily finds them out and will not buy their paper. In other words, groundless fault-finding in the long run does not pay, and ceases to injure the objects of it. So that, even where an irritable temper or personal griefs impel an editor to engage in it, he is generally conscious that, to insure success, there must be among the commodities he offers for sale, first and foremost, a tolerably sound judgment. His appreciations of men and affairs must be proved by events to have been on the whole reliable, and his charges must appear to have been supportable by facts, after making due allowance for the difficulty of getting at facts where one can neither send for persons nor papers. Of course, there are exceptions to these rules—anybody can cite half-a-dozen; there are newspapers which disregard them and yet thrive, just as there are defaulters who maintain their positions in society; but it is nevertheless true, taking the press as a whole, that a newspaper must be sincere and perspicacious to have influence, just as it is true that, taking society as a whole, honesty is the best policy.

How important this function of criticism is, is readily seen when we consider how completely the newspaper press has supplanted the other agencies by which public opinion was formerly moulded or directed.* * * Anybody who wants to address the public, in our time, has to get license from the editors, and there remains not an individual in the community powerful enough to set them at defiance.

Journalism is probably, to anybody who needs positive or palpable results, day by day, to keep his ardor alive, the most discouraging of professions; nothing but either strong faith or a great deal of self confidence is sufficient to satisfy a man that he is really doing more than increasing his list of subscribers.

A republic without a press is an impossibility, almost a contradiction in terms. The modern newspaper is the equivalent of the Greek agora, the only means possessed by the citizens of interchanging thought and concerting action, and Americans ought to be the last people in the world to talk of its uselessness. There is no country in which it is half so necessary. "The facts" are not always before the public, it is true, but principles are; the experience of past ages is; and whenever any government shows itself forgetful of these things, it is the duty of every editor, as at least representing his readers, to remind it of them.

JOURNALISTIC EDUCATION.—But the idea that a man needs to be specially prepared for it at college, we hold to be nearly as erroneous as the idea that he can be prepared for it in a newspaper office, though the first is a much more excusable error than the last, if, indeed, it needs any excuse at all. The purely mechanical work of a newspaper—the arrangement of the contents—is something for which, of course, more or less practice is necessary, but it is somethng to which the feeblest powers are equal. It bears about the same relation to the work of editing that battalion drill bears to strategy, and the proportion of really good editors it would produce to the number of those engaged in it, would be about that borne by great generals to drill-sergeants. Yet this is the only approach to special education that journalists need or can receive. Special education is required by men whose calling forces them to deal with a certain class of facts; a journalist's business is to reason on all the facts of life, of every class, or at least, if he does not reason on them all himself, to know whether other persons can reason on them or not. There is no recipe that will enable a man to do this. Good natural powers, strengthened by general cultivation, will, but nothing else. The more a man knows of everything, and the better he can make deductions from what he knows, the better journalist he will be, if he possesses also the art of expressing himself in a taking way, and possesses the orator's power of perceiving when he has said as much on any one theme as his audience will stand. The art of journalism lies in the expression; the science of it may be said to include all sciences, inasmuch as what it now undertakes to do is to help the public at large to think correctly on every subject of human interest. When we say this, we say enough to show the absurdity of establishing a special chair or opening a special class of journalism in colleges. As regards the expression or rhetoric of journalism, it is, or ought to be, taught to everybody. It is neither more nor less than the art of saying clearly and attractively whatever you have to say in as few words as possible—in other words, the art of being perspicuous and concise. There are certain rules which will help a man to do this, but they are taught in all the colleges. The teaching of them will enable anybody to speak and write better than he would without them, but can never teach a man to speak and write well in default of natural ability. In natural qualifications for journalism, as for other callings, men vary infinitely.

There are three fields of study, certainly, which are perhaps more likely to be useful to a journalist, as such, than to a man of other callings: history, legislative science—meaning by that the knowledge of the limits and powers of legislation—and political economy, or the knowledge of the working of the laws of human nature which regulate the production and distribution of wealth; but then these are fields which every man pretending to be educated ought to cultivate, no matter to what special pursuit he intends to devote himself. There is, however, nothing on which journals comment so much, or which they influence so much, as politics, and nobody can discuss politics properly who is not familiar with what has been done in that department of activity—who does not know what can be done in it, and what had better be let alone, and who does not passably understand the nature of the vast and complicated machinery of trade, now so large a part of the world's work. In short, no man can say he is qualified to be an editor, in default of actual trial of his powers, who has not received as good a general education as can be obtained. If, indeed, intellectual training be of any value whatever, it is of more value to the journalist than to men of any other calling, for various reasons. One is, that his work is one which is not, like the lawyer's, or doctor's, or scientific man's, submitted to any test by which its soundness or accuracy can be ascertained; his own judgment has, after all, in most cases to decide finally on the value of what he has done. "Sales" gauge the popular demand for his wares; but they tell nothing about the quality of his wares—the greatest ass often having the greatest number of readers. Another is, that his temptations to disregard intellectual standards and discard high ideals are greater than those of most men. He practises his profession in the marketplace, and is exposed alternately to the hootings or applause of a great and ill-informed multitude, and his judgment needs to be extraordinarily strong to resist influences of this nature. Lastly, deliberation and revision are almost completely forbidden to him by the very nature of his calling. Like the Irish witness who inadvertently swore the horse was fifteen feet high, and afterwards refused to substitute "hands" for "feet," whatever he has once said he has to stick to, and the importance to him, therefore, of saying the right thing the first time is enormous.

EDITORIAL PUFFS OF ADVERTISERS.—Referring to editorial puffs of financial or other advertisements, he asserts that newspaper editors can "maintain themselves free from taint solely by absolutely and entirely abstaining from all reference to any financial enterprise advertising in their columns. In no other way can any newspaper maintain its independence, its self-respect, its usefulness, and the confidence of its readers."

SELF-LAUDATION OF EDITORS.—The fact that the press shows so much of the commercial spirit has been often commented on by Mr. Godkin. "The editor," he says, is the only man who, pursuing an intellectual calling, looks for customers or hearers." A lawyer who offered a spring overcoat to anybody who paid him a retaining fee of one hundred dollars, or gave him that amount by way of professional remuneration, would lose caste, and the public would be rather shy of giving him their cases. A clergyman who announced that the deacons or vestrymen would present each taker of a pew in his church with a Dutch oven or a set of ladies' furs, would soon find his church empty. But an editor frequently professes to do the work of both a law-professor and clergyman; that is, expound the constitution, for instance, and save souls on the same page, and yet nothing is commoner than his offering goods of various kinds to persons who will listen to his teachings, or induce others to do so, and he does it with a perfectly imperturbable face, and with much puffing, both of his law and his gospel. * * * The press must, from its very nature, be more or less given to self-laudation, because it holds its own trumpet constantly in its hand, and it will probably never be in human nature to resist a temptation of this kind. If lawyers or doctors had the means constantly at their disposal of informing a great many thousand people, without expense to themselves, that their offices were amongst the few places in this world of sin and sorrow in which justice and health were to be found, we greatly fear we should hear of many more wonderful cures than we do, and the counsellor would have fewer laughs at the editor for his high appreciation of his own merits.

Mr. Godkin's ideas on editorial perspective have attracted much attention. They were originally set forth at length in a leading article in the *Nation*, the gist of which will be found in the following sentence: " An editor's duty is not only to lay the facts of the day before the public, but to indicate by the greater or less prominence he gives them the relations of each fact to other facts." * * * "The journalist's right to his title, then, depends altogether upon his sense of perspective. If he puts the unimportant news in the foreground and the important news out of sight, he has no right to exist."

One of the first duties of the press is not indeed to publish no false news—for this would be an impossibility —but to do its utmost to get accurate news, and, after it has got it, not to color it to suit the editorial taste or necessities. This again, when examined closely, is found to be simply a question of men. News is an impalpable thing—an airy abstraction. To make it a ponderable, merchantable commodity, somebody has to collect it, condense it, and clothe it in language; and its quality—indeed its whole value—depends upon the character of the men employed in doing this.

Nobody will assert that a newspaper should never assail a man's character. To lay down any such rule would be to deprive the press of three-fourths of its usefulness, and give a large body of knaves all but complete immunity. Nor should an editor be required to know personally the facts of every charge he makes. If every editor had to satisfy himself of the truth of everything he published, [newspapers would cease to appear. Nor is he bound to give the name of everybody who criticises the opinions or public career of public men. It makes no difference to anybody who writes the comments which appear in a newspaper on facts of general notoriety. But when an editor determines, for reasons of public policy, to denounce any man as a thief, or embezzler, or forger, or peculator, we believe the generally accepted and only sound rule is that he should be ready to produce the evidence of the truth of what he says, whenever called on by the accused person, before any tribunal whatever, libel suit or no libel suit.

MANTON MARBLE,

EDITOR OF THE "NEW YORK WORLD."

[From a published Lecture on Journalism.]

FUNCTION OF JOURNALISM.—As time flies, these historians of to-day become the best historians of the past. Said Bulwer :—" If I desired to leave to remote posterity some memorial of existing British civilization, I would prefer, not our docks, not our railways, not our public buildings, not even the palace in which we now hold our sittings,—I would prefer a file of the *Times* newspaper." Said Richard Cobden :—" Give me rather one daily *Times* than all Thucydides." These statements are rhetorical. We should claim for the journalist simply this :

1. That he is a merchant of news. He buys it everywhere—he sells it in any market not stocked with his commodity. Enterprise and industry get him, and other merchants, success and honor, and of like kind. Probity has the same reward in public confidence. Shrewd and far-sighted combinations bring to the merchant of news—or of flour, or of pork—profit and credit.

2. That the journalist has it in trust and stewardship to be the organ and mould of public opinion, to express and guide it, and to seek, through all conflicting private interests, solely the public general good. Herein his work is allied to the statesman's, the politician's, and takes rank as it takes tribute of letters, science and the law.

AN ORGAN AND MOULD OF PUBLIC OPINION.—What is *Public Opinion*, of which it is the highest function of the press to be the organ, mould and guide? First of all, it is not popular caprice. The daily ups and downs of the mercury in the thermometer are not the annual mean of temperature.

Public Opinion is the eminent dominant power in the modern free state, by good right, for its rise measures the ascendancy of democracy, its fall, the decadence. That irresistible tendency to equality of conditions, which De Tocqueville calls a providential fact, possessing all the characteristics of a divine decree, durable, constantly eluding human interference, as gravitation does, events everywhere, and all men contributing to its progress— democracy, justice between man and man, the final and consummate law of human society, operates most freely wherever three things take place: (1) where intelligence is free to be diffused among the masses; (2) where they can acquire property, and (3) learn political combination. The newspaper insures two out of the three. From year to year, the masses combine in societies, clubs, associations and parties. Newspapers are their constant political unions.

These tell each man what all others think and will do. A regulated, popular government, beyond the bounds of a single city community, was once impossible. These surpass Athens,—and collect the daily suffrages of our forty millions from a continent into one *agora*. Dr. Lolme says: "Through its assistance, a whole nation, as it were, holds council and deliberates." This public opinion, then, is not so much the supplement or a part of democracy as its essence and *modus operandi*. * * *

VALUE OF PUBLICITY IT AFFORDS.—In the mere *publicity* afforded by the press, is an immense public service, cheap as it seems. Mansfield said of the press : " It secures that publicity to the administration of the law which is the main source of its purity and wisdom." The ubiquity of Fouche's police made it believed that the Empress Josephine must be in his pay. The people's organ outdoes the police. Argus sees more than the Empress. Upon public abuses it turns the collected flames of its sun-glass and scorches them to cinders. Against the countless wrongs, the injustice and oppressions of individuals, it wages perpetual war, and is a better guarantee against their permanance than any institutions could be. Secrecy itself is unsafe in the fear of that unveiling. The press brings all society to bear upon the individual. The best and purest men work the steadier against this constant. pressure. Public opinion may not enforce a servile conformity in them. That is undesirable. But it hinders the committal of that which is indefensible, and makes men seek for sure ground of action, and a plausible defence for every act. A clever scoundrel could once repeat his crimes from city to city; but the press concentrates upon him the general gaze. There must be prevention in that. And as for punishment, the omniscience of a nation is more cruel and scathing than the ubiquity of the Cæsar, from whose imperial pursuit, De Quincy said, the pathless deserts of the Roman Empire were a transient security—wards of the one infinite prison.

Mere publicity makes monopolies rarer, and advances all the arts. Its equalizing power is obvious, but it raises the standards of merchants, manufacturers, and artisans by exposing to a wider competition the goods, or the skill, in any market. So that what we buy is everywhere better and cheaper for the newspaper.

Between the ancient and the modern state this distinction is chief. In the ancient, the state was everything, the individual nothing. In the modern, the individual—his rights, relations, interests and liberty—have come to be the common aim of every change. What security for the perpetuity of this difference is equal to that which gives to all the highest stimulus in the knowledge of what concerns all ?

ITS EDUCATING IN CITIZENSHIP.--The defenders of free institutions have always argued that nothing so nourished public spirit and developed general intelligence as participation in public affairs. Freemen are educated up to the level of good citizens by exercising the rights and privileges of citizenship. The local administrative institutions are the chief instrument of this educational process in its lowest branches. It is as jurymen, supervisors, committeemen, town clerks, registers, presiding officers, and secretaries, that we learn the $a\ b\ c$ of government. But the majority must learn mainly by the publicity of the press, wherein also we converse with statesmen, with Chevalier, Gladstone, and Wells, on finance; with Fish, Cushing, Bismarck, and Gortschakoff, on diplomacy, and learn the higher arts of government.

By and through the press our false democracy is made to approximate to the true democracy. The unheard of and disfranchised minorities make themselves heard through it.

* * * * * * * * *

The influence of the press upon legislation as an inspiration, assistance and supplement, is too large a theme to open here. Yet if the true end of legislation be to follow, not to force the public inclination—to give a direction, technical dress, and specific sanction to the general sense of a community—then we cannot discard that instrument which promptly points the angle of public inclination, and utters with precision and truth that general sense.

But observe how its publicity affords the widest basis for laws. Burke said: "Statutes and laws have not given us our liberties—our liberties have produced them," Neither have statutes given us our commerce, industry and arts. Out of them laws grow, crystallizing their complexities into rules. We add and alter laws yearly, adjusting them to new facts, fitting them for broader applications. Compare this prompt formative aptitude of legislation with the cherished abuses, the slow reforms of earlier eras. Admit that a representative government has worked wonders, but grant that the press was needed to complete the transformation. What security is thus insured—what confidence in humanity, what yielding obedience to law it has fostered; and how its gentle compulsion has made almost all men, each one to himself, a vindicator and officer for the enforcement of law!

Legislatures record; the press moulds; but see how beyond this function its duty stretches to that far wider sphere of general jurisprudence, civil and penal legislation, financial, political and commercial policy, all separate members of the comprehensive science of government —how it reflects the traditions, the prowess and the pride of states—how it enforces their unwritten codes!

In reply to a letter to a Western editor, Mr. Marble gave, in a condensed form, his views of journalism:

THE WORLD OFFICE, March 18, 1870.

DEAR SIR: "Is it not the proper aim of a public journal to get and publish all the news worth publicity, made intelligible by apt information therewith, instructive by philosophy of cause and consequence, conative by well uttered and iterated reasonings ; thus, at least, a journalist might serve his fellow-men, and for service have sufficient reward."

PARKE GODWIN.

"NEW YORK EVENING POST."

[EXTRACT from an Article on "Journalism" in OUT OF THE PAST.]

1. The community should require its editors to be intellectual men. By this we mean, men who should possess both power of thought and facility of expression. The first is needed because it is incumbent upon them to grapple with difficult questions; the second, because they are to make those questions plain to minds of every cast. All that interests men as members of a social and political body--the measures of parties, the relations of States, the merits of laws, the pretensions of artists, the schemes of projectors, the movements of reformers, the characters of politicians—all are, in turn, themes of newspaper controversy and remark. Politics, international and municipal law, political economy, moral and social science, and the art of reading individual character, must be understood by the editor—and not only understood, but explained. He must have that clear insight into general principles, and that familiarity with details, which will enable him to speak with clearness, originality and decision.

Topics, moreover, are often sprung upon him with the suddenness of surprise—topics in which are involved the happiness of immense numbers of people, who look to him for information and guidance. His faculties, fully prepared and rightly disciplined, must be at his command. He must stand ready, with argument, with illustration, with eloquence, to awaken the dull, to convince the doubting, to move the inert, and to instruct and interest the more enlightened. But, to do this effectually, he must be at once a patient thinker, a profound scholar, and a practiced writer. He must have accomplished his mind by the observation of mankind, by the reading of books, and by habits of quick and appropriate expression. He must, above all, be penetrated by that deep Christian philosophy which estimates all questions in their bearing upon the most exalted and permanent interests of human nature.

2. The community should require of its editors that they be firm and independent men. Force of will is no less necessary to them than greatness of thought. Few men have more temptations to an expedient and vacillating course. Regarded by many, and often regarding themselves, as the mere hacks of party, or mere instruments of gratification to prevailing passions, they are not expected to exhibit a fervent zeal in the prosecution of great ends. Like advocates paid by a client to carry a particular point, they are supposed to have fulfilled their obligations when they have made the worse appear the better reason. In many instances, if they have succeeded in embarrassing an adversary, if they have covered an opponent with ridicule, if they have given a plausible aspect a falsehood, if they have assisted a schemer in imposing upon credulous or ignorant people, if they have been faithful to the interests of their employers, they are clapped upon the shoulder as serviceable fellows, and rewarded with a double allowance of governmental or mercantile patronage. The notion that the press has a worthier destiny, seems hardly to cross their minds. That it should become a fountain of truth and moral influence; that it should take its stand upon some high and good principle, to assert it boldly, in the face of all opposition;

that it should strive to carry it out with the earnestness of a missionary, with the self-denial of a martyr, despising as well the bribes of those who would seduce it, as the threats of those who would terrify it, acknowledging no allegiance to any power but justice—in a word, be willing to face danger and death in the discharge of duty—is an intrepidity which, we fear, to most of the managers of public journals would seem to the last degree chimerical. Yet it is an end for which they should strive. No less than this should society require of them; nothing less than this can render them worthy of the trust which is committed to their keeping.

3. Journalists, again, must be required to imbue themselves with a just and Christian spirit. Few things are more to be deplored than the low tone, the unkind feeling which characterizes their intercourse with each other. We do not speak merely of those flagrant violations of decency which degrade the lower class of journals. We speak of the puerility, the violence, and the want of justice, which even the most respectable journals exhibit; we speak of their proneness to distort and to exaggerate, of their recklessness of fair-dealing, of their want of candor, and of their base subservience to particular classes. Indeed, so frequent have been their offences in these respects, that their dishonesty has almost passed into a proverb. "I only," said Jefferson, "believe the advertisements of a newspaper;" to which another distinguished man added, "and he ought not to have believed them." "He lies like a newspaper," would not be a far-fetched comparison. We are aware that it is urged, in extenuation of these faults, that they are to be ascribed to the circumstances of haste and confusion in which daily editors write; we know it is alleged that in other pursuits, law and commerce for instance, the average honesty of

those who follow them is not greater than that of journalists: but with all these palliations, with every wish to deal charitably, we must say that a large amount of moral aberration remains against them which admits of no excuse. What! shall we be told, because a man writes in haste, that he must therefore write falsely?—that because lawyers and merchants fall below the standard of virtue, therefore editors should be allowed to do the same,—editors, whose influence is so much more extensive, whose duties are so much more important? It is a shallow defence. Better relinquish their profession forever than sacrifice to it their integrity. Better drop the pen, and take up the axe or the hammer, than wield the former only to sap and extinguish public morals! No! we demand a more exalted morality at their hands. When a man assumes to direct the opinions and form the characters of his contemporaries,—when he voluntarily places himself in the attitude of a leader of the general mind— he should be compelled, by the force of public sentiment, to cherish habits of the strictest accuracy and honor. We require of the preacher of the pulpit that he should not degrade his office by inconsistencies of conduct; can we require less of the preacher of the press? Should a Channing, or a Hawkes, or a Dewey, or a Hughes, act in a manner derogatory to their sacred calling, would society overlook it? If a magistrate on the bench pollutes the ermine he wears, do we admit of any apology for his venality or corruption? Should a Taney, or a Story, or a Baldwin, or the meanest functionary of a county court, accept bribes from the parties to a suit, or be intimidated by popular clamor, or swayed in his decisions by personal feeling, could he avert disgrace? Could any circumstance of his position—press of business, want of time, haste—be pleaded in defence of his crime? Why, then, should we excuse similar defections in those who occupy higher places, and whose truth, consistency and justice are even more necessary than theirs to the good order, virtue and happiness of society?

We have spoken freely of the present condition of the press; we have spoken with equal freedom of what it might become. It is in no censorious spirit that we have pointed to its failings; it is with a spirit of benevolence and hope that we have indicated its duty. We are sorry that our strictures are deserved, but we are glad to know that instances exist in which they are inapplicable. It gives us pleasure to acknowledge that within the last few years the character of the American press has greatly improved. Were it not invidious, we could point to editors who, to the best of their ability, had striven to realize the ideal which we have depicted. We could refer to a Bryant, foregoing the applause that the world would willingly render to his great poetic talent and individual character, to become an example of the true, accomplished, unyielding editor;—to a Brownson, who prefers the fame of a candid, fearless writer, to the seductions of clerical supremacy; and to several others, still young and obscure, to whom the emoluments and honors of professional and political distinction have no blandishments, in comparison with those of becoming, as journalists, upright advocates of all that is good. But our object is not personal. We wish only to rescue Journalism from its infidelity to itself, and from the indifference and contempt of the public. We wish only to assert its claims, to vindicate its dignity, to exhort it to do its duty.

HENRY WARD BEECHER.

[Address before the State Editorial Reunion at Poughkeepsie.]

After expressing his pleasure at finding himself among so large an assemblage of editors, and a guest of this "beautiful old town," the speaker went on to say:

"I count it fortunate that a convention is called of publishers and editors in this fair and beautiful old town of Poughkeepsie, which no man, I venture to say, of good taste, fond of nature, ever visits, whether in winter or in summer, without making inwardly a promise to himself that he will come again and stay longer. I count myself fortunate, also, to be present again as an editor, and it carries me back to the earlier years of my life, when, in 1836, I began my public life as an editor, under the influence and example of that very valuable and very noble man, Charles Hammond, of the Cincinnati *Gazette*. It was while I was in the Theological Seminary that it was necessary that some one should take the place on the Cincinnati *Gazette* of the editor, who had gone to the General Assembly in Philadelphia, not the General Assembly elsewhere, and I took the place with no very great pride and no very great vanity, but still with such peculiar expectations that I remember I launched out and bought a gold watch and a superlative overcoat. For six months all things went well, at least in the office, however it may have fared with the readers, when the publishers broke, the paper was bought by a lawyer, and in the course of four or five weeks he informed me that he thought he could run it himself. My salary stopped, my watch went back. The coat they would not take, and I was left to pay for that as best I might. I have always felt a peculiar sympathy with poor editors from that time to this— (applause and laughter)—and if as years go on I feel myself called less and less to the platform and more and more to the pen and the editorial convention, I should not be ashamed to wind up my life as I began it, for I think that among the professions there is none that ranks higher than that which is yet to be a profession— that of journalism. The editor of the daily or weekly journal is in the nature of an encyclopædist: he passes over the whole realm of human thought, of human sentiment, of human feeling. He belongs to civic society in all its relations, and it is not meet that he should spin his web in a corner; that like some untimely spider he should have only an window attic, there to work and to feed.

A formal address, an essay or a miscellaneous address, as I am forced to give you to night, cannot be so profitable as those quick speeches, those inspirations, those discussions which take place over the very questions that are vital to journalism. Journalism, as yet, is a pursuit rather than a profession. It has no definite bounds; it has no common law or customs; it has principles, and yet they are held rather individually than by common consent. It is not shaped and drawn out into any form with acknowledged foundations and superstructure. That it is to be a profession, and like all other professions, to have its laws and its precepts, its maxims and its methods, there can be scarcely any doubt. It never will be a profession in the same sense in which law is. It has in it so much of necessity that is voluntary, that cannot be fixed, while the law spreads itself around about the different forms of civil society; it has a machinery fixed and bounded for it which professional journalism never can have. There are between 7,000 and 8,000 various journals published in the United States and Canadas, and for all moral and literary purposes the two great English-speaking nations are one. Of daily journals there are about 700 in Canada and the United States, and about 6,000 weeklies and 700 monthlies. Now, in so large a number as these, surely there is material enough to begin coalescing, taking counsel to make the outlines and the framework of the future profession of journalism.

The only bonds that connect papers with papers are very feeble, operating at long distances and for short periods of time. The great secular press is held together in bonds by chiefly political influences, but party feeling runs high for brief periods. Nor has it been found able to hold together, even in the same side, journals in such a way as that they should be fraternal or brotherly, for so soon as two journals come into such relations with each other that the profits are affected, the one by the other, the power of party is not strong enough to hold them in affinity; and they go into antagonism. In religious journals sectarian feeling is in the main the great bond that holds them together, but the same diversive influences operate there. Our religious journals have been known to be quarrelsome, and have been known to be envious and jealous, and even among sects there are diversions of opinions, and sects don't love each other as much as Christians should. But I think both secular and religious journals, if there be any distinction, are coming to the common ground of amity and of civilization, and of intellectual and moral elevation, much higher than they have had before. I take notice, for instance, that there is moral element in secular affairs that religious journals begin to recognize. Common life has in it a new element of morality and moral feeling that makes it religious. And so religious journals are beginning to talk about worldly things much to their profit, much to their advantage every way. And on the other hand, the secular journals are beginning to find that pure secularism is not wide enough—that the whole of manhood is not included in any such bounds as these, and therefore secular journals are beginning to reach out for moral influences, and take hold of moral principles.

"There is a great amelioration of feeling therefore, and a widening of sympathy between religious papers which indicates a general growth in one direction. Political journals are not so demoralized, I think, as they have hitherto been represented to be. I have for the last few years looked with some degree of particularity at the great leading journals of America, at a time when they were under the most fierce excitement. I am bound to say that while there has been much untoward, and much that was to be regretted, yet, on the whole, the tone of journalism, even in party heats and party struggles, has been vastly higher than it was immediately following our revolution, or in the earlier and classic periods of our national life. There has been less rudeness, less vehement violence; and on the whole, considering what human nature is, and what men are under excitement, political journalism has advanced. Whatever interests any member of the community interests all our great journals throughout the land. It is customary to speak of journalism in vague and general terms, and in terms, I think, somewhat extravagant. Thus I hear people say that the time is soon coming when editing will be a much more useful occupation than preaching, and that the newspaper is going to supersede the pulpit. Will the press, then, ever take the place of books or materially diminish them? I think that the press will be to books what the ocean is to ships; it will bear them up; it will give them a medium and an opportunity that they never have had, but it will never supplant them.

"Allusion has been fitly made here to the propriety of introducing newspapers in our schools. There should not be the slightest objection to that, but you never will take school-books out of the way. If you do anything you will do this. You will have more and better schoolbooks than you have now, and newspapers to boot, but you are never going to have such flat school-books as newspapers are. Our boys and girls will read more, and gather up scraps and fragments of information from newspapers, but the books will, after all, be the staple of instruction until such time as the living book is the only teacher, and that time should not be far distant, for that is the right teaching. If you turn from school-books to scientific works, although much may be done by the newspapers in the direction of science, they will never take the place of scientific treatise. It has been found by publishers that it is profitable to run a novel first through a leading paper, and that it sells afterwards all the more for its having been first in the papers. It is in the same manner true of scientific works. Let them be distributed in the newspaper and the demand will be equal or greater for them in the books.

Take classical and general literature. There no newspaper circulation will ever take the place of these. The library has nothing to fear. The book publisher has nothing to fear. The newspaper is to be the right hand and power to promote a wider book literature in this land, and when every single county paper has every principal family among its subscribers, books will follow newspapers, and books will never supersede them, nor will newspapers supersede books. And this is as it ought to be, for the newspaper is to be a new force not superseding any old one. Will the newspaper ever be a substitute for the pulpit? The pulpit will change. It has changed. It is changing, but it is not losing its root. It it is not losing its fruit. There was a time—and this is true of all institutions of civilization in the earlier periods of every community—when the functions were performed by fewer organizations. Once the pulpit was the home of learning; the lawyer, the doctor, the schoolmaster and the minister throughout the towns had all the culture, but to-day they do not by any means have it all their own way, and little by little the magazine teaches sometimes just as well as the pulpit, sometimes even better, and even the newspapers are coming up with matter and thought.

"The scientific books are coming up, and scientific knowledge is no longer distilled from the pulpit. The pulpit is being shut, not out, but it is no longer its function to distribute throughout the community all or most of the knowledge they possess. The church is more and more shut up to spiritual matters. Not that it has not the liberty when it pleases to make the applications of spiritual truth to human life, but there are other organizations and institutions to do these things, and less and less does it devolve upon the minister of the gospel. All the professions, then, instead of being in any sense weakened or suppressed by the progress of journalism, are to be rather strengthened—helped, not hindered. It would be well for those that have an over-sanguine conception of the power of journalism to consider that it derives its power from the community itself, and that the community is a greater power than any institution in it ever can be.

"We are apt to think of society as an aggregation of individuals. We scarcely think of it as it is, a vital organic whole, and we seldom think how much it is true that every institution and every organization in society is itself subject to the greater power of the whole. The will-power of the mass, the thought-power of the mass, the energy of enthusiasm that belongs to the mass, are more than a match for anything in the shape of an organ, in the shape of a book or paper. I don't believe, in the first place, that there is ever to be such an enormous concentration of circulation as many people think. I have heard sanguine publishers say there have been 400,000 papers published weekly of this, that, or the other magazine; why not 1,000,000? Why is it not possible for some great capitalized concern to print a paper in such a manner that it may have 2,000,000, subscribers? What king on his throne would feel like an editor then? Now, it sounds well. Engineers used to think that they could increase the speed of railway trains to even 100 miles an hour; but the resistance is in an inverse ratio to the increase, and engineers have found that there is a practical limit to speed. I don't believe there will ever come a time when a journal will exist with 500,000 regular subscribers year by year—*bona fide* subscribers I mean. There are natural limits to competition. The channels of community are so divided up that I do not believe there will ever be such a large circulation, but it is certainly in the power of every journal in the country to reach the whole man. Journals that suit the bassilar man will be largely confined to the bassilar part of the people in the community. The speaker insisted that nothing should go into the journal which is not fit to be read by every member of the family to which it found access. No respectable paper had the right to put in matter that addressed itself to the faculties that lay below the ears. It is the interest of journalism that these things be either shut up to the few or absolutely destroyed out of journalism. Ladies and gentlemen—I trust that, though I cannot speak from knowledge, I believe that you are most fortunate in your local journals. I believe that the gentlemen that have come together in this Convention will all return to their spheres of labor—many of them burdensome spheres—with a purpose to make journalism a profession, and a profession, too, in which truth, manhood, honor, justice, and all the sweet brood of Christian graces shall have their homes. God speed the day when throughout the whole length and breadth of this land journalism shall stand high up, not looking up to any other profession, but shoulder to shoulder, heart with heart, soul with soul."

F. B. SANBORN,

"SPRINGFIELD (MASS.) REPUBLICAN."

[Part of Essay read before the Boston Radical Club.]

THE readers of Mr. Frederic Hudson's entertaining history of "Journalism in the United States from 1690 to 1872,"—that is, from the birth of Franklin to the death of Greeley — have learned therefrom, long since, what the modern newspaper is, how it originated, and whither it is tending. It is a common saying in England that America is governed by newspapers, — and this by way of sneer, according to the charming fashion of Englishmen. But long ago Jefferson anticipated and met this reproach, when he said, "I would rather live in a country with newspapers and without a government, than in a country with a government but without newspapers." The alternative is seldom presented nowadays; indeed, it has been found easier to overthrow a government at Paris, Madrid, Mexico, or Rome, than to stop a well-managed newspaper. The steam-press, the electric telegraph, the enormous development of commerce and industry in the last half-century, accompanied as they have been by the swift growth of democratic ideas and institutions, social as well as political, have given newspapers a position and a responsibility which is but imperfectly understood, even by those who have the most to do with them. Journalism has been called the Fourth Estate (though what the other three are in America it might puzzle us to tell), and certainly it is somewhat in the attitude of the Third

Estate of France, as described by the Abbe Sieyes, in his brief catechism: "What is the Third Estate? Everything. What has it hitherto been? Nothing. What does it aspire to be? Something." Journalism in America is something, has been nothing, and aspires to be everything. There are no limits, in the ambition of enterprising editors, to the future power of the American newspaper. It is not only to make and unmake presidents and parties, institutions and reputations; but it must regulate the minutest details of our daily lives, and be school-master, preacher, lawgiver, judge, jury, executioner, and policeman, in one grand combination. We find it intruding and interfering everywhere. It reports everything, has an espionage as universal and active as any despot ever established, and makes its comments with that species of boldness which the undiscriminating call impudence, on all that happens, or is imagined to to happen, or is about to happen. It scorns to confine itself to the realm of the past and the present, but deals largely with the future. A German play represents in one of its scenes "Adam crossing the stage on his way to be created;" and much of the news gathered by our dailies is of this anticipative sort; imposing upon these active journals the necessity of contradicting on Tuesday the intelligence they have given on Monday.

Before De Foe, or Addison, Steele, Swift, Berkeley, Bolingbroke, or any of their witty contemporaries had engaged in journalism in the mother country, New England, according to the traditions, had seen the first American newspaper, the *Publick Occurrences* of Benjamin Harris, of which one number was published in Boston, September 25, 1690, "at the London Coffee-House, which Harris kept." Mr. Hudson reprints this sheet in full; its authenticity has been questioned, but, so far as can be seen, without sufficient cause. De Foe's kinsman, the bookseller Dunton, gives a brief notice of Harris, who was a printer, and like De Foe, had stood in the London pillory for some publication. His Boston sheet was harmless enough, but the magistrates of that city saw fit to suppress it, as they afterwards tried to suppress the *Courant* of the Franklin family, for its strictures on the Mathers and other Boston ministers.

In 1772, the Massachusetts General Court took notice of this impertinence of the Franklins in venturing to have a different opinion from the Mathers, and voted that James Franklin should be forbidden to print or publish the New England *Courant*, or any other pamphlet or paper of the like nature, "*except it be first supervised by the secretary of this province;* inasmuch as " the tendency of said paper is to mock religion and bring it into contempt; that the Holy Scriptures are therein profanely abused, the reverend and faithful ministers of the gospel are injuriously reflected on, *and the peace and good order of His Majesty's subjects of this province disturbed* by the said *Courant.*" In consequence of this vote, the newspaper was for a while published in the name of Benjamin Franklin, then a youth of sixteen. The rest of the story is well known; the two brothers quarreled, and Benjamin, at the age of seventeen, went to Philadelphia, where a few years later he established the first really good newspaper in America — the *Pennsylvania Gazette.*

When our revolution began, a hundred years ago, daily newspapers had become common in England, and were not unknown in America. Dr. Johnson, writing at this period, said in his tumid way, "Journals are daily multiplied without increase of knowledge. The tale of the morning paper is told in the evening, and the narratives of the evening are bought again in the morning," a description which may still apply in Boston, if not in London. A few of the London dailies now existing are as ancient as the Worcester *Spy*, which kept its centennial in 1870, and of which that worthy old printer, Isaiah Thomas, was the founder. The *Spy* was not a daily, however, for the first seventy-five years, but generally a weekly. In 1794 it had the pedantry, not unusual then, to print its motto — *The Liberty of the Press is Essential to the Security of Freedom* — in four languages, English, Latin, Greek, and French. At that time it was just about one-fourth of its present size; that is to say, its readers received in a week less than a twentieth part of the matter that the readers of the daily *Spy* now get. But, on the other hand, it cost but a dollar and a half, instead of the eight dollars now paid for the daily *Spy*, and only a fourth of its space was given to advertising, instead of about three-fourths, as now. Its news from Europe, in 1794, was nearly three months old, from Canada and Georgia more than a month old, and from New York a week, instead of coming twice every day from all these and a thousand other places, as it now does. Its editorial writing was almost nothing; and this was true of most American newspapers at that time. If principles were to be discussed or events commented upon, the task was usually left to correspondents, who, under various English and Latin names, maintained one side or the other of political and social questions.

The connection of poets and literary men of the highest rank with the modern newspaper is well known, and need only be alluded to. Had Goethe lived in England, instead of Germany, he would have been a newspaper editor rather than a theatre-manager, as he was at Weimar. In Paris everybody commences by writing for the journals. Sainte-Beuve and George Sand did so from the beginning; Thiers was and remains a journalist; and the *Revue des Deux Mondes* — the first authority in the world in matters of literature and philosophy — is but an exalted and glorified newspaper.

Thoreau's pungent criticism on the newspapers is not quite so true now as when he made it, twenty years ago. "I am sure," says he in Walden, "that I never read any memorable news in a newspaper. To a philosopher all *news*, as it is called, is gossip, and they who edit and read it are old women over their tea." "Read not the Times; read the Eternities." But even this philosopher admits that he read one newspaper a week, though he feared that was too much, and found that the sun, the clouds, the snow, the trees, did not say so much to him as before he desecrated his mind by letting in idle rumors and trivial incidents. And it is very true that to the serious thinker the murmurs brought by every day's report of the incessant stir of mankind are chiefly a disturbance and dissipation of his thought. But the journal of to-day is no longer a mere record of daily events; it occupies itself with the thoughts of men, the discoveries of science, the treasures of literature, and the acts of heroes.

There came a time after Thoreau had said these things when he was driven to the morning papers with as much eagerness as anybody; when, as he says, "I read all the newspapers I could get within a week." It was when John Brown lay wounded at Harper's Ferry, and his enemies, thronging about him, drew from him those answers that rang through the country for years, and still thrill the heart as we recall them. It was the everlasting reporter of the New York *Herald*, who then and there noted down the undying words that might else have been lost, or distorted in the recital of the base men to whom they were spoken. Then it was made manifest for what purpose the *Herald* had been allowed to exist all these years, —no other paper could have had a reporter there, and without him the conversation must have perished. All this was "foreordained and freely predetermined;" and John Brown, lying there on the armory floor, was the final cause of the *Herald* and its otherwise unaccountable editor. In those days the Times and the Eternities got printed on the same sheet, as they always do when a hero appears.

The triviality for which Thoreau complained of the newspapers, he was no less sensible of in the daily life of his fellow-men. "Nations!" he cries, "what are nations? Tartars, and Huns, and Chinamen. Like insects they swarm. The historian strives in vain to make them memorable." How, then, could he expect the journalist to do it? whose business is to record what he finds, be it trivial or momentuous, if it only be significant. And the great struggle of the editor, as of the historian or the essayist, always is to choose the significant fact, the event that really means something, and to give prominence to that. The telegraph and the innumerable newspapers have made the world one enormous ear of Dionysius— a perpetual whispering gallery; and of the confused mass and rumble of rumors, the poor journalist must snatch and print what he can, for it is quite impossible to give currency to everything. But the best journals now aim to furnish their readers not only the news of the day, but the thought and spirit of the epoch; and to some extent they do so.

Of late, too, there has been a perceptible increase in the courage of our journalists. The same thing has been happening in this country within a dozen years, which an acute Frenchman, Baron d'Haussez, who was one of the ministers of Charles X., and followed him into exile in

England, noted as going on in Europe forty years ago. "For a long time," he says, "the English newspapers limited themselves to studying public opinion; to follow in its wake was their sole aim. But lately the English press, following the example of the French journals, has jumped from the tail to the head of popular opinion; it seeks to mark out the course this opinion should follow, and aspires to direct it. The newspapers find fault with, denounce, menace one party and stimulate the other; and public sentiment is no less the slave of journalism in London than at Paris." Every observer of our American newspapers since the civil war began will see how well these remarks apply to them. Their tone has greatly changed; and though they are not yet models of courage, they are by no means deficient in boldness and confidence. They no longer deem it their highest duty "to feel round for the average judgment of their readers, and express that," as Wendell Phillips used to say: no, they have an ambition to lead rather than to follow; and instead of drawing steadily in the traces of party, as political newspapers did in the days of Jackson and Polk, they now try, every now and then, to form new parties, and raise new political issues; and sometimes they succeed. One reason for this change, which all must have noticed, is the vast change in the circumstances of our country and the features of American society. We have passed rapidly from a provincial to an imperial position among the nations, with all the attendants of our prosperous career,—fabulous wealth, increased culture, a prodigious diversity of tastes and interests, and a wide expansion of the horizon of individual ambition. These things stimulate us in all directions, and their influence is nowhere more keenly felt than in the field of journalism, where they are first noted and most frequently registered and compared.

Under the spur of such excitements, a new class of newspaper editors has appeared. In the book of Captain Basil Hall, an English traveler in this country in 1833, occurs this graphic sketch of the editors of that day: "The conductors of American journals are generally shrewd but uneducated men, extravagant in praise or censure, clear in their judgment of everything connected with their own interests, and exceedingly indifferent to all matters which have no discernible relation to their own pockets or privileges." How well this describes Thomas Ritchie, Isaac Hill, Thurlow Weed, and men of that stamp, a few of whom still remain at the head of newspapers they have founded or inherited! But the new race of American editors is different. In spite of Mr. Greeley's bucolic sneer,—"Of all horned cattle, a college graduate in a newspaper office is the worst,"—nearly all the rising and lately risen journalists in the country are educated men, many of them highly accomplished in scholarship or literature. Such as were not educated at the outset have oftentimes pursued their studies, and taken their degrees in half a dozen newspaper offices,— no mean school for acquiring a liberal culture. They are traveled men, too, familiar with foreign countries, and, what is quite as necessary, and less common, with their own; accustomed to meet and deal with people of all sorts, and especially with the able men of their region. Not a few of them, in the late war, enriched their minds with the experiences of army life, either as soldiers or as war correspondents; some are popular lecturers, others are cultivating literature with zeal and success; all, as a class, are alert of mind, with their faculties ready at command, and trained to steady service as much as any professional men in the land.

Moreover, journalism is drawing into its ranks every year more and more of the intellectual ability of the country; clergymen leaving their pulpits, lawyers their briefs, school-masters their desks, and scholars their studies, to ply the pen for the daily and weekly newspaper. Add to these the multitude who, without abandoning their old avocations, are correspondents or occasional contributors for the press, and the number becomes enormous, including, as it does, so many women of genius and culture. When Mrs. Child, that genial grandmother of feminine journalism in America, wrote her Letters from New York, and when Margaret Fuller went to the same city to help Mr. Greeley edit the *Tribune*, how daring and strange their venture seemed to their countrywomen! But now their successors may be counted by the thousand; and nothing so much surprises and delights a young editor as to find what rich stores of womanly talent and insight he can draw upon to enrich his columns. Every editor now rejects, for want of room, bushels of manuscripts from feminine hands that twenty years ago would have been sought out and proudly printed,—only, twenty years ago they did not exist.

And yet, with all this thronging of recruits to the rendezvous of journalism, the number of really able editors is small. Some years ago a journalist in another city was lamenting the poverty of Boston in this respect, and said, with real pathos, "Why, they've only got one good journalist in all Boston, and they're spoiling him in the pulpit!" Of course, things have changed for the better since then, in Boston—but hardly elsewhere. Brilliant and forcible and sensible as so many American journalists are, they seldom develop into marked superiority; each

has his foible, his impediment, and does not rise beyond a
certain level. Some of them remind us of the compliment
paid by a German prince to Wellington's troopers: he
liked the British cavalry, he said: "there were none better in the world,—*if they only knew how to ride.*" Mr.
Greeley, for example: how magnificently was he equipped
for journalistic service? how much he has done, too!
And, yet, he too often suggested that homely figure of a
cow who gives a good pail of milk and then kicks it over—
so furious, so ungovernable, were his whims. His great
rival, Mr. Raymond, certainly could ride, but he persisted
in riding nowhere; he would trot smartly northward, then
canter briskly southward, then amble easterly and west-
erly; but always came back at last to his centre of indifference. Unequaled in the details of journalism, he
lacked the steady force and moral purpose that alone accomplish great results. Mr. Dana, who, like Mr. Raymond, was for a while the associate and afterwards the
rival of Mr. Greeley, has shown some of the rarest and
most masterly traits of a successful journalist; but in
these later years he has wantonly sacrificed the best
parts of his reputation by a coarse, sensational and impu-
dent manner of conducting his newspaper. No other
names than theses three,—who are, on the whole, the
most famous of American journalists,—are needed to remind us how easy it is for editors of rare ability and opportunity to fall short of the lofty ideal of journalism.
Had Franklin lived in our day, and devoted himself to
the work of a newspaper as he did in his own century, he,
perhaps, would have come nearer than any other to the
true standard; but even of Franklin, it was said by Tim-
othy Pickering, that "he was never found in a minority."
Yet the ideal journalist must, like the greatest general,

sometimes lead a forlorn hope, and often must resist the public for the public good.

Courage, indeed, is the one quality indispensable for journalism of the highest order, and it is what our journalists still lack most. Of courage as an intellectual accomplishment, or a means of winning respect and deference, they have a much better perception than of its moral quality. They are, therefore, often bold and self-confident, audacious to the verge of insolence, and sometimes beyond it; but for that steady courage which accepts certain risks for uncertain advantages, and for that modest courage which dares more than it proclaims, they are not conspicuous. But it must be said that our newspapers, of late years, have one increased inducement and guarantee for a courageous course,—a much greater pecuniary independence than formerly. It grows more and more dificult each year to hire or buy a successful newspaper, because it can afford to hold its price high. Nor do newspapers now depend for success, except indirectly, upon their subscribers. It is advertising that supports them mainly, and a great subscription list is chiefly valuable, pecuniarily, to a great newspaper, as being certain to attract advertisers. This, to be sure, is only changing the burden of servitude, for an editor whose chief aim is to please his advertisers and retain their " patronage," as it is called, is but one degree less fettered than he who dodges and shuffles to please his subscribers. And it is important that newspapers should be the property, so far as possible, of those who have the editorial management; for without this security from monetary dictation, a journal may be as venal as if it were purchased outright. Neither is it well for the owners of a newspaper to have much other property actively employed in business ; else they will be tempted to use their newspaper columns to promote their private speculations. There is no more common mode of bribing editors and legislators, as we have lately seen illustrated, than by offering them an interest in schemes that depend upon public favor or special legislation for their success. The one excuse for all the annoyances and impertinences of which newspapers are guilty is their devotion to the public good; and a journalist who is detected feathering his own nest, or helping his friends to do so, loses at once his privilege as a public benefactor. Need we add that detection makes no difference in the offence? It is the one unpardonable sin against journalism to cloak private gain or personal malice with professions of public virtue.

Great as the temptations of a journalist are to enrich himself by subservient or corrupt courses, they are far less than his temptations to self-conceit, which is the main vice of modern editors, the sin that doth so easily beset us. To err is human; this is a common frailty in all occupations, especially such as are literary or political. We have an amusing instance in a religious poet of the seventeenth century, who had a picture of himself engraved, kneeling before a crucifix with a label from his mouth, "Lord Jesus, do you love me?" which was answered by another label proceeding from the mouth of Jesus, "Yes, most illustrious, most excellent, and most learned Sigerus, poet-laureate of his Imperial Majesty, and most worthy rector of the University of Wittenberg,—yes, I do love you!" The flattery which our journalists devise for themselves is less heavenly-minded than this, but no less gross.

Alcæus and Callimachus are nothing to the titles we bestow on one another, when in good humor; if you will take us at our own valuation you need be under no concern for the future of American literature. As Colonel

Diver remarked to Martin Chuzzlewit, when handing him the Rowdy Journal for his perusal: " You 'll find Jefferson Brick at his usual post in the van of human civilization and moral purity." The original Jefferson Brick has departed, no doubt, but he has left a family, and a numerous one, who have divided his mantle betwen them. Who is not forced to smile, sometimes, in the intervals of admiration, at the airs these gentlemen assume? as if uncreated wisdom had taken bodily form in their persons. They will allow us to know nothing which they have not told us; they give us epitomes of history after Tacitus, sketches of character after Clarendon and Kinglake, and systems of political economy as elaborate as Adam Smith's. And so positive, too, in all their knowledge! It should be the humble effort of a young student's lifetime to acquire the omniscience of an American journalist under the age of thirty-five. "I wish I knew anything," said Lord Melbourne, "as positively as Macaulay knows everything." Why wonder that our American bishops at the Œcumenical Council easily agreed to the Pope's infallibility? Had they not seen an infallible chair in every one of the five thousand newspaper offices in their own country?

Still, let us be just to these instructors of ours; it is no mean talent that they possess, nor, on the whole, ill employed. It is common to laugh at newspaper English, and the knowledge that is derived only from the newspapers. But, except in those masters of style which are above comparison, there is no better English than we find in the newspaper; and we can now fully appreciate what Horace Walpole meant in saying, a hundred years ago, " Every newspaper is now written in a good style; when I am consulted about style, I often say, 'Go to the Chandler's shop for a style,' "—that is, read any old newspapers you may pick up. And he adds a strikingly just remark: "Had the authors of the silver age of Rome written just as they conversed, their works would have vied with those of the golden age. Writers are apt to think they must distinguish themselves by an uncommon style; hence elaborate stiffness and quaint brilliance. What a prodigious labor an author often takes to destroy his own reputation!" It is because a journalist thinks more of his matter than of his manner, and seeks to make himself understood rather than admired, that he writes so well; and how well our best editors and correspondents write one can easily see by writing himself on one of their themes. These men and women are the lineal successors of Hobbes, who said if he had read as many books as the learned, he would have been as ignorant as they; of De Foe, whose "low style" is the admiration of all good critics; of Franklin, who acquired his art of writing, by no means inferior to Addison's, in a printing office; of the letter-writers and diarists, whose vocation has almost died out, except as they reappear in newspaper correspondents. Nor is it extravagant to say that the careful reader of a few good newspapers can learn more in a year than most scholars do in their great libraries; while the multitude of men and women are actually instructed so, more rapidly than in any way ever tried before.

At the same time, every able journalist, and nearly every mediocre one, is tempted to be a smatterer; he must have his say on every topic, and cannot be well informed about all. There was no royal road to geometry in Euclid's time, nor is there any railroad to universal knowledge now; to acquire it is impossible, and to come within sight of it demands much time and much patience, neither of which our journalists commonly have. The fancied necessity of scribbling something about every event and every intellectual and social manifestation is the plague of an editor's life, the ruin of his good manners, the cause of delusion, bewilderment and skepticism in his readers. Couple this with that other superlative folly, the rule never to retract an assertion or correct a mistake, and we have the cause of more than half the impertinence, error, and mischief of which newspapers are guilty.

A great deal is said about the slanderous character of the modern newspaper, and of its entire disregard of privacy and the right of individuals to be respected in their withdrawal from public notice. But in these respects our age is no worse than those before it. We have made error and slander more public by our inventions, but not more common, perhaps, nor more hurtful. In fact, the purely libelous industry of the press is probably less now, in comparison with its whole activity, than at any former time since pamphlets (*libelli*) began to be printed.

It is also true, little as we may think it, that our American new spapers are vastly improved in most respects from what they were thirty years ago, when Dickens saw, felt, and caricatured them. How we all winced under his satire in Martin Chuzzlewit, knowing so much of it to be deserved! This satire no longer stings us as it once did, because, notwithstanding the occasional efforts of the *New York Sun, Times,* and *Tribune* to rival the scarcely imaginary Sewer and Rowdy Journal of Martin Chuzzlewit's day,—notwithstanding the recent appearance of the interviewing reporter, that pest of society,—the moral and intellectual standard of our newspapers has risen a great many degrees in thirty years.

Nor is this the only change that has taken place. Since the death of Horace Greeley, and the events which preceded and followed it, there is no difficulty in perceiving that we stand at the close of a long era of American journalism, and are entering rapidly upon a new dispensation. The presidential campaign of 1872, and the death of Mr. Greeley, mark the end of partisan journalism in its old form,—that epoch of which the *New York Tribune* was the product and the survivor. "With the death of the founder of the *Tribune*," says Mr. Hudson, "party journalism, pure and simple, managed by accomplished and experienced editors, inaugurated by Jefferson and Hamilton, aided by such writers as Fenno, Bache, Duane, Freneau, Coleman, Cheetham, Ritchie, and Croswell, has ceased to exist, and independent journalism becomes a fact impressed on the minds of the people." To Mr. Hudson's mind, loyal as he is to the memory and the traditions of the *New York Herald*, this event is but a fulfillment of the plans and hopes with which James Gordon Bennett, in 1835, announced the first publication of his great newspaper—the first successful example of an independent journal in the United States. The *Herald* was disreputable enough in those days, and for many a long year afterwards; it has not yet achieved the best reputation in the world, with all its expeditions and discoveries, but it has been tolerably true to the purpose indicated in the first number. Its notorious faults have long kept its true and important mission from being fully recognized, and the proper credit given therefor. It has been the rude, low-bred, boisterous pioneer, preparing the way for the finer and better race of newspapers that are to follow in its track, with nobler aims, a keener sense of decency and responsibility, and a broader culture in the men who conduct them. Nor is it by any means impossible that the *Herald* itself may eventually become a newspaper of the kind just described.

Delighting in the great advances now making in American journalism, but not quite satisfied with any of the existing journals, there are a few persons so unreasonable as still to hope for a model newspaper, though they have never seen one, and though the most brilliant instances of journalistic success are generally coupled with grave and incurable faults. Such enthusiasts deem it possible to walk uprightly and deal justly with all mankind in the career of the journalist as much as in any other; that it is inferior to no other in the interests it protects, the need it serves, the high standard of character and performance it exacts.

> "It was not for the mean;
> It requireth courage stout,
> Souls above doubt,
> Valor unbending."

Not less does it require the deepest purpose, the most active spirit, the broadest thought and culture, the most tolerant heart. Journalism now is what the stage was in Shakespeare's time; its purpose, as Hamlet says of the "purpose of playing," "both at the first and now, was and is, to hold, as 't were, the mirror up to nature; to show virtue her own feature, scorn her own image, and the very age and body of the time his form and pressure." But literature, of which journalism is now the most alert and prolific form, has even a nobler aim than this, to describe which we must borrow the words, not of the tolerant dramatist, but of the more heroic moral poet, Milton. Its office, like that of poetry, of which it is so apt a vehicle, is also "to inbreed and cherish in a great people the seeds of virtue and public civility, to allay the perturbations of the mind and set the affections in right tune; to deplore the general relapses of kingdoms and states from justice and God's true worship; lastly, whatsoever in religion is holy and sublime, in virtue amiable or grave, whatsoever hath passion or admiration in all the changes of that which is called fortune from without, or the wily subtleties and refluxes of man's thoughts from within; all these things, with a solid and treatable smoothness to paint out and describe."

To succeed in all this, without doing injustice to the shipping list and the price current, to the last great fire, mammoth squash, Cardiff giant, new novel, or new religion; to discuss, besides, all the social topics, little and large, that have come upon us in the present age for consideration,—this certainly gives scope enough for the greatest activity and the best talent. Moreover, this ideal journalist, like the poet in Rasselas, must "disregard present laws and opinions, and rise to general and transcendental truths which will always be the same. He must therefore content himself with the slow progress of his name; contemn the applause of his own time, and commit his claims to the justice of posterity. He must write as the interpreter of nature and the legislator of mankind, and consider himself as presiding over the thoughts and manners of future generations; as a being superior to time and space." The reader, still subject to these limitations, is doubtless by this time ready to cry with Rasselas, "Enough, thou hast convinced me that no human being ever can be a *journalist.* It is so difficult that I will at present hear no more of his labors."

MARY L. BOOTH,

EDITOR OF "HARPER'S BAZAR."

QUESTION.—What do you deem the qualifications needed to make a capable editor?

ANSWER.—An editor's first qualifications are sagacity to discover what the public wants, and knowledge how to supply the demand. A good editor must have quick and sure perception, coolness in emergencies, the habit of ready decision, correct taste, and a judicial mind. To be fully equipped, he or she most also have the acquired qualities of thorough culture, extensive reading and wide literary experience. An editor must be an encyclopedist, and not a specialist. There is no kind of knowledge that may not sometime prove available in a newspaper office.

Q. Do you think women fitted for journalism?

A. Eminently so; especially in those departments of newspaper discussion which pertain to the family and to the needs of their own sex. Their acute and subtle intuition, and habits of keen observation, readiness of thought, and refined taste, fit them to succeed both as contributors and editors. They know instinctively how to choose what is readable, and to eschew what is tedious to the comfort of their readers. Of course, I speak of those who have had literary training, which they need as much as men. They are usually good at generalizing, and divine things easily. There are few journals that would not be more interesting for the aid of the feminine mind. Women are especially fitted for weekly and evening journals. Night work they will necessarily find difficult.

Q. As you have had ample experience in both branches, will you please state what you consider the comparative advantages of journalism and literature, more particularly as occupations for women?

A. That depends a good deal on the nature of the individuals who undertake either occupation. Bookmaking permits a woman to work at home, in her own fashion and time, in a careful and deliberate manner; and if she is fortunate enough to belong to the very small class of popular authors, she will probably find this the pleasantest and most lucrative kind of writing. But, as a rule, journalism holds out more immediate and surer rewards, and demands less preparation. For active editorial duties, women, like men, need cool judgment, ready decision, strong nerves and good health. As contributors, I have generally found them industrious, accurate, painstaking and faithful.

Q. Has not a great improvement been made in the status of women writers for the press of late years, and how do you account for it?

A. It is only within a comparatively short time that journalism has been regarded to any extent as a desirable occupation for women; consequently they have hitherto had no inducement to qualify themselves specially for it. With the opening of other avenues for woman's labor, this too was widened, and we see the result in the trained and capable women who are daily entering the field. That the pioneers were crude workers was due to their lack of training, and not to their sex.

Q. What department of newspaper work are women most capable of filling successfully?

A. As I have already said, I think they will succeed

best in literary and family journals. I do not believe that they are at present well fitted to conduct political journals, though their opinions are valuable, and should be given due weight in public measures affecting the interests of women. But political journalism proper, in the present state of society, seems to me so essentially masculine, that it is best managed by men, though in the golden age which we are all looking forward to, I dare say women will also take their part in it.

Q. What training have your assistants had, or do you think desirable that young women who aspire to become journalists should receive?

A. They must learn to discern quickly what will interest the public, and to write out their observations in good, terse, clear English. To do this, they must expect to waste reams of paper in unsatisfactory efforts, and to spend as much time in training as they would do in acquiring any other profession, law or medicine, for instance. The trouble is that women who have not education enough to be teachers, or practical ability enough to be anything else, turn to literature as a last resort, and expect to earn fortunes by their crude pen-products, when, perhaps, they don't even know how to write a letter correctly. Journalism seems to be regarded by a large class as a sort of refuge for those who have failed in every other avocation.

Q. Of what sex are the bulk of the contributors to the *Bazar*?

A. We have a great many contributors of both sexes, though I think that the balance is in favor of women.

Q. Do you think impersonal journalism is preferable; *i. e.*, that contributions should be signed rather than anonymous?

A. I think that a journal which relies for its success on

the quality of its articles, instead of the names of its writers, is likely to give its readers the best material. It also places the contributions of unknown or obscure writers, on a level with those of the most experienced, and puts them in a position to be judged without prejudice. In journals where the papers are signed, people are too apt to run over a list of the authors' names, and read only the writings of their favorites; young and unknown writers are not given due recognition; while editors are tempted by brilliant names to criticise too lightly the articles which they cover. Of course, I speak in the interest of the public, and not of the writers.

Q. Should not the press decline all favors, and refuse to give puffs?

A. Decidedly. Nothing degrades journalism more than the editorial bribery and "dead headism," great and small, which cannot be too strongly deprecated by respectable editors.

Q. What features, in your view, constitute the essentials of a complete journal, devoted to the field which the *Bazar* covers?

A. My best answer would be: the *Bazar* itself, which represents my idea, as far as I have been able to carry it out.

Q. How should such a paper be organized; should the responsible editor do any writing?

A. I think that the English idea, under which the *Times* and the other great London journals are organized —that the editor of a great journal has quite enough to do in inspiring and moulding the contributions of others, and making the paper harmonious in all its parts—is the correct one; though few editors have material at their command satisfactory enough to exempt them from the necessity of writing more or less. When an editor takes up the pen he abdicates his seat as critic, and becomes a special pleader on the subject of which he treats. His true business is to sit in judgment on the writings of others; to suggest or accept the subjects, scrutinize the reasoning, adapt the articles to his needs, and fit them into the harmonious whole of which they form a part. There are plenty of writers who can seize an idea and put it into proper form, but the suggestive and judicial faculties to which I have referred are exceedingly rare.

Q. Is not the common impression that the *Bazar* is merely a fashion journal unfounded?

A. I don't think that it is thus regarded by those who know much of the paper. It seems to me that a journal which numbers among its constant contributors the best writers of light literature, both of Europe and America, which treats, in the course of each volume, of almost every subject that would be likely to interest the family circle, and which contains some of the finest art illustrations published in any newspaper in the country, can hardly be ranked by any one as a mere journal of fashion. A considerable space is devoted to fashion, as a subject peculiarly interesting to women, but this is only one department out of many in a paper designed to interest men, women and children.

Q. What response do you receive from your readers in the shape of inquiries and criticism on the *Bazar*?

A. We have inquiries on all sorts of subjects, and plenty of friendly eulogies, with some intelligent criticism, and occasional advice from tyros, in illustration of the old adage that "editing a paper is like stirring a fire; everybody thinks he could do it better than the one who holds the poker."

Q. Do you believe in recompensing contributors by

the yard, or is not the plan of paying for quality rather than quantity more satisfactory in its results?

A. Journals usually find it necessary to have some standard of price, especially for prose; but it is certainly wise to make this elastic enough to give way at discretion, when an opportunity offers to secure a brilliant article, or one that will attract attention and be of signal service to its readers.

Q. When did you begin writing for the press, and what has been your professional experience since?

A. I don't like autobiographies, and will only say that, contrary to the usual custom, I arrived at journalism by the way of authorship, having published numerous works, original and translated, before undertaking the charge of the *Bazar*. However, I had for many years contributed more or less, but always anonymously, to various journals, and had also a good deal of editorial experience in a quiet way. I was known to the public, nevertheless, solely as an author and translator.

Q. Please sketch the history of the foundation and objects of *Harper's Bazar*, and the results that have followed it?

A. The first number of *Harper's Bazar* was published November 2, 1867. I have edited it from the beginning, and can, therefore, speak with knowledge of the objects which it had in view. It was designed to furnish to the public a first class illustrated weekly family journal, which should be both readable and useful, and which should contain something of interest for every member of the household, and especially for the ladies thereof. As the care of the wardrobe belongs exclusively to them, it has paid particular attention to the department of fashion, giving practical patterns and illustrations, and chronicling the leading styles, while it has endeavored to discourage extravagance and folly, and to commend only what is sensible. But prominent as the fashions appear at first sight, they form after all but a fraction of the *Bazar*, which is filled with fine art illustrations, numerous humorous cuts and other engravings, together with stories, poems, essays, miscellany, juvenile literature, etc., from the best pens, both of Europe and America. It is only by looking over a volume of the paper that one can form an idea of the numerous subjects treated therein during the year. Care is taken to exclude everything of a political or sectarian nature, as well as all objectionable matter, and to make a paper which may be read aloud with pleasure and profit to the whole family. Financially, the *Bazar* is reputed to be the most rapid success ever known in journalism. A newspaper is generally expected to lose money in the beginning, until it gains an established footing. The *Bazar*, on the contrary, has paid handsomely from the very first number, a thing almost unprecedented in journalistic annals. This result is explained by the need that existed for just such a journal, and by the very liberal manner in which the efforts of the editor have been seconded by the wholly exceptional facilities possessed by the publishers for carrying out the designs of the paper.

GEORGE W. SMALLEY,

LONDON CORRESPONDENT "NEW YORK TRIBUNE."

THE LONDON TIMES. — Mr. Watterson has put his finger on some of the weak places in English journalism; its strong points appear to have attracted less of his attention. In the case of the *Times*, criticism of a certain kind is easy and inevitable. Every journalist sees and feels that the *Times* is deficient in certain qualities which have contributed a great deal to the success of the penny press. It is not sensational, either in the good or bad sense of the word. If you look through the *Daily News* or the *Telegraph* you will see almost every morning some current affair treated with an evident effort to make it attractive to the reader, or to the possible reader—to help sell the paper, as its manager would say. No matter what is uppermost, a great strike, a review, a ministerial crisis, a railway accident, there is a marked difference between the way it is treated in the *Times* and the way it is treated in the two leading penny papers. The *Times*' account is likely to brief, sure to be formal, reads like a Parliamentary blue-book, and has almost an air as if published on compulsion, or as if the thing were a bore, and to be disposed of as quickly as possible. The necessary information is given, and little else. The *Telegraph* and *Daily News* will perhaps fill a page or two with the very same subject, written up and written out till in quantity it almost equals a three-volume novel, and in its romantic interest surpasses it. If there be no news, a topic that is timely answers as well—seaside life, for instance, which just now is in season. A correspondent consults his guide-book, discovers, if possible, some place that has not been described before, and describes it as if it were something between Venice and the Sandwich Islands. The process is understood in America; perhaps was borrowed from there. If I explain it to American readers, it is only to give them a clear notion of what the *Times* does not do. Whether it is a good or bad thing to do is not the question.

There can, however, be no question that the *Times* leaves undone some good things which American journals have long done, and which of late years the apparent carelessness of the great journal about news is difficult to understand. It was not so in other days. Part of its immense reputation was built up on its success in collecting intelligence, and stories of its enterprise and lavish outlay are still current. False economy cannot be the secret. It still sends out its correspondents with —as the correspondent of another journal rather too pompously said of himself—the rank of an embassador and the pay of a prince. But the chances are that that very correspondent, with his incomparable opportunities, will be beaten day after day by men who are no abler than himself, nor even more energetic. If Forbes himself had been on the staff of the *Times*, he might never have become famous, nor journalism have been enriched by his unequaled energy and unsurpassed genius. A man does about what he supposes is wanted of him. Had Forbes remained on the *Morning Advertiser*, to which he was attached during the first weeks of the war of 1870, neither he nor his paper would have profited by the occasion. It happened to him to be discovered by the manager of the *Daily News*, whose appetite for news was sharp, and whose sense of the enormous difference between to-day and to-morrow was singularly keen. Under his inspiration and direction it was that Forbes' great exploits were achieved, and it was from Mr. Robinson that the whole staff of that journal came to understand that the first thing they had to do was to beat the *Times* and the *Telegraph;* that a telegram or a letter might be worth a thousand pounds to-day and not a thousand farthings to-morrow.

The misfortune of the *Times* was that it had nobody to teach its correspondents that lesson. Of course it was not a matter of inspiration merely, but of minute instruction, of provision for improbable contingencies, of organization, of what men call good luck—which is the logical result of such qualities and efforts, and the only kind of good luck a journalist can safely believe in. The manager of the *Times* is an able man, but his is the ability of a generation which knew not the telegraph, and when the special correspondents of to-day were in their cradles. I I do not forget Russell in the Crimea, nor his brilliant services, but his triumphs were won almost in the absence of competition, and his success was not due to superior energy alone, nor to that mainly.

Yet it is not to be supposed the *Times* was content with the part it played in 1870 and 1871, or indifferent to the successes achieved by its younger rivals. If cotemporary gossip can be trusted, it was anything but indifferent. It made extraordinary endeavors, but made them too late. Its principal achievement was an account of the entry of the Prussians into Paris, some six or seven columns long, which it published next morning, although there was then no telegraph between Paris and London. I say although. I might say because, for it really seemed as if the *Times* managed this because it had to be done in the old way, and fell in with the traditions and customs of the paper. Dr. Russell, with one or two colleagues, witnessed the entry, left Paris by special train in the evening to Calais, thence by special steamer to Dover, from which again a special train brought them to London about three in the morning. They wrote *en route*, and their story was easily put in type for the morning's paper, which goes to press at 5 o'clock. This performance was also a good illustration of the kind of influence which the *Times* can bring to bear when it chooses. Other London papers attempted the same thing, and there was a keen rivalry about it, because it was believed that the entry of the Prussians would not be made without a serious conflict, or at least a disturbance; so much faith did people still put in French bluster. The circumstances were peculiar, for Paris, though it had surrendered, was still held by its French garrison, the Prussian lines still surrounded it, and the country which the railway between Paris and Calais traverses, was partly in French and partly in Prussian occupation. The confusion of jurisdiction, the disorganization of traffic, the difficulty with which a traveler could make his way with the strongest credentials, were incredible to anybody who had not tried it. The *Telegraph*, which had been used to having its own way in Paris, did its best to get a special train. It offered any price, but this was a case in which money was powerless, and it failed. The *Times*, after trying through the usual channels without success, went to Baron Rothschild, who owns a large part of the stock in the Northern Railway, and told him they wanted the train and must have it. They got it, and there was not another paper in Europe which could have got it in that way, or in any way.

Influence of that kind is only one among many which the *Times* possesses, and can use when it sees fit; its supremacy in certain respects is not merely without parallel, but is unquestioned. Men covet the honor of serving it. Its correspondents hold a position apart. Doors fly open to them at which the representatives of other journals knock in vain. Dr. Russell's personal position is, from a variety of causes, such as no other correspondent is likely to attain, or to attain for a long time. He knows all the kings and princes and prime ministers in Europe who are worth knowing, and his acquaintance with them is old enough and familiar enough to give him a sure footing in the highest society. I need scarcely remind you that when the war of 1870 broke out, the privilege of accompanying the Prussian headquarters was granted to Dr. Russell and refused to every other European correspondent. His acquaintance with the Crown Prince of Prussia and other magnates of that Court may partly explain that signal favor, but there was something behind it. There is reason to believe that Count Bismarck had at that time decided that it was expedient the war should be reported for one European and one American journal, and no more. For Europe he chose the *Times*, for America the *Tribune*. Afterward the restriction was relaxed, but it is safe to say that if it had been maintained for Europe, there never would have been any question that the *Times* was properly selected. Be its faults what they may, it remains the leading journal of Europe, and if the choice had been left with its rivals in London, or to all the English papers together, it would have been the same.

Which only makes it, I repeat, all the more wonderful that a paper in such a position, and possessing such advantages, should ever allow itself to be beaten in news; still more, allow itself to be beaten constantly; and most of all, being beaten constantly, should retain its supremacy. But it is to be borne in mind that these conspicuous and frequent defeats have only been endured for a comparatively brief space of time. Three years are no great period in the life of an old journal, and it is only within the last three years that competition has been so keen. Nor is the English public even yet so eager for news as the American. It has had to be educated, and the process of educating the public is a slow one. There is a most remarkable proof of the carelessness of the English about such matters. When the *Daily News*—always an able, but not always a prosperous paper—had taken the head of the English press in its war news of 1870, and had kept it almost unchallenged for many weeks, there grew up a belief that it had outstripped its penny rival, the *Telegraph*, in circulation as well as intelligence. This belief became so general, that the *Telegraph* was at last stung into publishing a statement of its circulation, certified by the most eminent firm of accountants in London. It appeared that instead of losing it had gained, and gained very largely. Its daily issue for the last six months of 1870 averaged over 190,000 copies—a very large increase indeed over its usual circulation. This is, after all, not very surprising. People buy more papers in war than in peace, and the sluggish as well a the enterprising profit by the excitement. I don't doubt the *Times*' circulation increased also, though Jupiter never condescends to impart information of that kind to the mortals over whom he rules. It may be disrespectful to touch on such a topic, but I shall venture to say that common report fixes the daily issue of the *Times* at rather less than 60,000 copies. The *Daily News*' circulation must have been more than twice 60,000 during the war, and is probably not far from 100,000 now. With respect to the *Times*, however, an old habit, born of the days of dear papers, when threepence really meant something, survives.

It is very largely lent as well as sold. The same copy goes through several hands, being bought in the first instance by a local news-dealer, and sent by him to different subscribers successively in the course of the day, the one who gets it first paying most. Then it is posted in the afternoon to some country or provincial, or perhaps colonial reader. This is so common that the proportion of readers to copies published is considerably larger in the case of the *Times* than of any other paper. That it may stand this wear and tear it is printed on paper which is stouter and better than most of the paper on which American books are printed. I may add that the accuracy of its proof-reading is something admirable.

Mr. Watterson thinks the *Times* dull and weak, and wonders at its influence—or would wonder did he not find the people who read it also dull and weak. There I must part company with him altogether. Undoubtedly, it lacks the sprightliness and vivacity, the personality, the positiveness, and many other spicy characteristics of the *Courier Journal*. But then it is with newspapers as with almanacs. They are calculated for a particular meridian. It is quite possible the *Times* would not be adapted for that of Louisville, neither do I think the *Courier Journal* would do for London; which is no more reproach to one paper than the other. Mr. Watterson's mistake is in applying the same standard to both.

IMPERSONALITY IN THE LONDON PRESS.—Mr. Watterson says English journalism is "impersonal," meaning that journalists as individuals are obscure, and expresses the astonishing opinion that "the English press is conducted by scholarly dummies, who, dwelling in London, to which the press is confined, are able to live reclusive lives, and who, being for the most part the employés of men who publish newspapers as they would traffic in breadstuffs, are not paid enough, or permitted to display a costly and offensive individuality." Of the errors—not errors of opinion but of fact—with which that sentence abounds, I will deal with one at a time. Who are the scholarly dummies who lead the life of a recluse? I pass over the argumentative answer which would be complete, that no important paper could be long conducted by a recluse or scholarly dummy and continue to be important. I will keep to facts and persons. The editor of the *Times* is Mr. Delane. I make no apology for mentioning him by name or for writing freely about him. Mr. Delane is as much public property as Mr. Gladstone, and Mr. Watterson's notion that there is any impersonality or mystery or secrecy, or state of general ignorance about the editorship of the *Times*, or of any other important journal, is very wide, indeed, of the truth. Mr. Delane was never before, I will venture to say, accused of being a recluse. I believe I spoke of him in my last letter as a well-known figure in London drawing-rooms. Few men are better known, or better liked, or more often seen, or naturally enough, more courted. Mr. Watterson will perhaps admit that I am likely to know something about the matter, but he may say that a change for the better has occurred lately in the position of journalists. No doubt the profession stands higher in public esteem, and is to stand far higher yet; but what I say of Mr. Delane has been true during, I suppose, the whole of his thirty years' editorship. We have, at any rate, the best possible evidence that it was true in 1860. How is it that Mr. Watterson never heard of that extraordinary debate in the House of Commons, in 1860, in which the relations between the *Times* and the Ministry were brought in question by Mr. Horsman? Lord Palmerston was then Prime Minister, and I will quote what he said :

"My right honorable friend has stated that he did not know what the influence was which drew Mr. Delane, one of the editors or managers of the *Times*, to me ; and if by that statement he means to imply a wish on my part to exercise any influence over the line of conduct which is pursued in the case of that journal, I can only say in answer to this charge, in the words of Mrs. Malaprop, that I should be but too glad to plead guilty to the soft impeachment, and to know that the insinuation which it involves was really founded on fact. (A laugh.) If there are influences which, as the right honorable gentleman says, have fortunately led Mr. Delane to me, they are none other than the influences of society. My right honorable friend has observed, in that glowing address which he has just delivered to us, that the contributors to the press are the favorites and the ornaments of the social circles into which they enter. In that opinion he is, it seems to me, perfectly correct. The gentlemen to whom he refers are, generally speaking, persons of great attainments and information. It is, then but natural that their society should be agreeable. My acquaintance with Mr. Delane is exactly of that character. I have had the pleasure of meeting Mr. Delane frequently in society, and he has occasionally done me the honor to mix in society under my roof. That society was, I may add, composed of persons of all shades of politics [cheers], of various pursuits; and I need hardly say I feel proud when persons so honor me without undertaking any other engagement than that which Mr. Delane always makes good—of making themselves agreeable during the time of their stay."

A model speech in its way ; equally honorable to Mr. Delane and to Lord Palmerston. No private house in London was more famous than Cambridge House during Lady Palmerston's reign and so long as Lord Palmerston lived, and its owner's description of it was perfectly correct as far as it goes. Every celebrity was to be met there. It would have been surprising, indeed, had Mr. Delane been excluded; still more surprising had the fact of his visiting there been supposed to put him under any obligation to his host. The only suggestion of that kind I ever heard came from a disappointed contributor to the the *Times*, who complained that an article had been mutilated; a good story at Lord Malmesbury's expense cut out because Mr. Delane liked to dine at Malmesbury's, and an attack on the Jews suppressed for fear of its costing him his *entree* at the Rothschilds. Both those are pleasant houses, but Mr. Delane could do without both better than either could do without him. No man's position is more independent.

Mr. Walter's name is as well known in connection with the *Times* as Mr. Delane's. He is one of its owners, and the largest, and being also a member of Parliament, the double relation is sometimes a little delicate, but always managed with discretion and good faith. The family keeps possession of the paper as of an entailed estate, and it goes down from generation to generation. Mr. Walter is an able man in business and otherwise, a moderate Liberal in politics, and takes a certain constant share in the affairs of the *Times*. He cannot yet be forgotten personally in America. Mr. Mowbray Morris, late manager of the *Times*, whose malady is, I regret to say, hopeless, was long in high repute as such. It is understood that Mr. John Walter, jr., will be his permanent successor. The gentleman who holds that post temporarily has signalized his administration by some changes and some successes—notably by the Spanish correspondence, in which the *Times* has fairly surpassed in its old way all the other papers; two of its men turning up at Cartagena and on board the English fleet at the critical moment, and doing a dangerous duty with marked ability and no brag.

So when Mr. Lowe, now a Cabinet minister, was a leader-writer on the *Times*, his connection with it was an open secret—was indeed so public, that ill-natured people were found to suspect that it continued, in one way or another, after he took office. As in Lord Palmerston's days, the information of the *Times* in Cabinet and other Government matters has usually been singularly early and accurate, and they have a way of not printing it as news, but using it in a leader; so that, in fact, you must read the leaders before you can be sure you have gleaned the real news out of this paper. But if I were to mention the names of all the men who in one way or another, during the last twenty years, have been connected with the *Times*, and are known to have been, I should call the roll of half the statesmen and soldiers and writers and great lawyers of the day. They may not have been on the regular staff, but this journal has always known how to get what it wanted written on the topic of the moment from the man most competent to do it. The secret of these occasional contributors is sometimes kept and sometimes not. It depends pretty much on whether they wish it kept, which they do not always, for however great a man may be in his own profession, writing in the *Times* adds a certain luster. You may often hear particular leaders attributed to such and such outsiders, and you would not always be wrong if you inferred that the rumor was set going by the writer, and not by anybody inside the office. Men holding high office, however, can scarcely afford a luxury of this kind, and some men of high place in literature are extremely unwilling to have it supposed they write for the papers. I remember that serious offense was once given by a letter printed in New

York, describing an annual dinner given by a certain journal to its contributors. The mischief lay in publishing the names of the principal guests. The guests themselves, however, were not angry; it was the proprietor who was angry in their behalf, fearing lest they might dislike to have their presence on such an occasion known, and not write for him any more. They never heard of it, probably.

Not to go beyond the regular staff of the present, or a very recent period, I may name Russell, Dasent, Courtney, Oliphant, Dallas, Sampson, Abel, Gallenga, Phillips, and many another as men whose places on the *Times* are, or were, as well known in London as—well, say as the members of the existing government who are not members of the Cabinet. I have purposely chosen from various departments of the paper. In what sense can this be called "impersonal" journalism? In one, undoubtedly, that the name of the contributor never appears, that it is always the *Times* or the *Times* correspondent says this or that, never Mr. A or Mr. B, individually. But that is not what Mr. Watterson means.

Of other papers this is true to the same extent, or a proportional extent. Everybody knows, or if he does not know and cares to ask, will be told by the first person to whom he applies, that the editor of the *Daily News* is Mr. Frank Hill. Mr. Hill is a much younger man than Mr. Delane, and his control over the *Daily News* dates back not more than three or four years, but the fact of his becoming editor of that paper gave him instant celebrity, which is the point I beg Mr. Watterson to note. Since then, Mr. Hill has made his mark in society as a brilliant talker as well as a brilliant writer. There is no shrewder observer of men and things, nobody more familiar with what goes on in the world, with the talk of clubs, and especially of that best of clubs, the House of Commons; no man who at the same time is more intimate with Radical leaders, or knows better from contact with the world how far it is safe to carry his paper on a new path. I must admit he is a scholarly person, if that be a reproach to him, and I may add that no man, unless he possesses, to use Lord Palmerston's phrase, great attainments and information, could gain or keep an important place on an important London paper. Nor is the manager of the *Daily News*, Mr. J. R. Robinson, altogether a myth or a mere name. Readers of these letters know him well enough already, for I have said something of his services, and of the rare capacity which has enabled him to outstrip all rivals in the organization of the news department of his paper. His success was the talk of London in 1870. Or is Mr. William Black, the author of "The Daughter of Heth" and "The Princess Thule," a shadow of a name—the most successful of recent novelists, and one of the most successful and valued of journalists. Or Mr. Forbes, the war correspondent of 1870–'71, with all a soldier's knowledge of war, and taking place by the side of Russell as a descriptive writer? Or Mr. Justin McCarthy, with his double fame in England and in America? Or Miss Martineau? Or Rae, or, Hilary Skinnen, or Pigot, or Clayden, or Walker,—all men of high rank on the same journal,—which of all these is to be classed as an unknown recluse, and as the victim to "impersonal" journalism?

As for the *Daily Telegraph*, its management and editorship have always been kept to a great extent in the hands of one of its proprietors, Mr. Levy. I may almost say I never went down to the House that I did not see Mr. Levy there. His personal relations with Mr. Gladstone, and with Mr. Gladstone's lieutenant, Mr. Glyn, lately first Whip, now Lord Wolverton, are notoriously intimate. His name figures often in the *Morning Post* in the lists of guests at fashionable parties. Lately there was serious question of making him a baronet, and I suppose his elevation to that rank is only a question of time, a rank to which it is not the custom to elevate dummies, scholarly or otherwise. Under Mr. Levy, Mr. Thornton Hunt held the chief post until his death, and he went to his grave followed by a train of mourners distinguished alike by their love for him and their honorable place in the world. Mr. Hunt's successor is Mr. Edwin Arnold, a scholar no doubt, for he has published a book on the Greek Poets, but a man of most energetic mind and wide acquaintance with affairs. You can turn to his biography if you like in "Men of the Time," where also you will find Mr. Edward Dicey's, another eminent contributor to the *Telegraph*, and Mr. George Augustus Sala's. Lately there was Mr. Felix Whitehurst, Paris correspondent, and in his way certainly the most renowned of them all, an *habitué* of the Tuileries in the Emperor's time. My complaint of the London press, or criticism on it, would rather be that society is allowed far too great an influence upon it; that too many of its opinions are derived from incessant intercourse with a world which, after all, is not the universe, nor even England; that the editors and writers on London journals mix so much in fashionable life that they sometimes lose sight of the life which is unfashionable; that, on some questions, they let the judgment and interest of the upper ten thousand outweight the judgment and interests of the millions below. Most truly did Emerson say of the *Times* that it gives the argument, not of the majority, but of the commanding class. I know of no daily paper which speaks for the majority, not one to which you can go with any certainty of finding the true thought of the laboring classes sympathetically and fully stated. They are not a newspaper-buying class. To the appeals of the press in behalf of existing institutions, they might answer as Victor Hugo's Communist answers the poet pleading for the Library against the torch, and recounting the literary treasures it holds—"I cannot read." Toward that class the press is rather philanthropic than just, and to representing it it makes no pretense. If the journalists who are, to quote Lord Palmerston once more, the favorites and ornaments of society, would leave society sometimes to take care of itself, would quit, occasionally, the club for the cottage, the *salon* for the factory, the lobby of the House of Commons for the council-room of the other Trades Unions, they might really speak the voice of the people of England instead of echoing, as they too often do, the selfish cry of its prosperous minority.

JAMES GORDON BENNETT.

THE extent of the service which Mr. Bennett rendered to the press may be judged from the following list of the changes and additions which he effected in daily journalism during his life:

His primary object, as set forth in the prospectus of the *Herald*, was to make a perfectly independent journal; and this he accomplished just so far as he aimed to do.

Mr. Bennett introduced the cash system into periodical publishing, the only safe mode of carrying on a newspaper, and which saved him from immense losses, from bad debts, such as had ruined many of his predecessors, and injured most, if not all of his cotemporaries.

Instead of giving the preference to large single advertisements inserted for long periods, with the customary discounts, he encouraged small notices, especially those classed under the head of "wants," which paid far higher rates proportionately than the large yearly or half-yearly cards, while they helped to extend the circulation of the paper. This was a stroke of financial genius, and did more than anything else to establish the prosperity of the *Herald*.

Editorial puff-notices of advertisements were never given in the *Herald*. This practice, which few other newspapers have been independent enough to follow, though it is the only right rule of newspaper management, has been maintained by the *Herald* for the past twenty years.

Again, since 1847, the *Herald* has omitted all illustrated or displayed advertisements. Its pages have a uniformly neat appearance and its typographical arrangement is excellent. Soon after that date a regulation was also put in practice that no advertisement should be received for more than a single insertion, and this has also been rigidly enforced.

Next in importance were the measures introduced by Mr. Bennett to collect news of all kinds for the *Herald*. These, by general consent, surpass those undertaken by any other newspaper, and placed their inventor in advance of all his rivals in respect to energy and enterprise.

The practical utilization of the Magnetic Telegraph was hailed by Mr. Bennett as a means of widening the sphere of journalism, "no better bond of union for a great confederacy of states could have been devised," he wrote enthusiastically at the time. "The whole nation is impressed with the same idea at the same moment. One feeling and one impulse are thus created and maintained from the centre of the land to its uttermost extremities."

He was perhaps the first to arrange to have regular correspondence from the leading cities of Europe and other foreign news centres. Occasional letters from abroad had appeared in several American papers before the *Herald* was established, but there was no such thing as an organized correspondence bureau, such as most of the leading metropolitan papers now maintain, until Mr. Bennett set the example in 1838.

As a result, American newspaper readers now know the details of every important event which occurs in many countries, about which they were formerly grossly ignorant.

Mr. Bennett began with the first issue of the Weekly *Herald*, in 1836, summaries of the news for the period covered by each issue of that edition. This was afterwards made a feature of the daily *Herald*, and has been widely copied into other journals.

In the Spring of 1839 the *Herald* reported for the first time the religious anniversaries annually held at that period of the year, and in 1844 it began to give reports of sermons preached in the different metropolitan churches each Sunday. Both of these proceedings gave great offence at first, but they have now become habitual with all newspapers.

Bennett introduced a new style of writing into American journalism. Instead of the long, heavy and often ponderous editorials common to most papers like the *Globe* and Washington *Intelligencer*, he substituted short, crisp and pointed articles, written with French vivacity, added to American vigor and boldness. His original and entertaining style naturally found many imitators, and is now practiced by hundreds of journalists.

It must thus be admitted that in many of its features the *Herald* anticipated the present ideal journal, and that the American press is much indebted to its editor for the improvement.

JOURNALISTIC TRAINING.—Mr. Bennett's theory of journalistic training was simple, namely, that his own paper was the best school for journalists. It having always been designed that his son should succeed as editor of the *Herald*, he was carefully trained by his father. Mr. Bennett is one of the most thoroughly educated young men in America, having studied in Europe under the best masters. He speaks several modern languages, and has traveled extensively, while he can set type and run a printing-press, an accomplishment possessed by Horace Greeley, Thurlow Weed, and many of the elder editors, but one which probably none of the younger generation of journalists are master of.

When Mr. Halstead, of the Cincinnati *Commercial*, offered to buy the *Herald*, Mr. Bennett declined to enter into negotiations, on the ground that his son, who has since succeeded him in the proprietorship of that paper, possessed qualities that would give him the highest rank in journalism.

NEWSPAPER PERSONALITIES.—In May, 1831, the *Herald* contained a calm and dignified article upon the mode of conducting a newspaper, in which it was asserted that "there is no existing cause for personal invective between the conductors of the press in their support of men or measures," and it was complained that "the want of union of individual respect and courtesy among editors of established character" injures the press. It further said, "We declare solemnly, that we take pleasure in seeing every editor prosperous, that is, every editor whom public opinion deems worthy of support." And it animadverted strongly against those persons who foment personal quarrels between journalists; adding, "We are thus played off between battledore and shuttlecock—used by all, to be proscribed and thrown off by all."

IMPERSONAL JOURNALISM.—In the early days of the *Herald*, and up to within a few years, its editor seemed to take special pleasure in talking about himself and his private affairs in the columns of that journal. His amusing and boastful garrulity was a marked feature of the *Herald*. His marriage, the increase of his income, and the growing prosperity of his paper, were all paraded so as to give spice to the paper, and with a naive disregard of what the public thought of such revelations. Of late years, however, quite an opposite course has been pursued in the *Herald*. For nearly ten years a dignified silence has been maintained in its columns in respect to the private affairs of its conductor, and the impersonal tone of the London *Times* has been adopted. When Mr. Bennett's house on Washington Heights caught fire, and was nearly destroyed, the *Herald* made no allusion to it; neither did it refer to the change when the younger Bennett's name was placed at the head of the paper as "manager."

A FEW extracts from the estimates of Mr. Bennett, made after his death by certain of his cotemporaries, will aid in forming a clear conception of his life and labors. Mr. Dana observes that "It was the day-dream of his (Bennett's) life that by keeping the *Herald* in the vortex of New York business life, and by enlivening it with a wit that his successors have not even understood, much less emulated, he might make it the journal of the future; and he did not hesitate to say as much. In a pecuniary sense he was prodigiously successful."

It is commonly said that the great success of the *Herald* is primarily due to the enterprise and talent it has displayed in the collection of news. This remark contains some truth; but it is not the essential truth by any means. The chief elements which have given to the *Herald* such popularity are of a more intellectual and a more personal character. These elements are Mr. Bennett's genius, his wit, his extraordinary independence of mind, his originality—amounting often to a fascinating kind of eccentricity, and his moral courage. These it is that have made the *Herald*, and to these its industry and its expenditures as a newspaper, however remarkable, have been subsidiary.

An invaluable service which Mr. Bennett has rendered to the press has been to emancipate it from the domination of sects, parties, cliques, and of what is called society. Before him a really independent newspaper was unknown, and now there is a number of them, and they are increasing. Mr. Bennett's mental independence and moral courage were alike absolute and uncompromising. There was nothing which he so much hated as the idea of being owned, managed, or dictated to by anybody. Before everything else it was his rule, his policy, his religion, to follow the conclusions and promptings of his own mind; to do and to say what he himself thought proper. He revolted at every scheme to shape and influence his action. Flattery, however cunningly administered, he despised; and those who imagined they could use him for their own purposes were sure to be convinced of their mistake in a way as surprising to them as it was diverting to the public. This fidelity to his own ideas and his own ends was not qualified by any necessity for much social intercourse, or for coöperation with other men, or by any regard for conventional assumptions. The greatest magnate was no more to him than any common man, and he castigated the one just as readily as the other. Accordingly he had few friends, and of those, still fewer were intellectually his equals. Even in his early life, before he had begun the *Herald*, he does not appear to have cared much for companionship; and yet he was never misanthropic. His manners were courtly and elegant, without pretention and without affectation, and no man could be more charming to those admitted to his society. He was always liked by his employés and assistants, but he never sought for advice, and those who pressed their counsels upon him never gained much from their efforts.

Of all Mr. Bennett's qualities, that which was most universally appreciated was his wit. This was peculiar and incessant. Though unlike the wit of any other man, everybody understood it. It was never labored or far-fetched, and its jollity and apparent good nature, even when employed in the destruction of an adversary, made it delightful. For years this wit constituted one of the principal attractions of the *Herald*, and when everything else failed, it could always be relied upon. Mr. Bennett's moral courage was also equal to every test. The *Herald* was never afraid, and never cowed before the most formidable adversary.

Mr. Bennett's mind was intuitive rather than logical, but it was so shrewd, so suggestive, and so fruitful of ideas, that it is not too much to say that he was a man of genius. His culture was that of experience, observation and reflection rather than of much study or reading. He was not learned, in the usual sense of that word, but he possessed an extraordinary stock of general and often of recondite information. He had a strong tendency to paradox, and his delight in whimsical views of men and things make his conversation as entertaining as his writings. He was essentially skeptical. He knew men by instinct, and saw through their motives at a glance, especially the bad ones; and he was rarely taken in by an impostor. Credulity he despised; the merely commonplace was nauseous to him; a sham excited his scorn; fools were his playthings; and solemn, respectable humbugs he loved to pounce upon and tear to pieces. And so he lived his life and fought his battle, misunderstood, feared, assailed, hated, and courted as few men have ever been; and yet through the whole of it walking in his own path and acting according to his own uninfluenced will and opinions as few have ever been able to do.

It is easy now to say that Mr. Bennett would have been a greater or a better man if he had possessed a more confiding heart and more delicate moral sensibilities; if his mind had been believing rather than skeptical; and if he had been the follower of a party or a creed rather than their gay and laughing critic, using parties and creeds for his own pleasure, even when he seemed to favor or to serve them. But those who dwell upon these defects should remember that in his domestic relations he was most affectionate and generous; and that in his relations to others he was always honest and truthful, never defrauding or deceiving any one. And who can affirm that if he had been constituted otherwise than he was, he would have suited his day and generation so well as he has done, or that he could have played so large or so useful a part upon the stage of the world.

Mr I. B. Chamberlain, of the *World*, ranks Mr. Bennett as first among that class of American journalists who seek to float on the current instead of directing its course, as Mr. Greeley was first among those who have made newspapers great controlling organs of opinion.

Mr. F. B. Sanborn, in reviewing Hudson's "History of Journalism," remarks: "We call the New York *Herald* a very bad paper," said Horace Greeley, before the English Parliamentary Committee in 1851—and he spoke the sentiment of the better portion of his countrymen then and for years afterward. Theodore Parker, in 1859, alluded pungently to "those two 'escape pipes of secular and ecclesiastical wickedness,' the New York *Herald* and *Observer*," and it was not until after the civil war began that Mr. Hudson's newspaper fairly rose to respectability.

"No good cause was without its support," says Mr. Hudson, with a natural enthusiasm for his own newspaper which does credit to his heart, "no bad cause was without its denunciation." But it seldom supported the good cause until it no longer needed support, and it abstained from denouncing a great many bad causes till the majority of its readers knew from other information how bad they were. Since 1861 this has been changing, but it is not unkind to say that neither the character nor the reputation of the *Herald* lost much by the death of Mr. Bennett. He was a man of prodigious power in his way, and Mr. Hudson does well to recall the better features of his career; but the blemish on his book is his amiable inability to deal out exact justice to his former chief—" the Napoleon of the American press," as he is styled.

The editor of the *Nation* remarks " That Mr. Bennett did journalism a great service, every one must admit. That he did not render it this service without at the same time doing it great injury, and that the stage in which he left it is not to be forsaken and left behind, no one, we suppose, can rightly deny. Indeed, Mr. Bennett lived to see—or lived so long that he had the opportunity of seeing—that the *Herald* order of journalism is already in great part superseded. If to buy the news and sell it were all of journalism, the *Herald* would not now be held in contempt by all men—and they are an increasing number—who believe that the true province of a great journal is to buy and sell, not news alone, but news accompanied by such comments as shall help the general public to understand the intelligence each morning spread before it, and shall be of a character to assist " right reason and the will of God to prevail.' 'The *Herald's* method in journalism,' says one of our generalizers, 'is to lay before the people all that happens; this is God's teaching.' God, however, is not his own interpreter, and the best journalist is not he who dumps most facts before his public, nor yet he who by his comments aims to acquire to himself power and influence in politics or in the gold market, but he who, exercising power in virtue of intelligence and right feeling, uses it to advance the general good with no thought of his own aggrandizement, or even of his journal's, and with much thought for the public. The lesson of Mr. Bennett's career, laborious and successful as it was, is not in the most important respects a good one. In his domestic life, and in his relations with his co-workers on the paper which he idolized, he was greatly liked—even loved. We have known many instances of his great and thoughtful kindness to those who served him. But he has left behind him a bad example as well as a good one, and to-day men who can imitate his scurrility and audacity and shamelessness, but not his acuteness, his generosity, his enterprise, his genius for finding out not only the bad and mean things, but also the good things, about which the people wanted to know immediately, are doing much to make our profession a disgraceful one, and to give us an impish press as he gave us the Satanic."

The following is part of an editorial estimate of Mr. Bennett's career, taken from the *Tribune* of June 6, 1872, the second morning after his death:

"Mr. Bennett will not be judged in future by what he was, but by what he accomplished. The passions, the hates, the controversies of the past, will all fade away from memory in another generation. But the *Herald* will remain the permanent and visible proof of what there was in the heart and the intellect of its founder.

"Viewing his life from this point of view, it was completely successful. He had no other aim than to make

a great and lucrative newspaper. In his days of poverty
and privation, he boasted with gay defiance that, in spite
of all the malice of his enemies, he would one day make
the *Herald* produce $30,000 annually. He probably
thought this prophecy exaggerated, but he lived to see it
dwindled into absurdity by its tenfold accomplishment.
He attained this great result by no trick, no luck, no accident. There was never seen a more logical and necessary issue of a given course of action. He was a man of
extraordinary capacity. He has written so little of late
years that elderly people have forgotten and young people never have known that no journalist in the country
excelled him in the power of commenting upon current
events in the way most acceptable to a large majority of
readers. He had a good temper and a geniality which
were purely professional, having no relation whatever to
his toilsome and sombre life. At a time when drunkenness was the rule among people of his craft, he was as
frugal and abstemious as an Arab. An iron constitution
enabled him to do the work of three ordinary men, without either fever or fatigue. To these qualifications was
added a gift which is common enough now, but which at
the time when he began his career was so rare that it par-
took of the exceptional quality of genius. He understood the value of news. He may almost be said to be
the inventor of journalism in its latest and highest development as a means of disseminating all accessible
contemporaneous intelligence. He was the first journalist who went to meet the news half-way. This was the
sole secret of his success. All the sensations, scandals,
and fierce wranglings of his earlier years did very little
to advance or retard the march of his great newspaper.
When he began that long and desperate battle with a
hostile fate in the dark Wall Street cellar, the victory was

assured to him beforehand by his inexhaustible energy and his infallible journalistic instinct.

"By adhering to certain true principles of journalism, he made the greatest material, that is to say, pecuniary success, in that profession, which the world has yet seen. This is perhaps as much in the way of example as the world has any right to expect from any one man. Beyond this, it certainly receives nothing more than warning from the founder of the *Herald*. He attempted no more than the establishment of a newspaper. Others have followed him in the same path with equal success, and now the only journalism which looks to the future for a constantly widening sphere of power and influence is that which aims not only to gather and edit each day the whole world's history for the preceding day, but, so far as possible, in addition, to lead and train the honest thought of the world. This is an immense plan, impossible to be accomplished perfectly by the present resources of any journal. Even to approach its fulfillment will require all the energy, all the sagacity, all the varied ability, all the personal probity of the great journalist who died on Saturday, together with a public conscience, a personal earnestness, a freedom from private ends, and a respect for the dignity of human nature, which he considered outside of the sphere of journalism."

JAMES GORDON BENNETT, Jr.

The present proprietor and editor of the *Herald* inherits the opinions of his father, and follows the traditions of the paper, as may be seen from the annexed expressions of his views on journalistic topics, as contained in late articles in the *Herald*:

The Greatness of Journalism.—Commenting on the nomination of Mr. Greeley by the Cincinnati convention, the *Herald* said: We see in this a tendency on the part of the people to regard the journalist as a master. The profession which once was despised now wins respect from our people, has open to it the highest prizes of citizenship. We see due honor and propriety in this, but at the same time we must dissuade all journalists from treading the thorny and perplexing path by which Horace Greeley has reached a nomination for the Presidency. The time will come, and we think swiftly, when an editor will see no ambition higher than the fulfillment of his duty as a journalist.

Morals of Journalists.—Without discipline and a certain degree of decision and firmness, no respectably established newspaper can run long without corruption creeping in somewhere, and the whole machinery finally becoming rickety and out of order. Indeed, we are not sure but it would be a good thing for the proprietors of all leading papers to unite in a league to refuse employment to persons accused, upon well established grounds, of bribery and other serious malpractices while in the discharge of confidential and responsible duties in newspaper establishments. It is very true that newspaper writers in this day are exposed to more temptations than ever fell to the lot of the earlier knights of the quill. There are the stock-jobbing tempter and the gold operating tempter, and the cotton speculating tempter of Wall Street, the breadstuffs and provisions tempter of the Produce Exchange, the railroad grant tempter, the old fossil claims tempter, the job contract tempter, the patent street pavement tempter, the street railroad tempter, but, above all, the tempter par excellence—the very Beelzebub of bribe offerers—the unscrupulous politician, who with plethoric wealth at command, tempts some poor newspaper subordinate from the strict paths of rectitude. There are some people, however, who make no disguise of their weakness in the matter of bribery and openly boast of the achievements in that line; but these are of the seedy, irresponsible, Bohemian class, who are obliged to live by their wits so long as that feeble capital lasts.

Now, while it is mortifying to be compelled to read these charges of bribery and corruption bandied between our cotemporaries, we want to ask what does the great public care about them? What does a great reading community like New York care whether this man of the *Sun* has taken five thousand dollars from a tempter like Boss Tweed, or that man of the *Tribune* has taken one thousand dollars for some twaddle or another, or the other man of the *Standard* has become the victim of misplaced confidence which others reposed in him—what does the reading public of New York, we repeat, care about all these abusive charges, these criminations and recriminations which now disgrace the columns of city papers?

We warrant that, after the first titillating sensation arising from the fun of the fight is over, the people as a mass feel humiliated at witnessing these demoralizing newspaper quarrels.

DAILY JOURNALISM NOT A SCIENCE.—We believe that it is impossible to reduce daily journalism to a science. Journalism, properly understood and wisely developed, is the reflection of events which are created almost hour by hour of thoughts and opinions that change and take shape in the mould of these events. Based upon the shifting sands of perpetual change; following rather than leading the philosophy of daily life as we hear and read of it in all quarters of the Earth, journalism must catch the current as it passes. It must be instantaneous, quick almost as the electric flash itself. The capacity to accomplish this may be skill, method, enterprise, discipline, genius, if you will, but it does not belong to the sober ranks of science. The secret of power in journalism, after all, lies most in the impersonality of the journalist. If the managers of newspapers would only stifle the ambition to unite their individuality with their professional successes, whatever they may be, they would be pursuing their grand mission clothed with a tenfold influence. Egotism has so taken hold of our editorial system in this country that the majesty of the press is often reduced to the infinitessimal proportions of the writer, which is a great pity, because the newspaper press is a mighty engine, working with a mystical and sometimes latent force through all the channels of civilization.

IMPERSONALITY OF THE PRESS.—Whatever may be said to the contrary, it is nevertheless a fact, that the old system of considering the editor of a paper the embodiment of its opinions and suggestions, is giving way to a grander and more comprehensive idea, the offspring of the progressive spirit of the age. Now the newspaper press brings to its aid those tremendous powers, steam and electricity—the godfathers of our gigantic lines of telegraph, railroads, ocean steamships and other press auxiliaries, that were not dreamed of in the early days of American journalism. Hence it is natural that a great newspaper should drop its individuality of former periods and become what the character of the times demands—the great oracle of popular sentiment and the untiring vehicle of universal intelligence.

JOURNALISM OF THE FUTURE.—From these suggestions the whole broad field of American journalism rises before us, past and present, and with its probabilities and possibilities of the future. In this general view of the subject we may say that Francis P. Blair, Sr., of the Washington *Globe*, represented an epoch of American journalism which is among the things of the past; that Mr. Greeley, in the *Tribune*, represented an epoch that is rapidly passing away, and that the new journalistic era that is now dawning upon us will mark still another advance with the advancing spirit of the age. The journalism represented by the old Washington *Globe*, the Albany *Argus*, and the Richmond *Enquirer*, was that of kitchen cabinets, party regencies and juntas. The *Globe*, from Washington, gave the cue to the whole Democratic press of the country, while the Albany *Argus* and Richmond *Enquirer* each regulated the party of its section, the one in the North, the other in the South. The *Globe*, however, was but the organ of the kitchen cabinet, and the *Argus* and *Enquirer* were the mere mouthpieces of a controlling regency or junta. This was the dominating American journalism of the political period represented by Jackson and Van Buren. The independent press came next upon the stage, in the modest but popular form of a penny paper or two, in most of our great cities, and from the pressure of these enterprising newspapers those previously omnipotent central party organs were driven from the field or stripped of their influence over public opinion. But, at the same time, personal journalism under this new dispensation, in the New York *Tribune*, for example, was more broadly developed than under the old party dominion of Blair, Ritchie, and Croswell. The *Tribune* became the organ of Mr. Greeley. He was the *Tribune* and the *Tribune* was Greeley. He possessed those strong intellectual qualities, that marked individuality of character, those distinguishing and popular eccentricities which made the *Tribune*, and which, whatever the modifications, are indispensible to the success of a personal journal. To similar causes are due the success of the *Herald*. Indeed, such has been the partiality of the American people for those exceptional intellects capable of impressing themselves upon the public mind in everything they discuss, that Parson Brownlow, at the head of a small weekly newspaper in the mountains of Tennessee, brought it into general notice and won for it an unexpected success. Nor is this a new thing, nor is it limited to this country; for in England, Cobbett, in his day, and in France under the late Empire, Rochefort was a marked success in personal journalism. From similar striking individualities Dickens, so successful as a novelist, would doubtless have been equally successful as the writer of the distinguishing editorials of a newspaper. But with the extension of the facilities of the telegraph our metropolitan newspapers are inevitably tending to that impersonal journalism which is most fully represented by the London *Times*. The news from the four quarters of the globe, which is now gathered for a daily metropolitan paper, embraces so many subjects for editorial discussion that a number of competent writers are required to cover it. Hence the disappearance, more and more, of that marked individuality, even of the *Tribune*, of late years. With the death of Mr. Greeley that journal must necessarily be reorganized upon the rule of impersonal journalism. And we speak from the results of experience in giving it as our opinion that this is the true system for a great daily journal, and the road to the highest success for "the age we live in," with its enlarged and still widening telegraphic facilities. The *Herald*, the *Tribune*, and the *Times*, with the loss to each of its founder and builder, have lost all their character as personal journals; but they are each established on that solid foundation of success which invites them to this new departure of impersonal and independent journalism, so distinctly outlined by Mr. Greeley on his return, from that "other line of business" to the conduct of the *Tribune*. There is enough, too, in the example, the system, and the policy of the founders of each of these journals to guide their successors in office, independently of that personal journalism which has at length for us been overreached by the telegraph.

THE following account of the inauguration of Mr. Bennett's most brilliant enterprise, the Stanley-Livingstone expedition, is so characteristic of its author as to deserve recording. It was given by Mr. Stanley in a short speech at the banquet at Paris in his honor: Before referring to my humble self, I will speak to you of meeting with James Gordon Bennett, Jr., who telegraphed to me to come to Paris from Madrid to receive some very important instructions. I arrived by the express train and called immediately on Mr. Bennett, whom I had to knock up; he rose, and my name found me a ready welcome. Asking me to be seated Mr. Bennett informed me that he had matters of serious importance to communicate, and whenever he spoke thus it was always preparatory to something really worthy of attention. He began by saying it was his wish for me to find Dr. Livingstone. I really thought he was joking, and to find out if he was in earnest spoke of the expense likely to be incurred in sending me to Central Africa in search of Livingstone. "How much do you think it will cost," he asked. "Probably two thousand pounds," I replied. Bennett then said, "As I want to find Livingstone you can draw a thousand pounds; two, three, four, five if requisite, but only find Livingstone; get what news you can from him; perhaps the old man is in want, then relieve him; perhaps he will require your aid, give it him, and don't fail to let us know if Livingstone lives." Who could withstand such generous reasoning as this? I said, as many of you would have said, "I will find him if human nature permits me to do so; if not I can but die." On parting he said, "I wish you good evening; God be with you." "He will," I said, "on such an errand; good night." That very evening I left.

In response to an invitation to attend a press convention of the Ohio Editorial Convention, early in 1872, the

Herald laid aside its impersonality so far as to say : " We must confess that we do not like the personal publicity which some members of the press on occasions like this and at other times are prone to encourage. It is dangerous, and demoralizing to the profession. The journalist should be like a sensible actor, who, when he is off the stage, discards stage dodges; in other words, he should resemble discreet business men, who "sink the shop" when they are out of it. In short he should be impersonal. He has a responsibility to bear before the public which should impel him to do his office work in the sanctum, and when he is abroad he should be as modest and quiet as possible, making no pretensions to superiority in any respect over any other class of men."

After commenting severely on the arrangement for supplying visitors to the convention with free passes, it continued: "It is the mission of the newspaper press, aided by that mighty lever, Public Opinion, to move political worlds, make and unmake statesmen, cause crowns and dynasties to tremble, reveal and lay bare corruption in high places, inspire enthusiasm in religious communities; that it is becoming more potential in all that works the moral, social, political, religious—indeed all practical improvements of mankind—than any other agents under the sun ? There are newspapers in existence that do as important a business, and with as much promptness and regularity, as many of the first banking and commercial houses in the world. Their credit and standing are as good at home and abroad as those of any of the famous banking and merchant princes we hear so much about, while personally they are more independent in conducting their business affairs.

"Becoming thus so powerful an engine in promoting the welfare of mankind and in influencing the human mind, is it not humiliating to see decent newspaper men stooping to barter away their independence by accepting a " deadhead " ticket for any purpose whatever? For ourselves we desire to have it distinctly understood that we do not thank railroad or steamboat companies, or hotel keepers, or theatrical managers for " deadheading " any person representing himself to be an employé of the *Herald.* All our attachés are gentlemen, who, when on office business, are prepared to pay their way; all others may be set down as imposters."

GEORGE P. ROWELL.

NONE of the preceeding statements in this volume consider, except indirectly, the business side of journalism, and, therefore. it has seemed fitting to give some account of certain features of newspaper publishing by an acknowledged authority on such matters. While part of his remarks are intended specially to interest the advertising class, yet they also treat of the principles which effect most, if not all publishers :

The usual methods of attracting business are well known, and are to a certain extent effective. Every dealer has a sign to show his name and trade. A handsome display of goods attracts casual observers. Better than these are the commendatory words of customers who are pleased with their transactions. A word in favor of a business house is often worth much. If one person's good words are worth something, the commendation of ten will be worth ten times as much, and of an hundred, an hundred times as much. Life is short, and it is every man's ambition to make a fortune. Everything is sought which will tend to hasten the happy time when that fortune can be counted as made. The way is: to be prepared to serve the public, and then let the public know what you can do so that they may hasten to become customers. Every man, to a greater or less extent, prefers to trade where he has formerly traded. The shrewd business man is therefore anxious to secure the first possible order from every man who has an order to give. The earlier the first order is secured the better prospect there is of making a regular customer at an early day.

A man intending to do business, having prepared himself to suit customers, must next let every possible or probable customer know that he is so prepared. How to do this becomes the question. In a very small place he may tell all the people what he can do. In a large village a printed handbill, poster or circular, properly distributed, will be efficacious, but whoever is in a place large enough to support a newspaper, will find that the cheapest medium through which to address the public.

The local newspaper is taken by the best people in every locality. It is the only advertising medium that is bought and paid for by the persons whose attention the advertiser is desirous of attracting. The attention of the subscriber to a regular newspaper is invited to an announcement in it without any officious solicitation, almost without his knowing it. Every man is conscious that he thinks much more of the paper for which he pays than of any occasional copy of a gratuitous sheet or circular which is thrust in at his door. An advertisement in his own paper attracts his attention and secures (to some extent) his confidence, while the same notice under other circumstances would pass unheeded. The great point, the strong reason why the newspaper is the best advertising medium, is because it is paid for by the recipient. The subscriber pays the actual cost of manufacture and distribution. The publisher can therefore give publicity to an advertisement at a much lower price per hurdred or per thousand than could be afforded under other circumstances. Nothing can compete successfully with the newspaper as a general advertising medium.

A clothing store may be advertised in all sections of the country from which visitors come to the town where the store is located, the same rule will apply to trunk or harness makers, jewelers, or dealers in any article in which reputation has anything to do with price, and which may be sent to a distance at a comparatively small cost. A dealer in such goods, located in New York, may advertise in papers circulating in every state in the Union, If located in Boston he must confine his cards mainly to newspapers having a circulation in New England (excluding Connecticut, whose trade goes to New York) and in the West. If in Chicago or St. Louis, he must try the West and Northwest. San Francisco merchants may use the press of the entire Pacific Coast. It is plain enough that the attraction must be very strong indeed, that will carry New Jersey trade to Chicago, or Kentucky and Indiana trade to San Francisco.

A trade in those articles which require to be personally inspected by the purchaser, can only be built up, profitably, in the regions from which the people are in the habit of visiting the locality of the advertiser.

Money can only be procured at reasonable rates where it is more abundant than is needed for home use. It will be observed that railroad bonds are not advertised by shrewd operators, to any great extent west of Illinois, or in any of the Southern States. In New England, New York, New Jersey, and Pennsylvania is most of the unemployed capital, and these are the fields in which to advertise. Cheap lands and colonization schemes are advertised in the older and more thickly settled States. Anything which seeks money for investment must appeal where the money is to be had.

Schools require but few customers, and these may be drawn from any section of country: only the children of the rich and cultivated are sent away to school. A school should be advertised in papers of large circulation, among people well-to-do and intelligent. Daily papers, the religious press, the magazines, weeklies of the large dailies, the literary, the high-toned and high-priced journals, and (possibly of more value than any others, compared to the cost,) local journals issued in neighborhoods from which the school now has or formerly had pupils; there is no place where it will pay so well to advertise a school, or in fact anything else, as in the place where it is already favorably known. Advertise before each term from one to three months.

To advertise books, newspapers, etc., use first the standard papers—dailies, weeklies of dailies, magazines, literary papers. As a rule, book advertisements should receive no more than from one to six insertions. The more solid the book, the smaller and more select the list of papers should be. The more flashy the book, the larger and more varied should be the list, and the advertisement may be inserted for a longer period. The remarks about books apply equally well to newspapers. It has become customary to advertise newspapers in December mainly; sometimes in July, or a few weeks before. All the leading journals issue their announcements at these periods. It is a question whether it would not be more efficacious to take some other time, thus securing greater prominence by avoiding the flood of similar announcements.

A large class of advertisements are intended for the eyes of persons seeking profitable employment. Such are usually headed "Agents Wanted," and are used by publishers of subscription books, dealers in patent rights, new machines and sundry notions—are generally set up in small space, and pay best in papers having the largest circulation, without much regard being had for the character of the circulation, beyond the acknowledged fact that country readers are more easily induced to try a new thing than are those in cities. Advertisements of this class pay better than any others (except medicine advertisements) in country newspapers.

Local or country newspapers are favorite mediums for those who wish to make sales in particular localities, because the circulation of a village newspaper is generally confined to a circuit of a few miles around the office of publication. The county newspaper is hardly known in adjoining counties. In these mediums the advertiser makes every subscriber available. Our meaning can be best illustrated by an example: The *Weekly Tribune*, published in New York City, will insert a ten-line advertisement ten weeks for $200; but in the State of New York the *Tribune* has few more readers than the Albany *Weekly Journal*, in which ten lines for ten weeks will cost but $20. In Western New York, the Rochester *Weekly Union and Advertiser* has as many readers as the Albany *Journal*, and in the Rochester paper the advertisement will cost but $5; while in Brockport, in Western New York, the circulation of the *Republic* exceeds that of all the other papers combined, and will do the advertising for $4. For the advertiser who only wishes to sell in Brockport the *Republic* is worth more than the *Tribune*—hence it will be seen that judgment must be used in the selection of papers. To reach sections the local journals are the best. Let us suppose that it is desired to appoint agents for a certain book. Each agent is to control certain territory, towns or counties. It is desirable to dispose of the whole country as soon as possible. It would be best to advertise for one or three months in all the advertising mediums of large circulations, whether local or general in character. Soon agencies are made, and some States are sold entire, in others counties and towns are sold. It will no longer do to advertise in papers of a general circulation, but in those only which go over the unsold territory.

To sell patent rights, sewing machines, notions, patented articles, pictures, &c., &c., use the country weeklies on the "List System," and all the weeklies of over 10,000 circulation, particularly the religious and agricultural papers. Contracts should usually be made for one or three months; generally for the shorter time. To sell seeds, plants, agricultural implements, &c., use agricultural papers, and the larger circulating weeklies which have a practical every day life character. Such go mainly into the country, and are read by the most substantial classes of the agricultural population. To reach factory operatives, youth, the fancy—for sale of light literature, photographs, cosmetics, beautifiers generally—use the story papers and the lighter class of illustrated weeklies. For horse, sporting and turf advertisements use the sporting journals and the leading dailies.

It is a pretty well established fact that a patent medicine, or other proprietary article, cannot have a permanent sale unless meritorious. Advertising, we are often told by druggists, will sell one bottle of a worthless preparation, but it will not sell another to the same man. Although it is true enough that any preparation which could be sold once to every person in this country would make the fortune of the advertiser, yet it is best to start with a good thing, something that wherever best known will be in greatest demand.

On yearly contracts the country press offers by far the cheapest advertising mediums. On short time contracts the papers of large circulation give greatly more service for the money. He who would become a successful advertiser must keep out of his mind two ideas which are very prevalent. 1st. He must not think because a paper has a very small circulation that it is of no value as an advertising medium. 2d. He must not think because a paper has a very large circulation that too high a price cannot be demanded. It is an unfortunate thing, perhaps, but it is nevertheless true, that there is no standard price for advertising. We have known a man to make a rule of offering publishers one-half the price they demanded for inserting his card, and he often paid very high prices indeed. Many a publisher who has space to spare will not refuse an offer of forty dollars for inserting a column one year, although his published price is one hundred.

Of late the style of advertising by reading notices has come greatly into fashion. The most successful advertisers at the present time use a sheet of fifty-two notices, a new one for each week, and generally four standing advertisements, which are to alternate once in three months, or perhaps a new one to go in each week, so that the entire lot may have one insertion every month. These are all printed on one sheet, together with the notices, with printed instructions, generally calling for regular insertions in the weeklies and alternate days in dailies (on the ground that a contract for alternate days will be taken for about half the price for every day, and that in all but the best seasons, the publisher having plenty of room, will prefer to insert every day rather than take the trouble of changing). These sheets are sent to publishers, who are offered a certain price to insert both the advertisements and notices. Some publishers make a practice of charging for the standing advertisements according to the scale and putting in the notices gratis. Others, for equally good reasons, charge for the notices according to the scale rate, and put the advertisements in gratis. Occasionally a publisher wants pay for both. In any case, unless the original offer is accepted, the matter goes back to the advertiser, with a rate named for either the notices or the advertisements separately and for both combined. The advertiser then accepts the proposal he considers most advantageous. So much discrepancy exists among publishers regarding the comparative value of standing advertisements and local notices to be changed weekly, that every shrewd advertiser has felt himself compelled to provide copy of both sorts.

Whoever would secure advertising at a low price should not be in a hurry. The best advertisers know that there is not much difference in the value of the various seasons, and although they often use the argument to hurry up a dilatory contractor, or in complaining of omissions to a publisher who has been remiss, they are generally content to make contracts when they will be taken lowest, and never to seem in a hurry. The true rule for a patent medicine man is to always advertise when space is offered low enough, and never to pay a high price when there is reason to believe that by waiting the same service can be had for a smaller sum. A yearly contract runs through all seasons, no matter when it is begun.

Advertisers are frequently disappointed at the time which it requires to receive answers to their advertisements. A card appearing to-day in a New York daily brings answers to-day and is forgotten in a week; while in the weekly of that daily it will be a week before the paper comes out, from one to ten days may elapse before the paper reaches the subscriber, and as many more days go by before the reply to the advertisement can come in. Mowing machines are sold in June and July, garden seeds in March, April and May, but advertisements for these articles must be ordered in time to appear in the papers and for orders to come in and be filled before the day of actual use. A school which commences its term September 15th, should be advertised in June, July and August.

Almost every advertiser has his theory about the proper season for advertising. Some say that there is no use of trying to force trade when it is dull; others say that trade is good enough at certain seasons, and they only want more trade in such and such months. Hence they advertise at that time only. Some regard must be paid to season, without doubt, and advertisements should be so worded as to be seasonable; but people read the newspapers about as much at one time as another, and if at certain periods an advertisement is not likely to be quite as productive, that fact keeps competing advertisements out of the newspaper columns, and consequently gives the whole field to the man who *does* advertise at that time, thus making the dull season in truth a season of plenty. We would not recommend a druggist to advertise "Ice Cold Soda" in January, nor should "Arctic Overshoes" for the retail trade be pushed with much energy in June; but outside of a few articles which have their seasons, it is admitted by the most experienced advertisers that the best time to advertise is all the time.

Nothing is more common than the complaint, "My advertising did not pay me because I commenced too early"—meaning it was stopped too soon; or "My advertising was so late when it appeared in the papers that the season for advertising had gone by." A good reason why advertisers should be in the papers all the time may be found in the fact that, as a general rule, contracts by the year cost a very much lower price per month than when made for a shorter time.

An advertiser should use only those newspapers whose

circulations are in localities from which it is possible for him to secure trade. Questions of freight, local prejudice and competing markets are to be considered. An advertiser doing a trade in a country town may advertise in his local papers and in the papers circulating on lines of road leading into or through his place of business, while it would hardly pay to insert cards in distant towns, where customers, before reaching the advertiser, must pass through larger places, offering facilities for supplying his wants to better probable advantage. Every inexperienced advertiser should begin small, and move cautiously, feeling the way, as it were. Goods which can be sent by mail or in express packages, may be advertised indiscriminately, even if but a comparatively small amount is to be expended; but bulky articles, which involve heavy freight charges in the delivery, should not be largely advertised in fields where the goods have not been previously placed on sale. It would be plainly absurd for a manufacturer of a new mowing machine or cooking-stove at Albany, N. Y., to advertise his goods in Minnesota or Northern Michigan, without first arranging to have the goods placed on sale in those localities. Of course a limited amount of advertising would not be injudicious, if done with the intention of causing inquiry, for the purpose of preparing dealers to take an interest in the new candidate for their favor.

As a general rule, the highest-priced advertising mediums are the cheapest in the end, but it must not be concluded from this that a paper is a good advertising medium because it is high-priced. The old-established journals of large circulation demand prices that seem excessively high. *Harper's Weekly* demands $2 per line of space for each insertion of an advertisement. Several papers demand prices varying from 50 cts. to $2; and for small advertisements, to be inserted but a few times, they, as a rule, give greater circulation for the money than can be otherwise obtained.

So thoroughly has the advertising public become impressed with the fact stated above, that there has of late been a large increase of the advertising patronage of the few highest-priced advertising mediums. To such an extent has this been carried that prices have been so much advanced in many of the choicest mediums that they are no longer cheap. We know of but one weekly paper charging 50 cts. per line, or more, which gives 1,000 cirlation for each cent per line, while there are many which take advertisements at from 10 to 20 cts. per line, and give more circulation for the price than is named above. At one cent per line per thousand copies issued, *Harper's Weekly* and the *Weekly Tribune* must print 200,000 copies weekly to be worth the $2 per line which they demand.

It must specially be borne in mind that while high-priced papers charge the same price for each insertion, and allow but small discounts on the largest orders, lower-priced papers allow very large reductions of price on long advertisements continued by the month, quarter or year.

Supposing the New York *Weekly Tribune* to charge $2 per line, and to print 200,000 copies weekly, this gives for one week 1,000 circulation to an advertisement of 100 lines for one dollar. If continued three months it is customary to deduct say ten per cent., giving 1,000 circulation for 90 cts.; for six months deduct one-eighth, or 87½ cts. for 1,000 circulation; for one year a deduction of one-fourth is made, or 75 cents for 1,000 circulation. Other high-priced papers make deductions in about this ratio. An ordinary country paper, with 1,000 circulation, will insert 100 lines one week for, say $5, or five times the *Tribune* price for the same circulation. For three months the country paper will demand say $15, which will be ten per cent. higher than the *Tribune's* net charge per thousand; for six months the country paper will be satisfied with $20, while for the same circulation the *Tribune* will demand $22.75. For one year the *Tribune* must have $39 for 1,000 circulation of an advertisement of 100 lines, while the country paper will take the same for $26. Unreasonable as it may seem, it is true that what are known as country papers have no fixed schedule of prices for yearly advertisements of the size named above—sometimes as low as $8, $10 or $12 per year will be accepted. Any one can see that at these prices they cost at from one-fifth to one-third the price demanded by high-priced papers like the *Tribune*.

In estimating the value of newspaper circulation it may be taken as a safe rule never to pay more than one cent per line for 1,000 circulation of a weekly journal. In a monthly magazine more may be paid; also in some papers of especial value, which, from their character, are likely to be more extensively read or more generally preserved for future reading than would ordinarily be the case. Another point of great consequence to the advertiser is the amount of advertising in a journal. Where a paper has but one column or less of advertisements it is worth an extra price, because it makes those few so much more conspicuous than they would be among ten times as many. Daily papers are not considered worth more than half a cent per line for 1,000 circulation. Every observer will have noticed that a daily paper is not kept as long as a weekly. It is not as thoroughly examined by the family, and furthermore, a successful daily paper usually devotes two-thirds of its space to advertising, while no well-managed weekly will admit more advertising than can be accommodated in one-third of its columns. When we place one cent per line as a price for 1,000 circulation in a weekly, half a cent for a daily, and two cents for a monthly, we state the maximum figure which an advertiser can afford to pay for any extensive line of advertising. In special and unusual cases he may afford to pay more, but he must generally secure his business at a lower price. To do this it is best to make yearly contracts.

Some advertisers will only advertise in those journals which are patronized by others in their business, on the ground that their more experienced rivals have decided on these papers because they have been found to pay; other advertisers have taken the ground that papers which do not receive the general run of advertisements possesses an especial value over others, on the ground that their readers are fresh and more easily attracted by the promises which the advertiser purposes to set forth in their columns.

As a general rule the value of a newspaper is fixed by its circulation. This value is influenced by various causes, which we will enumerate: 1st. If devoted to a specialty, as a class journal, it is worth an extra price to those advertisers who would appeal to that class. 2d. If particularly well printed it is worth more than if poorly printed, but as it is also worth more to the reader, the circulation is likely to fall off while the poor press work is continued; consequently it is wise to treat with great caution all claims of large circulation put forth in favor of journals which are poorly printed, either by fault of printer or pressman. 3d. The amount of advertising affects the value. Many publishers point to crowded columns as a proof of value, but the truth is the fewer advertisements which appear in any paper the more those few are worth to the advertiser. This rule applies only to general advertising, and not to those classified advertisements which appear in some large daily journals, which, becoming a characteristic of the paper in question, are a part of its value to the reader. While on this point we may state as another reason for an extra value on some newspaper columns (4th), those which classify. A paper which carefully classifies every advertisement, gives it, in effect, extra display without cost. In the Chicago *Tribune* we may find half a column of advertisements, each one occupying from three to ten lines, announcing that Messrs. A, B & C, are some other individual or firm have a horse, a carriage, or harness for sale. Any one wishing to buy finds the heading " Horses and Carriages for Sale," and reads all the announcements; hence in the Chicago *Tribune* a five-line advertisement of a horse for sale becomes as conspicuous and as sure to attract the eye as would the same announcement displayed in one-fourth column of space in a paper which does not classify. Hence, whenever advertising is to be done, if of a nature calling for classification, it should always be placed (other things being equal) in the paper which classifies and shows in its columns the largest list of similar notices ; for where such advertisements are constantly appearing it is proof that the public look for them and that they attract the expected attention.

5th. We maintain that the practice of always obtaining a fixed price, proportioned to the value of the work, and the same price from all men for the same service, is an important element of value in any newspaper, and one which is thoroughly recognized by experienced advertisers.

Where a man must advertise, the actual circulation of

a paper is sometimes of not very much importance. A patent medicine vendor who has sold $50 worth of goods to a village druggist, on condition that he shall put his advertisement into the local paper, must, to carry out his agreement, make the best contract which he can, and will frequently pay for 600 weekly circulation in one town twice as much as he pays for 1,000 in another. The only paper in a town of some importance, or the best paper in a good district, can frequently demand prices to which their circulations do not justly entitle them.

To cover sections with a little advertising, use the leading papers issued at the metropolis of the section referred to. There are one or two journals in Boston which circulate quite evenly throughout all the New England States. In Western Massachusetts is one paper that circulates up and down the entire valley of the Connecticut, through three States. In Hartford one weekly has subscribers in almost every town in Connecticut.. Rhode Island has a leading daily which is said to cover the State. Maine has an agricultural weekly of this character. New Hampshire has another, while neither Vermont nor Massachusetts can be reached throughout all their sections without resorting to the local press. Two different weekly papers in Albany go to almost every town in the State of New York. In Toledo and Cincinnati are large weeklies reaching all through Ohio and Indiana. Chicago has an agricultural and one or two religious weeklies and one or two dailies which may be relied on to reach the Northwest. St. Louis has two political dailies and weeklies and one religious journal all of which are freely read in Missouri. Three dailies on the Pacific Coast will reach some readers in every town. In Louisville we find papers which circulate through Kentucky and Tennessee. At Memphis and Nashville are those which reach Western Tennessee and Arkansas. Galveston governs Texas; so New Orleans reaches Louisiana and Mississippi. Mobile, with one daily and weekly, provides fairly for Alabama. In Georgia and the Carolinas we have no papers that can be said to reach all sections of those States. Richmond has one or two dailies and as many religious weeklies which are largely read in Virginia; but neither Maryland nor Pennsylvania can be reached to any general extent without resorting to the local press.

Advertisers should generally write their own advertisements. The man who cannot do this is not fit to advertise, for if he don't know what he wants to say to the public, how can he suppose it will pay him to expend large sums of money for the purpose of communicating with that public. An advertiser without experience often writes the best advertisement, and many a notice is sent out which is made up on principles entirely independent of English grammar, and sometimes of all rules of orthography, yet expressing the meaning in a manner which cannot be misunderstood, and showing the plain, straightforward, honest intent of the advertiser in such a manner as to make it a most telling card. When an advertiser can write his own advertisements to suit himself it will be time enough to employ others to assist him, and he will frequently derive great advantage from such assistance. He must never forget, however, that as his own money pays for the insertion, he must use his own judgment in deciding what to insert. There is one rule which has been found a good one by which to write an advertisement. It is to first write out, no matter at what length, all that is worth while to say; next examine it critically, with the purpose of ascertaining how many words can be stricken out without injuring the sense. It is not rare to see a six-line advertisement which could be expressed in five lines.

An advertisement should not be flowery—nothing need be said in it for ornament. It should be plain and honest. It should claim nothing which is not strictly true, but should be sure to claim as much as is true. Whenever the case will admit of it, it is well to put in the words "send stamp for a circular." A good pamphlet or circular setting forth the merits of the business is a good thing to have, and to whoever may be sufficiently interested to write for it, it will pay to forward one. Whatever a man invests a stamp to obtain he will be sure to look at when it comes to hand.

The object of display in an advertisement is to attract additional attention. If this object is not obtained, the price paid for the additional space required for the display is wasted. If a more conspicuous card, that is a card which will attract more attention, be seen quicker, or catch the eye at a greater distance while occupying three inches of space with proper display, than when filling four inches with type selected with bad judgment, then the advertiser can well afford to pay the cost of the inch of space saved to the judicious compositor, who, by his taste in setting up, shall produce the more effective result.

Advertising costs a great deal at best, and he who will make money by advertising must so arrange as to secure the best effect with the smallest possible expenditure.

An advertiser of much experience has said that an advertisement should be so arranged that the first glance conveys the idea, the theory being that catch words or lines convey to the mind of the interested reader the idea of the thing he needs, without his having the power to overlook it, and that he is then sure to read the whole advertisement, no matter how small the type in the body thereof. Some carry this idea so far as to use diamond type for the filling up. This is not wise. Pearl is the smallest type which should ever be used in a newspaper, while agate is as small as it is safe to try in any but a few of the best printed journals.

No paper which is fully equipped ever uses a larger type than nonpareil for advertisements. Any larger type is a waste of space, and no prosperous journal can afford to use it a single month. Nonpareil is a favorite type on account of its measure, 12 lines making one inch, the space adopted by nearly one-half the publishers of the country as the "square."

It may be as well to state here that the term " square " is indefinite, and before making any contract for so many "squares" of space, the advertiser must in the same agreement have the size of the squares designated, as so many lines nonpareil or agate.

The object of placing an advertisement in the columns of a newspaper is that it may be seen, and whatever contributes to make it more easily seen adds to its value. When choice positions cannot be obtained, and it is desirable to advertise in newspapers already filled with conspicuous cards, it is often said, with truth, that a modest announcement, set up in the usual style, stands a poor chance of being seen. An electrotyped design (cut) attached to the advertisement will frequently attract attention, from being conspicuous, or for its oddity, its beauty, or for some peculiarity. No matter why it attracts, so long as the fact remains.

Some of the most effective cuts which appear in newspaper columns are made up entirely from type.

Next to representations of the articles advertised, the most popular cuts are trade marks.

SUPPLEMENT.

ILLUSTRATED JOURNALISM.

DAVID G. CROLY.

QUESTION.—I should like to learn your ideas in regard to illustrated papers—what you think of the future of the illustrated paper?

ANSWER.—Oh! that description of journal undoubtedly has a great future before it. The time, I think, is coming when every large city in the world will have its daily illustrated paper devoted to the pictorial reporting (if I may so phrase it) of all the current events of the day.

Q. It would be a curious thing to enquire how literary and pictorial art would affect each other in such journals. How do you expect that such illustrated papers will differ from ordinary papers?

A. Well, I think it safe to assume that the paper will naturally take its tone and quality from the pictures. A paper of this kind will instinctively, as it were, avoid much of the news which other papers give a great deal of space to; for instance, market reports and commercial affairs in their dry, statistical aspect—and, in fact, all topics which are not susceptible of illustration. Of course those who project such journals will at first be disposed to follow the old types—to accept the old traditions of journalism. But this will be a mistake, as will afterwards appear to them; and the picture being the leading feature, the journal in all its news, critical, and editorial departments, will insensibly take an artistic tone. I don't mean that it will be perpetually parading the cant terms of art. That high tone which is inseparable from constant association with works of art of superior quality, will imperceptibly enter into and flavor, as with a delicate aroma, all the literary matter of the journal. For instance, if artist and reporter are sent out together to sketch and describe any particular event, they cannot but influence each other's minds in regard to what they see. They will suggest a thousand new points to each other; and I think the reporter's account will gain in brilliancy and the artist's picture in completeness from this contact and interaction of the two minds.

Q. Your conception of it is certainly a very expansive one?

A. Well, obviously domestic events must receive the most attention. "News" is what newspaper readers want now; "news pictorial" is what they will want then. The great crimes, the terrific accidents, the society-shaking scandals must be illustrated. As these appeal to the emotions rather than to the judgment, their pictorial illustration will be most welcome to the public; and the picture paper of the future will occupy the field that the novel and the story paper now does. Lamartine once said that the newspaper would ultimately engross *all* literature—that there would be nothing else published but newspapers. Startling as this assertion may sound, one really can believe that when daily illustrated papers are common, they will engross *much* of literature. If the conductors of daily illustrated papers are wise, they will approximate their journals to that type which has been so very successful—the weekly story paper—with this differentiation, that in place of fiction they will delineate actual occurrences. Indeed, I foresee a great diminution of weekly journals—perhaps their utter extinguishment, if the conductors of illustrated daily journals understand their business. The women, the idlers, the loungers in society, who are not interested in business or politics, will eagerly seek after a paper which gives them the pleasant stimulus of pictures of remarkable current events; and which delineates the poetic and romantic aspects of the life we are daily living.

Q. Yes, and then there is the humorous side of things?

A. Undoubtedly. A daily illustrated paper has peculiar facilities for making that a prominent feature of its pictorial news; and humor and artistic wit ought to color a good many of its illustrations. I should warn the managers of such papers, however, against following the heavy English style of humorous illustration. Let them invent a piquant style of their own, based on the light, fantastic art of the French. In that direction lies success for American humorists.

Q. What are your views in regard to printing, itself? Do you think it likely that any revolution can be effected in that mechanical department?

A. I should not be surprised if the recent application of steam to lithographic printing, and the improved mechanical processes which have made the issue of a daily illustrated journal possible, may solve the question of type-setting, by substituting photolithographic work for printed sheets. Mr. T. L. De Vinne, one of the best mechanical printers in this country, has demonstrated that the most admirably contrived type-setting machine can never save more than fifteen or twenty per cent. of the cost of setting type; that of the *five* operations into which type-setting can be analyzed, only *one* is susceptible of a saving in time. The great cost of type-setting is the one great obstacle to cheap publications and cheap literature; and any process which will give us printed results—good, legible reading matter—without the intervention of printed types, will cheapen and popularize literature to an amazing extent. It really seems as if ultimately the question of the mechanical part of bookmaking would resolve itself into a question as to the relative rapidity of working of the scribe and the compositor. It is now well known that even ordinary writing is performed in less than half (most probably one-third) the time that type-setting is performed in. A reporter goes into the office and writes out from one to two columns after twelve o'clock at night: but it takes a great many more than one or two compositors to set up that one or two columns of matter. In fact, I believe a compositor can set up a line of nonpareil of about nine words in one minute; but in ordinary writing we certainly write double that number per minute, and I suppose a professional scribe who set to work steadily at a manuscript would write at least twenty words a minute, in a clear and elegant character. It seems possible, therefore, by the new processes I have described, to put literal matter upon the stone and have it ready to get off impressions at a cheaper rate than to have it set up in type and got ready for the press. Sennefelder, driven by poverty to seek some cheaper method than printing of giving his ideas to the world, invented lithography! How strange if in these latter days his dream should be realized, and all literature be henceforth lithographic sheets.

Q. You open up a vista of grave possibilities?

A. Well, if what I suggest is possible, you can see at once that the days of type-setting is numbered—or, if not so exactly, yet it will be dispensed with in an immense majority of cases, in favor of a cheaper mode of producing printed sheets. I should not be at all surprised if imitation manuscript books again came into vogue, and the profession of the scribe revived again. You know they formed a very important class in Rome; and

Disraeli the elder (I think it is) suggests that it was the fear of depriving this large and useful class of men of the means of living that prevented the introduction of printing among the Romans. They actually had the idea in their very hands, for hundreds of stamps were in use among them for multiplying letters and names upon pottery. We shall have reproductions of the beautiful styles for chirography employed in the ancient missals, and all the charming accessories of grotesque borders, and elaborate initial letters, and little quaint vignettes and tail-pieces, such as were in vogue in the best epochs of bookmaking. Instead of taking our manuscript to the best printers, we shall take it to the most noted scribe; and he will re-write it for us in the fashionable character; and then we shall get it photographed and transferred to stone, and out will come the dainty volume, delightsome to the eye as well as to the inner sense. And by this method we may effect another revolution in bookmaking, which I think is highy desirable.

Q. What is that?

A. I have discovered, (and with all due modesty I claim this as an original idea of my own) that reading matter made by the impression of blackened types upon white paper is extremely injurious to the eye; and the great amount of myopia, amaurosis, and other diseases of the eye which afflict the civilized world is due to their constant use of white and black printed material. These effects, of course, have been slowly operating through many generations, until now really healthy eyes are extremely rare; and there are more people with impaired vision than they themselves really suspect.

Q. What then would you substitute in the place of ordinary printed matter?

A. With our present system of type-setting it would

be impossible to effect the reform I desire, which is a reversal of our present tinting of the page. I would print the whole page in color, and leave the letters light. In all nature we have the dark back ground and the light object upon it. There is the deep blue sky, and the light cloudlets upon it. There is the dark brown earth, or the green grass, with the bright flowers upon it. There is the dark grey rock, with the pale green, or orange-colored lichen upon it. White, as in the snows of the Arctic regions, the cliffs of the Pyrenees, and the sands of the desert, has ever been found injurious and destructive to the human eye, which is accustomed to the blues, greens, browns, greys, and the dark neutral tints of nature.

Q. Well, what reformation do you propose?

A. I should say that if we were to pick out the object that is seen at the greatest distance in the universe, then *that* would indicate to us what would be the proper contrast of colors for page and letter.

Q. And what may that be?

A. The Chinese, when they invented printing, first incised the characters upon the block (reversed, of course) then covered the block with dark ink, then impressed it upon the thin yellow paper which they have used from time immemorial, and so the page came forth with light yellow letters upon a dark back ground. We find the analogy to this in nature—the object that can be seen at the greatest distance is the bright star upon the dark background of the universe. There is no fatigue in looking at the constellations traced in lines of fire upon the dark pages of night. It would follow, therefore, that a golden or yellow lettering upon a back ground of dark blue is that which would best suit the human eye. Curiously enough, since I first published my ideas upon this subject, a gentleman who found blindness gradually creeping upon him, tested his ability to distinguish colors and characters in the different stages of his disease, and he found that the dark back ground with yellowish or golden tinted spots upon it was what he could distinguish longest and last before total obscurity supervened. You will find the case recorded in the *Boston Medical Journal.*

Q. That was very remarkable?

A. Why yes; don't you see that even uninstructed sign painters adopt the same principle in their business. They give the sign the black back ground, and the golden lettering; and we know that these are the signs we can read most distinctly, and at the greatest distance in the streets. But we cannot affect this combination of dark pages and light literals with our present typographical processes. You must put up with a dark ink upon a light back ground, because there is no white ink of sufficient body to make a distinct white impression from type upon a dark page. Well now, with this new photolithographic process, it is possible to make the combination which I claim is the natural and proper one, that of bright lights upon dark back grounds; and hence the books of the future will bloom like a garden of flowers. We can make letters and pages of any different combinations we please. All we require is to employ different colored light papers, and different colored dark inks, and the taste of the workman of the future will be exercised in devising the most charming combinations of colors to suit and stimulate the tastes of his patrons.

[The above was written out before the *Daily Graphic* was started. The writer has since asked Mr. Croly whether, from the experience he has acquired in that enterprise, he finds reason to modify any of the views he formerly entertained. He states that he has only one change to make, and that is, that the public does not seem to care so much for mere news pictures—illustrations of actual events—as he supposed they would. A well conducted picture paper goes into families; and parents object to illustrations of unpleasant subjects—as, for instance, pictures of hangings, or persons rendered notorious by some great crime—being presented to their children. While a paper, which illustrates some great public horror with excessive realism and particularity, may have a temporary large sale; the fact that it is accustomed to publish such pictures would greatly injure it in respect of home circles, which are, after all, the best patrons of pictorial journals. The public seems to crave something higher and better in a picture paper than in a non-illustrated sheet. Portraits of beautiful women and famous men, charming and striking scenery, sketches illustrative of the affecting, the interesting, the humorous phases of human life, all that relates to the love of the husband, wife and children, for parent and friend—these are the subjects that find most acceptance in families, and are the most attractive themes for an illustrated daily paper. These are the experiences both of editor and artists of the *Daily Graphic;* and there cannot be the slightest doubt that the spread of illustrated journalism tends greatly to elevate the tone of the press. In this respect art is true to its mission as the principal factor in the civilization of mankind.]

THE MOTIVE AND METHOD OF JOURNALISM.

INTERVIEW WITH D. G. CROLY IN 1873.

Q. A short time ago I saw an article in your name in *Putnam's Magazine* which interested me very greatly. I have called on you to make some further inquiries regarding your views on the theory and practice, the motive and method of journalism?

A. I had promised myself that I would write a book on this very subject; but the demands upon my time have been so great that as yet I have been unable to do so. I think I may claim, without presumption, to have been the first in this country who insisted that journalism has a theory and practice which it is desirable to reduce to form; so that young journalists may understand the business they wish to pursue.

Q. Could you give me, in brief, your general conception of the newspaper?

A. I think the mistake of recent writers on this subject has been in having some conception of an ideal journal—a purely *a priori* notion—and in supposing that there was but this one ideal of the newspaper. Now, the fact is the ideal journal will very likely be a periodical with a number of impossible virtues. Instead of there being one kind of journal to describe, there are really many varieties; hence, the features of any particular journal would not be practicable under all circumstances. The various successful journals of this country have each peculiarities of their own. They differ, as stars differ from one another, in appearance as in glory. In each city you will generally find some one journal which leads the rest, and which, consequently, is the type of paper which suits that locality. In New York it happens to be the *Herald*; in Philadelphia it is the sober *Ledger*; in Cincinnati the *Commercial*; in Chicago the *Tribune*; and so on. Now, all these journals differ widely; and there is little reason to suppose that the type which is successful in one locality would be successful in another.

Q. What other mistake?

A. Another mistake is in descanting upon the ethics of journalism. The primary necessity of a man's existence is, first of all, that he should be born; and in the next place that he should live. His character and morals are subsequent considerations. Clearly the seed will not flourish unless it is planted in the right kind of soil, and hence business considerations are those which are first in order in establishing a journal. If I was asked to plan a journal for any particular locality, I would enquire what part of the field is already occupied; and what part appears to be void. Is any particular party unrepresented? Is the general news-field inadequately gleaned by existing journals? Do the other journals lack editorial ability? Are local interests receiving due attention? All these considerations would have to be thought out before a journal was started in any particular locality. Abstract considerations as to the temper, tone and moral purpose of the journal, while they occupy the first place in all discussions about journalism, necessarily occupy the last place in the minds of those who are investing money in such enterprises. And the danger in schools of journalism will be in putting them in charge of broken-down parsons, or "brilliant" newspaper leader-writers—persons whose heads are filled with all sorts of high notions and fine spun theories which would be shivered like glass at the first rude contact with the realities of competitive journalism. The students will probably be well drilled in composition, and well lectured as to morals and manners; but will be left in ignorance of all that relates to the business and editorial functions of a journal, which, after all, is of most immediate importance.

What the press of this country wants, is not so much trained writers, as trained editors. I do not think that sufficient discrimination is made between the two by the general public. It certainly is not clearly kept in mind by those who write on this subject. The editor requires the judging, suggesting, selecting, discriminating faculty. The writer, he who exercises his mind in expression, is very apt to be a mere phrase-monger; and to lack the capacity to make a really great and successful paper. I think it will be found, on a careful review of the history of any of the leading newspapers, that their success was due mainly to the business capacity of those who founded them. Journals should never be put in charge of mere writers. The men who come to the front, and who are most thought of when the merits of a journal are discussed, are, of course, those who show the most brilliancy in writing; but "able journalists" in that sense very often make a mess of it when they attempt to conduct a newspaper. This is because they lack business and editorial talent. The London *Times*, the New York *Herald*, the Philadelphia *Ledger*, the Cincinnati *Commercial*, the Boston *Herald*, represent far more business and editorial ability than they do mere facility of literary expression. Indeed, the best written journals are by no means the most successful. You remember how two of the greatest *litterateurs* that ever lived, Goethe and Schiller, jointly started the *Horen*. They were supported by the best writers of Germany, and yet that journal was a most conspicuous and disastrous failure. "In spite of the most flattering promises," says Carlyle in his *Life of Schiller*, " and of its own intrinsic character, the *Horen*, at its first appearance, instead of being hailed with welcome by the leading minds of the country, for whom it was intended as a rallying point, met in many quarters with no sentiment, but coldness and hostility." It did not, in fact, live two years, and I venture to say that if all the best literary men in this country united in contributing to a particular journal it would nevertheless be a failure, unless it was directed by very superior business and editorial talent.

Q. In what way, then, should a paper secure the highest success if not distinguished for high literary ability?

A. Good, strong common sense in all its departments is what a newspaper (as every other business) most requires. It is unfortunately very often the case that those who are most capable persons in a literary point of view are lacking in these essentials.

Q. Suppose, for instance, I had ample capital, and wished to start what I aimed to make the first journal in the City of New York. How would I go about it?

A. If the aim was to found the journal with the largest circulation and influence, it is very evident you must study several things. In the first place, the character of the papers already in existence, and the features in each which have proved most acceptable to the public. Next, you must consider what new features would be likely to prove popular in addition to those already recognized by the existing presses. And then, again, you should carefully analyze the population you address, with a view to meeting their wants.

Q. You think, then, that a purely original paper, a

paper entirely different from anything that the community has been in the habit of seeing, would not take well?

A. No. Men are creatures of habit. An essential type of paper prevails everywhere; and the mass of journals are mere modifications of this original type. All English papers emulate in a manner the London *Times*. Even in the British Colonies—in Australia and Canada—the same kind of journal (in appearance, at least) in the favorite. In this respect newspaper projectors are right; for, after all, we like best that which we are habituated to. Hence, in starting a new journal, the appearance and the general features of the existing type of paper should be borne in mind. But as every year makes changes in the social and political condition of the people, especially in this country, it is fair to infer that there are some new fields to occupy which it would be wise for the projector of a new newspaper to recognize. The newspaper of the future will contain many features not now contemplated as within the scope of journalism.

Q. Apropos of this matter of the theory of a newspaper, I see that many periodicals scoff at the notion, and are disposed to ridicule people who are endeavoring to systematize journalism into some definite theory?

A. I know it; but then the least reflection tells us that we can do nothing without a theory, not even the most trivial act. All our actions are the result of forethought—that is, we theorize about them before we do them. Everything connected with a daily paper involves forethought; this is required in all the departments, and in all their ramifications. In regard to novelties in journalism, I may say there is a number of features I could point out which would seem to me to be entirely within the scope of the daily journal, and which are now overlooked in all existing periodicals.

Q. Then, as to the analysis of the population you address. What do I understand you to mean?

A. Simply this, a paper started in the City of New York has a *possible* audience of one million of readers. Now, it will be my business, if I aim at the very highest mark, to form some sort of judgment of that audience. It is very evident that of this million of persons the great bulk are poor laboring men and women, to whom even pennies are an object. Hence, the first business element of success in a paper wishing to address a very large audience in the City of New York would be the fixing of its price at the very lowest, the minimum. Next, it would be necessary to remember that this vast population, consisting principally, as I have said, of men who live by their daily labor, would not have much time for reading, and very little general culture. Of the million of possible readers, perhaps 50,000 may be college graduates; 100,000 would be men and women of rather superior education and intelligence; while the rest would be such material as our common schools turn out year by year—persons who know how to read, write, and cipher; whose literature at the best is the story paper and the cheap novel; and who, in one way or another, casually read the daily journals.

Q. Do I understand you, then, as advocating a low grade of newspaper, aiming only to meet the wants of this class, which you say lacks all special culture?

A. I have profound faith in the strong common sense of the ordinary man. The people composing the working classes, dealing, as they do, with realities in their daily life, are not in the long run much deceived by newspapers which distrust their intelligence. I find that all the cheap papers which have succeeded in this or any other country have been noted for the accuracy of their news, and for the intelligence and common sense of their comments. Such papers as the New York *Sun* (when under the management of the elder Beach), the Baltimore *Sun*, Philadelphia *Ledger*, are very good types of this class of paper. What the working classes do *not* want is fine writing; they like plain common sense expressed in clear language—yes, and if you please, common place observations with homely illustrations. We can never please them by shooting above their heads into the regions of transcendental didactics; and I doubt if a workingman is entertained with the finest quotation from the poets of which he does not apprehend the drift and cannot perceive the application.

Q. But would not a journal after this conception prove a very dull affair? Are we to drive the educated class from journalism altogether, both as readers and writers?

A. I was coming to that point. To make a successful study of the great newspaper audience a man has to be something of a psychologist. He must understand some of the leading mental peculiarities of the mass of people. Now, as human beings prize above all things their own freedom, one of the things which would strike most forcibly a newspaper audience would be the journal's independence; its perfect freedom from all political and social entanglements and alliances; that self-reliant attitude which would enable it to say the just word for or against all parties and all prominent persons; the courage to speak one's mind to one's friends as well as to one's enemies. From this it necessarily follows that the paper which aspires to the largest circulation cannot be a party paper; for the very best party papers that ever existed have not been truth telling papers. If they do not actually tell falsehood, they are bound to suppress the truth when it is calculated to do a little mischief to those on their own side. No amount of literary ability will compensate for this want of integrity in dealing with public men and measures. Another great element in the popular mind, and one that must be catered for in a journal aiming at a wide circulation, is the sense of humor. Next, after the news of the day, in importance, I should estimate that the detecting of what is humorous in current events would be one of the most acceptable features in a journal. The *Sun*, I think, is a striking example of the value of this humorous way of looking at ordinary events. The appreciation of humor is one of the commonest of faculties; but humorists themselves are rare; and it often happens that newspapers are conducted by business men or solemn editors who exclude all the fun which should bubble through the columns of a real live journal. Undoubtedly the most popular feature in the old *Herald*, as it flourished under the elder Bennett's management, was its pregnant wit and broad humor.

Q. But was not this wit and humor somewhat tinged with malignity? Was it not objectionable from its attacks on individuals?

A. In a moral point of view—yes! In a newspaper point of view—no! While I am willing to attribute all the ordinary virtues to the great mass of people, there is no disguising the fact that human nature, as developed in newspaper constituencies, has some very unpleasant features. The cynical philosopher tells us that we can regard the misfortunes of our friends with great equanimity. A boil on another man's neck does not trouble us much. It is rather a source of mirth. And when a newspaper attacks humorously, forcibly, and even malignantly, some prominent person, the reading public is apt to roll it as a sweet morsel under its tongue. Those brutal personal attacks upon prominent people which characterized the early career of the *Herald*, while it may have detracted from its general character, and weakened the force of its criticisms when they were just, certainly helped to widen the circulation of the journal. People like to laugh at the grotesque misfortunes of their fellows, and this is how the general public looked upon the victims of the elder Bennett's ferocious wit. It is to the very great credit of the junior Bennett that the personalities which disfigured the early pages of his father's paper are now entirely excluded from its columns. Yet I candidly confess that if the same sense of humor had sparkled in the columns of the *Herald* in these its latter as in those its former days, I do not think that there would have been the opening for the success of the New York *Sun* which this journal has undoubtedly achieved. One, if not more, of the writers on the *Sun* is a born humorist, who, if he had not been an editor, would have been a Mark Twain or an Artemus Ward. It is this infusion of wit, with a flavor of bitterness and wrath, which excites and attracts the mass of idle people. And here let me remark, in defence of journalists, in this and some other respects, that they are, I think, far better in moral tone and in the avoidance of personalities than their constituencies warrant. They are not so bad as they might be, the public willing. The cause of this, however, may perhaps be traced in the circumstances of the proprietaries. Most great newspapers are owned by rich men or rich corporations: the editors are known and have a social standing; hence there is a tendency to suppress improprieties of expression and damaging personalities, which makes the tone of our papers superior to that of the public they address. But the very great success of those journals which have indulged in humorous and malignant attacks upon individuals shows how large an appreciation of this sort of thing there is in the public mind. Then, all our papers are remarkably clean in respect to impure news.

Q. Will you please define what is properly " news " for a daily journal?

A. That is a question which comes up very often, and is the basis of a great deal of absurd criticism on the matter given in the daily papers. You must bear in mind that the journal is the history of current events; that to please a popular audience it must consult their taste. Now it happens, unfortunately, that disquisitions on scientific topics, unless these topics are of immediate and obvious utility, or in some way strike the imagination vividly, possess very little interest for the mass of people. Current history, like all the history of the past, deals with exceptional phases of human nature — with wars, unexpected national complications—with social ruptures and convulsions—in other words, with the New Thing—and not with the usual thing. There is, it is true, a newer kind of history, which deals with the progress of nations, with the philosophical ideas which underlie the course of events, with the development of manners, the growth of religious ideas, and those higher themes connected with the history of the race upon this planet. But after all, the popular histories, those which mankind take most delight in, have been the doings of great kings, the intrigues of courts, the amours of princes and the issues of great battles—in other words, with exceptional occurrences. Now, as our population is not composed mainly of philosophers, students or scientific men, but is a busy, practical working community, which wants to be interested and amused, to know what is going on, to laugh or cry over passing occurrences of a humorous or pathetic nature, it is obvious that we must deal with this reading community as we find it. To tell the laboring man, when he takes up the paper, of the discovery of a new bug, or of an improvement in the steam engine, of the resolution of nebulæ into distinct stars, or of a new generalization in psychological science, is like talking Arabic to him. He can take no interest in such matters, because it requires a long time to form even a general idea of the sciences into which these facts can be fitted, and he has neither time nor inclination for any exercises of the kind. He therefore will not look at the paper which devotes its columns to such topics. What the public likes first of all is a fight of some kind. Hence a great war is of the most absorbing interest, and the paper which tells best about the exciting scenes in some conflict of nations will be the most widely popular. And next to a war the most popular source of interest would be a prize fight, wherein two well-known names contest for the supremacy. Then comes horse races, yacht races, boat races, and, above all, the periodical contests of great political parties—anything which excites the combative element of human nature—anything where men, or horses, or dogs, or parties have a set-to. That is the kind of entertainment which public taste demands. Man is as yet largely animal, and a newspaper which appeals to his understanding alone, or to his literary taste merely, may get the applause of the good and the wise, but it will inevitably go into bankruptcy as a business speculation. Mr. Greeley achieved his reputation as a good fighter, and the strong spice of independence in his character made him attractive to the general community.

Q. Still I think there may be a department in all journals for the brief and attractive exhibition of all the newest discoveries in science and the arts?

A. Yes, but, as I have said, only those which appeal to the imagination or minister to the immediate wants of man should be attended to. The discoveries in the solar spectrum, phenomena connected with earthquakes and tremendous storms, the exploration of unknown regions, the ascent of prodigious mountains—all such things as these appeal strongly to the imaginations of the mass of readers, and is very interesting reading matter to the general community. For one, I own up to a sense of impatience when I hear these constant discussions touching the morality of the press—the necessity of doing this and that—for advancing science—for administering to a high and pure taste. It is well enough to keep these things in mind; but the newspaper editor has to view human nature from a very different standpoint to that of the scientist or the moralist. He must never forget that primarily man is a very combative animal; that he has a sexual organism which controls his whole life; that it is the marvellous, the unnatural, the unusual, which most strikes the common mind; and that man is an animal who likes to be amused. With these four points in view—man's combativeness, giving him a keen relish for contests between men, horses, vessels, political parties, nations—his amativeness, which so influences him as to make whatever relates to this master passion of his nature a matter of supreme importance—his curiosity and credulity, influenced greatly by a love of the marvellous, and by a keen interest in whatever is remarkable, striking, or unusual—and lastly, his sense of the ridiculous, his willingness to laugh at what is comical, or grotesque, or merely unlucky—in these you have the conceptions which should underlie the conduct of a great popular journal.

Q. Do you care nothing then for literary skill, for the ability to write able articles, for high tone, for appeals to the understanding?

A. Oh, yes; I certainly would not neglect them; they

have their place as important adjuncts to a successful journal. But I deny that they are of the first importance. The body is to be considered before the mind—the framework before the adornments of the structure.

Q. What do you think of literary criticisms in daily journals?

A. They have no place there, with this exception: certain books are events in the history of literature; they excite public curiosity, and are sought after by the community; and they are proper subjects for notice in a daily journal. Hence, while novels generally merit no attention, the productions of any great popular author, a a novel, for instance, by such a man as Disraeli, a book by a great statesman or noted public character, or a remarkable anonymous work like *Ecce Homo*—anything which is out of the course of events, which piques public curiosity, or marks an epoch—all these are proper subjects for journalistic comment and criticism. And in this particular department I should certainly advocate the employment of the highest literary ability.

Q. Then how about style and literary taste in getting up other matter?

A. To me it is very obvious that from the success of certain journals in which everything like literary Art is studiously disregarded, and the non-success of other well-written journals, the general public cares very little about good writing—I mean "good" in the sense of being a very fine and well studied style. Strong common sense; humorous or sparkling comment upon current events; a plain and distinct statement of the case at issue, will satisfy a far larger number of people than the most brilliant article written upon indifferent subjects. Leader writers on the press have naturally magnified their own calling—have sought to create the impression that what the public mainly desired was an elegant and fine-strung style in the comments upon the news of the day. The facts are certainly against this theory.

Q. You surely do not underrate literary skill in the conduct of a paper?

A. No, I do not—I rate it very highly; but it is that literary skill which can best adapt itself to the common sense of common men; that really strong sound writing which any cartman or servant girl can understand; and which is clearly high literary art. Read the Pilgrim's Progress, and the sermons of John Henry Newman, and you will understand the style I allude to. That is the kind of writing we need. Cobbet and Greeley were masters of a good newspaper style.

Q. Since these are your views, I do not doubt that you have a criticism to urge against some particular kinds of writing that are found in editorial columns?

A. I have. Some very able journals, conducted by literary men, have, I think, greatly erred on the side of elaborate discussion of points of constitutional law and the subtleties of party doctrine. Lawyers, I fancy, as a general thing, make very poor journalists. The forensic habits of rhetorical display and casuistical reasoning, the references to precedent, the elaboration of legal lore—all these things were at one time in favor with the American public. This was in the old days when party journals were much more in vogue than they are now. In the early history of the Republic, when the foundations of our institutions were] being laid, the discussions between Federalists and Democrats had a very great attraction for the slower and more thoughtful community which then inhabited the United States. But the change brought about by steam and electricity, the mighty and overpowering interests of the present, the multitudinous activities of modern life, have made men impatient of these fine-spun discussions; and that class of journalists which indulged in them (once so common in the South— old Father Ritchie might be taken as the type), is now obsolete. Nor do discussions upon international law interest more than a very small proportion of the community—as the sale of books devoted to that branch of study clearly shows. And questions of constitutional law, vitally important as they may be in the interests of the nation, have but small attraction to the mass of readers of newspapers. These discussions are no doubt needed—but by a person who wishes a large circulation for his journal they must be carefully avoided, or at least made use of only when popular attention is turned to them by national, political, or international exigencies. What the editorial column wants is fair and plain statement, and either wise or witty comment—sometimes, but rarely, explanation—never argument, never a process of reasoning except that which is slightly constructed and merely incidental.

Q. How might a daily journal be best arranged?

A. A great newspaper should have an organization like that of an army. It should never be owned by a joint stock company, but always by an individual proprietor. The misfortune of a joint stock company is that when business men have an interest in the concern they more or less, consciously or unconsciously, dictate its policy. All editors naturally resent this interference, as they know it is pregnant with mischief. The wisest business man is sure to blunder when he undertakes to control an organ of public opinion. The proprietor of a paper, to my mind, should have nothing to do with the details of the paper; he should be the Mikado and have his Tycoon, to whom he should issue his general orders, but never interfere with details. The Tycoon should be the general of the army, unembarrassed by aught except general instructions, and free to do what he deemed best for the interests of the paper he had in charge. Like the general, he should have his subordinates, responsible to him alone, and each supreme in his own proper department. No newspaper can be run by a commission; councils of war never fight. A newspaper in which half a dozen persons have equal or co-ordinate authority is sure to produce a commonplace result. Men's actions, following the law of mechanics, move along the line of least resistance. A newspaper must do surprising things—striking things. These can never be accomplished by joint action. It is always the individual who acts thus.

Q. I confess that in looking over some of your remarks it seems to me that they give rather a low conception of the functions of journalism. Has it no mission as an educator of the public?

A. Journals, in the present stage of humanity, must be, in a certain sense, representative. Newspapers which undertake to lead public sentiment generally fall into a ditch. Public opinion is formed not by newspapers but by the progress of events—the results of international contests, the fighting of battles, the condition of the crops, the movement of public affairs, the fluctuations of the money market—all the moral and material events of the day have a certain effect upon the minds of communities. An editor might as well attempt to regulate the perturbations of the atmosphere as to control the public opinion which so many elements combine to form. The great journal is that one which appreciates what the effects will be, and gives voice to the public consciousness and the public reason upon the events of the day. The value of a journal in its editorial department is not that it expresses the opinions of the individual, of Mr. Smith, or Mr. Brown, or Mr. Robinson, but that it gives voice to the best views of the best minds in the community. If an inhabitant of Jupiter could come down upon the earth, the journal most interesting to him in New York would be, first, the one which told him of all the occurrences of the day, and in the next place, that which best represents the average sentiment of the people about him. He would not care for a partisan journal, no matter how great its ability, if he knew that it was an advocate of a line of conduct, irrespective of the opinion of the community, nor would he want one which gave a distorted or one-sided account of current history. The fact is, the public journal to-day occupies an anomalous position. The spiritual power, once wielded with such splendid effect by the papacy, is, if not dead, certainly in a very demoralized state. The public journal has usurped the place of the Pope. It gives voice not indeed to the anger or satisfaction of the God, but it expresses or tries to express the average human sentiment upon the general conduct of affairs. An editor is a kind of bastard Pope. His business is to pass judgment upon public occurrences, and to do so in view of the highest and wisest morality of his time. An editor who lacks independence of judgment, whose views of politics are low, who is an aspirant for office, or a politician in any sense, or whose aim is simply to make money, he indeed descends to an extremely low level, and his journal is justly an object of public contempt. No ability will compensate for want of a high standard of integrity in matters national and political. In the war against corruption in New York city, those journals which paltered with the facts, which failed to realize the public indignation at the successive revelations of fraud, suffered, and very justly, in the estimation of the people. I have heard a noted editor tell how, after he had opened a war on the corrupt members of his own party, and had been signally beaten (the time not being yet ripe for the overthrow of the iniquitous organizations), he was puzzled what to do. On the one hand he was strongly urged by the people in his own office not to lower his flag, but to keep up the moral tone of his paper, and give no quarter to the persons whom he knew to be public plunderers. A noted politician and friend of the editor, on the other hand, remonstrated with him upon his then recent course of attack against those parties. Said he: "This will never do. You have made a good fight, and you have been beaten. The party organization is now in the hands of your opponents. There can be no success in political life unless a man gives up his prejudices, and acts, if need be, for public ends, with his former enemies." The editor succumbed to this view of his duty presented by a man whom he knew to be pure, and whose aims were lofty, though all his life he had been a politician. Incontestably this distinguished gentleman was right from the politician's point of view; but he was grievously wrong from the journalists', in view of the spiritual function of the latter. The public will permit no journal to lower its flag on any question of pecuniary honesty. The editor of whom I speak, however, unfortunately made this alliance with his enemies; and when the facts came out indubitably proving the guilt of the scoundrels whom he had before been fighting, he carried on a weary battle in their defence, with a most disastrous result to himself and his paper. So impressed was I personally with these views of the duties of journalists, that in my "green and salad days, before my judgment ripened," I proposed that an agitation should be started having in view the enactment of a law forbidding editors of public journals from becoming candidates for office, or in any way profiting by the success of party action. But without any enactments, and in the natural course of things, those journals have been most successful in this country of which the editors have taken this very position. Mr. Raymond and Mr. Greeley's willingness to accept office always stood in their way as conductors of great journals. The success of the elder Bennett was largely due to the fact that no office, no pecuniary reward, would swerve him from any course which he undertook. The most powerful controllers of parties have been editors like Thurlow Weed who would never accept office. Hence, instead of putting a low estimate on the integrity and honesty of public journalists, I realize the fact that a high moral tone, a sense of strict integrity, and great personal independence, are absolutely indispensable to the conduct of a really great paper. Indeed, there are no qualities you can put into a paper that can compensate in the public mind for a doubt as to your personal integrity, or a suspicion that you do not deal with public events, and noted men with entire and unreserved honesty. I believe the time is coming when we will have a real spiritual power composed of scientists mainly. Indeed, to-day, Huxley and Tyndall, and men of that stamp, are the real priests, are believed implicitly, and followed without hesitation. But as yet the scientific body is not organized for any useful social function; and until they are, public journals must in a measure take their place, and be the spiritual directors of the public. It must be moral in the highest sense, but the editor, at the same time, must recognize the whole nature of man—his combativeness, his sexuality, his credulity, and his love of humor, as well as his moral sense.

Q. How about "sensationalism," so called?

A. Somebody has defined sensationalism to be "commonplace in a fit of delirium tremens." I judge that sensational writing is due to a perception on the part of editors that the public like what is unusual and startling. If your sensation has a basis—if it stands on a fact, a real occurrence, the incredible is a very popular feature in the daily journal, for men like to be surprised, startled, waked up. But if your sensation is based on a falsehood, it will certainly damage the journal. No newspaper can afford to deal in lies, or at least the fictitious sensations must be very few and far between, and the general statement of the news must be trustworthy. On the other hand, a tame and spiritless account of an interesting fact is damaging to a paper. A journalist should treat current history as you would treat past history. I see no harm in a reporter or a correspondent describing a fire, or a great mining accident, the foundering of a ship at sea, with such illustrations as would vividly picture the scene.

Q. How about reformatory business and sectarian journals?

A. Any one who proposes to start a paper to ventilate certain views of his own—to change the face of society—to get people to adopt different theories of life and religion from what they now hold, must expect to do it at his own cost. All journals having mainly in view the education or betterment of mankind are from the start business failures. It is painful to see earnest, enthusiastic men and women, conscious of a noble purpose, sure that if their views were adopted society would be bettered, starting journals, expecting the public to change their opinions, and pay for the privilege of doing so—I say it is sad to see how often these amiable people fail. Temperance, free trade, women's rights—in fact, educational and reform papers of all kinds, can never be expected to pay expenses. They are always a loss to those who invest money in them. It is not always so with sectarian or religious papers which represent established views. These do not seek to change people's opinions, but conform to opinions already estalished. Hence they have their *clientele* already formed. But then the constituency is necessarily limited to their own sect. Journals started to propagate opinions of any kind are utterly useless in a business point of view. This is another reason why party journals are generally business failures—they appeal to their own party, and the party alone reads them. But then this party is already converted; their opponents, on the other hand, sedulously avoid reading arguments which seem to them fallacious. The most extraordinary spectacle which it is possible to conceive is that presented by the party journals on the eve of a great presidential election. Each of them is frantically shouting to their respective audiences arguments intended for the opposition, which the latter never reads, or deliberately dodges. The mass of the people are far wiser than newspaper writers suspect them to be during the active period of the presidential contest.

Q. You spoke of the bad effects of the business department upon the conduct of a daily paper. What do you mean?

A. Simply this, that as a general thing the better business man the publisher is, the worse off is the paper.

Q. That seems to be paradoxical. What am I to understand by it? Surely a good business faculty can never be an injury in any affair where it operates?

A. Well, no, not to the business itself; not to the newspaper perhaps immediately, but it operates injuriously to the distant, the permanent prospects of the paper. The business man deals with the transient, the immediate—not with the permanent, which lies in the distance. The publication department in a journal corresponds to the nutritive department of the animal economy; it should no more give the law to the editorial department than the human stomach should give the law to the brain of man. The proper distribution of power will always subordinate the purely business and financial departments to the demands of the editorial department. The command must lie in the intellectual centre of the organization. One of Mr. Bennett's wisest reforms was in making himself the publisher of his own paper, and not permitting any influence " down stairs " to control the course of the *Herald*. The business department in his establishment is to take in and pay out moneys; with the editorial or any other columns (except of course those of advertisements) it has nothing to do. The business man should never be the adviser or councillor of the editor. If he is a good financier it is his function to economize, to fight all bills, no matter how necessary they may be, and to accept any kind of advertisements that will swell his immediate receipts. It is he who, if he can, will gladly degrade the editorial columns by the puffery of all manner of questionable financial enterprises. Anxious to swell his weekly receipts, he will do all, and more than all his rivals were doing, to get what he calls " business." Now, as it happens that precisely those business enterprises which are the most objectionable are those which most desire editorial endorsement, the publisher is always eager to have these swindling operations favored with editorial approbation—and he too often succeeds. He is not immediately made to feel the injury, the loss of character, which a paper sustains in business circles by this puffery of swindling railroad schemes, or bogus petroleum companies, or quack doctors; all he cares for is the $100 or $1,000 which is added to his weekly cash account. I think that all papers with publishers are more or less injured with this disposition on their part, especially if they are able, capable men. Another peculiarity in regard to the publisher is, that if the paper belongs to a stock company it will in time infallibly become his property. The editor-in-chief, or the chief proprietor, is very apt to be a trifle jealous of his managing editor or chief writer; he is conscious of his rivalry at every point. He totally overlooks the fact that the man "down stairs," knowing the financial condition of the paper better than any one else, and handling all the funds, is in the best position for securing the property in time. When stock is for sale, it is the publisher, and he alone, who knows what to give for it. And so papers are more and more representing the business, rather than the general interests of the community. I should say this kind of proprietorship will in the long run prove disastrous, though here and there a wise owner seems to learn to forget the shop and attend to the wants of the community at large.

Q. Is there not a field for special journals—those which aim to represent distinct business interests?

A. Yes; it is in this direction also that journals are differentiating. Very great interests, such as the financial, the commercial, the marine, the real estate, and the like, are now having their own special organs; and as these special papers multiply, they, being able to supply the demand for information in these domains of human activity so much better than the daily journal, which undertakes to cover the whole field, the latter should retire, to a great extent, I think, from these peculiar departments. In London, the local news is now taken charge of by special classes of journals, leaving the larger questions that affect men in their political, business and social relationships to be dealt with by the great dailies. I think that to-day the New York papers pay too much attention to local matters. A city with a million of inhabitants is too vast to be mainly interested in the ordinary business which occurs in its own immediate vicinity. It should be the universal human interest that should be the guide to the editor in selecting news—not because it happens to refer to New York rather than to New Orleans. Of course, there is local news of special interest which bears on the business or pleasure of the whole community. But what I mean is, that little local meetings of societies and trades have no place in a paper which has the whole country for its constituency.

Q. You said but now there was no room for reform papers—those which try to educate people to certain new theories. Do you think then that papers should only represent the ettled convictions upon religious and political topics of a community, without reference to the new notions which are everywhere struggling for expression?

A. I am satisfied it would be wise for some one paper to give a chance to the new ideas of the age—not perhaps in the form of advocacy so much as in allowing them to be represented. I think the warmest friends of the *Tribune* are those who were attracted to its columns, in the early days of its history, by anti-slavery discussions, socialism, and the general reformatory discussions of that time. I have always thought it a mistake for the *Tribune* to "go back" on the Woman's Rights people. In the definition of news which I gave in the early part of this conversation, I said it was the "new" that was interesting—all manner of new views—social, scientific and literary—these all have place and function in the daily. Indeed, the ordinary orthodox notions of society cannot be recognized as news at all; but the proceedings of any new fangled sect, with grotesque observances, or entirely novel theories, are far more entertaining reading than notices of the old-fashioned Calvinistic, Episcopalian, or Methodist churches. There is a real want of this to-day in New York City—for a journal which, without committing itself to the vagaries of new light follies, would give attention to the radicals, the reformers, the revolutionary scientific views which are so marked a feature of this age. But editors are timid; they do not like to offend their orthodox readers—although even to these the proceedings of the new fangled philosophers are more entertaining reading matter than are the occurrences of their own councils and synods. The social surroundings of editors are such as make them averse from giving publicity to the notions of people with novel theories of religion and manners.

Q. How do you account for the general failure of workingmen's organs? The working classes form by far the largest proportion of the community, and are, after all, the main support of all the papers; yet why is it that papers devoted to their interests are almost universally failures?

A. I hardly like to say what I must on this subject; for it will seem like a reflexion on the great body of the community; but the fact is, these papers fail because the projectors do not realize that workingmen have an animal nature; and well intentioned reformers, seeing the objectionable condition of the laboring classes, and knowing they suffer many grievances, start a journal to enlighten them as to their condition, and to demand certain reforms which would benefit them. Now the workingman, dealing as he does with realities, has very little taste or temper for abstract discussions. He can understand why his wages should be raised, why the hours of labor should be shortened ; but in what way a derangement of the currency affects him he cannot be made to understand. The evils of land laws are entirely beyond his comprehension—though he may admire articles which prove to him that he pays too much rent. The whole series of questions which have entered so largely into the discussions of political, economical, and social reformers are entirely outside of his daily life and sympathies. He sometimes tries to take an interest in them and understand them, having been assured that they concern him closely. He attends those socialistic gatherings where Mr. Bounce and Mr. Buffer launch thunderous periods against governments and landlords ; but finally he yawns, finds that it is beyond his comprehension, and starts for the nearest alehouse to get a drink. There is one class of workingman's journal which is very successful, of which *Reynold's Journal* in London is a type. It sympathizes with workingmen, and represents their prejudices as best it may ; but it fills its columns with news which could not very well be read in the family circle. The projector of this paper recognized the fact that the average workingman is an animal, with but little intellect, and who can be interested in such news as appeals to combativeness or sexuality. Hence the prize fight, the *crim. con.*, the seduction, is the kind of mental pabulum which that class of the English population craves—and that is the news which *Reynold's Journal* supplies ; and it has an enormous circulation among the very poorest classes of the community. It is to the credit of the working-women of England, that while they run up to an enormous circulation the *Half-penny Journal* and *Cassel's Magazine,* which often reach half a million of copies per week, it is nothing more harmless than the romantic side of the love relation which they crave. The servant girls and dairymaids, the workingmen's wives and daughters delight in reading the love scrapes of dukes and lords, and support immense establishments which supply them with that kind of literature. But the journals which have been established to discuss the land laws, co-operation, and such matters—the working-man will none of them. They bear no relation to their daily life; and the benefits they promise are so remote, that workmen decline to purchase any such. In this country the working class is not so distinctly a caste by themselves as in England; and, therefore, they cannot be so well appealed to. Besides, they are of diverse nationalities; and have little community of action or feeling. They can join a trade strike, because the benefits of that are obvious; they can demand a legislation which limits the hours of labor, that also is a matter of palpable benefit; but they turn a deaf ear to all appeals to join labor parties or support journals established in their interest. Then, among Americans, the ambition is to get out of the working ranks. The Yankee mechanic, if he can't be a boss, wants to be a policeman, or a huckster or to keep a small store, or become a ward politician, or "go west on a farm." Hence, among American artizans it is only the poor residuum that is left—the unenterprising, the debauched, the poor in spirit. I judge that all this will be bravely altered in a few years, as the trade associations have succeeded in raising the price of manual labor so far above that of clerks—for it was once the ambition of all young men to become clerks, and then great merchants. But now, in the altered circumstances of manual labor, a father will insist upon his son's becoming a tradesman, and not a counter-jumper. But until these ideas take hold of the community, there will be little hope for labor parties, or for the establishment of a journal devoted to the interests of the laboring man. In these conversations I may have expressed seemingly diverse views as to the morality of the average reader. Men in masses are always instigated by higher emotions than when they act individually. It is Macaulay, I think, who points out that the audience of a cheap theatre in the slums will very often be composed entirely of the vicious classes; but the thief, the burglar, the pimp, the felon will always sympathize with the heroine in her troubles under persecution, though it is probable that every one of these fellows would be quite willing to enact the role of the ruffian of the play in his own private career. But men's sympathies acting in unison are generally right; while individuals are very often coarse, sensual, vicious, in their modes of life. Hence, a paper may be in disrepute; the moral sentiment of the community may be against it; but, at the same time, as the journal addresses the general reader it will have a large circulation. Hence, the success of *Police Gazettes* and of obscene picture journals, as well as of *Reynold's Miscellany.* I am quite aware that these views are not very popular; the conception of the newspaper reader, which I have constantly kept in mind, is not that of the writers who usually discuss these matters; but, I think, common sense people will see that it is a conception which is much more likely to be the true one.

Q. Do you expect that the papers of the future will be any better morally than they have been in the past? I notice those who write about journals are expecting the advent, some day, of a higher type of journal, morally speaking; and that the model paper is yet *in futuro?*

A. I judge that, as human nature will remain pretty much the same throughout many generations yet to come, the papers will not differ very materially from what they have been in the past. As I have said, I believe the moral tone of papers now is somewhat ahead of what public taste demands. New York is destined to be much larger than it is now; it will contain a great many more people; but I see no reason to believe that the Manhattanese will become fonder of philosophy or develop a higher literary taste. Crowds will come here from the ends of the earth to enjoy themselves or to do business; and the papers which cater to their tastes will represent very nearly the literary pabulum they require. I should say there is room in New York for a very much worse paper than it has. Let a paper get into the hands of an editor with a very malignant temper, with some wit, with a good knowledge of human nature, unscrupulous as to means, uninfluenced by public opinion or social ties, and the public of New York would sustain him in his ferocious sallies, even if he published the vilest paper that was ever seen—I mean vile in the sense of irresponsibility, of pandering to vicious tastes, of malignity, and of sensationalism in its worst phases. There is "ample scope and verge enough" in New York to-day for just such a paper; and, it would be surprising indeed, if that want were not supplied in the future. It is lucky for society that editors, like other men, are approbative animals—they crave the good opinion of the best rather than of the worst part of the community; and hence, are under strong social restrictions not to pander to vicious tastes. The worst of men are under some such restrictions; but I should tremble to see a paper issued by a really strong man who was also vile in his tastes and unscrupulous in the material he employed to cater to the wants of the public. It is natural in Americans, in viewing the unexampled progress of their country, to be hopeful, to suppose that every everything is for the best, and to believe that every change will bring about better results; and so in speculating about journals they would naturally suppose that a higher and better type would be developed from what had gone before. But this does not follow. Until I can see a higher moral tone developing itself in the community, I don't understand how we can have better journals than are now published.

Q. This is not a very hopeful view of the case; and if it is true, as some allege, that religious faith is slowly dying out, that the community cares only for the growth of material wealth and influence, and that pleasure is more and more pursued for its own sake, and in its grosser forms, why then it is not unlikely that these lower tastes will be gratified by some unscrupulous and able man?

A. I fear very much that some such thing is likely to happen. I think it inevitable that with the growth of our city the journals will gain independence; that with the enlargement of their constituency they can afford to be superior to cliques and parties; and that aiming to please wide circles of readers they can disregard the little schemes of the politicians who have too often influenced the conduct of the great journals. I may add here, that a wide acquaintance with the foremost men of the country is a serious hindrance to the efficiency of an editor. It is impossible to be the critic, when you are the personal friend of the men who play their part upon the public stage. If you are upon sociable terms with the eminent men in literature, art, politics, and business, and enjoy the atmosphere of clubs where most of them assemble, you are restricted in a thousand ways from that independent and impartial criticism of the works and actions of such persons which is within the power of an entire stranger. The elder Bennett, I think, had a great advantage over his son, in being what is known as a "social pariah"—in keeping himself to himself—and in declining to have any visiting relations with prominent men in the city. He was not entangled in social restrictions, nor were his employés embarrassed with fears of treading on the toes of his personal friends—for he had none. I do not think his son is in quite as independent a position; and his assistants are, no doubt, sometimes in trouble in dealing with persons who are friends of the editor-in-chief. One of the advantages which Catholic priests possess over other ministers, is their celibacy, their avoidance of all social ties and obligations, by which they are enabled to devote their whole time to the church. So it should really be with editors. Careful avoidance of all personal entanglements is desirable if the paper wishes to be really independent.

Q. But is it not desirable for editors to know the views and opinions of politicians—the men who control party machinery and action?

A. Not at all. The most grievous error in connection with any newspaper establishment is the affiliation of its editors with any of the so-called statesmen or politicians of his party. The methods of the politician and of the journalist are radically different—that of the former is secretiveness; the editorial function, on the contrary, is to publish everything to the world. Editors always come to grief when they are influenced by the leaders of parties. The great object of the politician is to be secret, to work out his plans in the dark; the aim of the journal is to open things, to let in light, to tell the truth. The statesman wants to make a certain impression, to accomplish a certain end, and to do so he is necessarily evasive; he arranges his machinery behind the scenes; he cannot afford to have personal antipathies; the man he quarrels with to-day he consorts with to-morrow. But the critical attitude which the journalist is bound to assume, the necessity which impels him to display the whole course of current events, and to express opinions about them, makes his alliance with the statesman a source of perpetual weakness and embarrassment. The editor deals with public events as they arise. His judgment of what is going on, if he understands his business, is far better than any politician's. He deals with the same problems as the latter, but the object he has in view is far higher. The whole history of journalism in this country is a palpable warning against party dictation and the influence of party leaders. The journals which have succeeded are those in which the editors were wise enough to keep aloof from their own party managers—to give the law to them instead of taking it from them. The most serious embarrassments to which political journals have been exposed have resulted from their connection with noted politicians. Wherever you see a thick and thin partisan paper, you see a poor and weak one—and necessarily so.

Q. You have indicated that any one who wishes a large circulation for his paper must fix the price at the minimum—by which, I take it, you mean two cents in New York city, as being indispensable for the largest circulation. Should all papers try to get along at that rate?

A. Let me explain. One of the most serious mistakes of persons who start papers is in endeavoring to furnish them all at the same price. I believe that there is to-day room for a daily paper in New York city at ten cents a copy. People differ widely here as regards means; and there is a class of people which would buy the dearest paper in preference to the cheapest, provided it had some peculiarities which pleased them. I find the American people have to-day the highest priced wines, the costliest hotels, the most extravagantly rich dry goods, the fastest and costliest trotters, and, in fact, as Jim Fisk used to say, "Give the American people just what they want and they don't care for the price." Now, a daily newspaper with certain special features to satisfy the demands of fashionable, clever, ostentatious people, and which would cost ten cents a copy, would be no tax on—say, for instance, wealthy fellows who pay a good deal more for cigars and drinks several times a day. Certain rich ladies would prefer to see a costly morning journal upon their breakfast tables, and it would be a matter of emulation to buy such papers on the railway cars. Of course I don't suppose a paper of that kind would reach a circulation of more than 15,000 copies, but that would pay very well. Such a paper should not depend on advertisements —should try to get along without them—except such announcements as were in themselves in the nature of news. Mr. Bonner did a wise thing in excluding all advertisements from his *Ledger*, and, strange as it may seem, a daily paper, sufficiently costly, could get along very well without them. Thus it would be rid of another entanglement which seriously embarrasses all newspapers depending on advertisements to meet current expenses.

Q. Wouldn't the ten cent paper require to be very different from the make-up of an ordinary popular journal?

A. Certainly. In the first place it should be as admirable, typographically, as the modern printing art could possibly make it. Its literary character ought to be of the very highest order of excellence. It should have the best contributors on all current topics, and it should give their names. Naturally appealing to a more cultivated class, its art criticisms, its lecture notices, its treatment of dramatic and musical topics, and its comments on current affairs should be equally distinguished for force and brilliancy. It should avoid the ordinary ruck of local and merely routine news, and aim at the highest standard of taste in all its discussions. But it should never overlook the social element, these matters which affect human beings in their domestic relations. The temptation in all such journals would be to be too purely intellectual and artistic, to the neglect of those materials which lie nearest to the hearts of men and women. It is this too exclusively literary character which detracts so much from the merits of papers like the *Nation*. There is a craving in the social instincts which, as all literature shows, is that which publishers have always found it to their profit to minister to.

APPENDIX A

COLLEGE TRAINING FOR JOURNALISM.

It having been reported that steps were being taken to introduce a course of special study at Cornell University, N. Y., and at Washington and Lee University, Va., adapted to qualify young men for the profession of journalism, application was made to the heads of these two institutions of learning for information on the subject. In response, the following communications were received from President White and General Lee's representative :—

THE CORNELL UNIVERSITY,
PRESIDENT'S ROOMS,
ITHACA, N. Y., *May* 29*th*, 1875.

DEAR SIR,

I regret that absence from Ithaca has prevented an earlier answer to your letter, and that pressure of duties upon me during the closing examinations and preparations for commencement of this University year, forbid my giving the requisite thought to the subject you mention.

I can only say that in view of the importance of the profession of journalism, and of the very serious deficiencies in it, as now conducted, which every thoughtful man in this country must deplore, I have long wished to established general and special courses in our colleges and universities with reference to those contemplating journalism as their profession in life.

Our effort here has been purely tentative, and circumstances have as yet hindered us from carrying out our programme fully. Its general features, as we hope to carry it out within a few years, are as follows :

Firstly. To make the body of the course with reference to journalism out of the three existing courses in Literature, Arts, and Philosophy ; but giving especial prominence to studies in history and the various modern literatures, with especially close study of the constitution and general history as well as literature of our own race.

The next feature contemplated is the giving of instruction in Phonography, that the student may have means of self-support at the beginning of his profession, and the advantage in the practice of it which such knowledge would give.

The *third* feature is practical instruction, but on the usual basis of laboratory practice in courses of scientific instruction in the University Printing Office, so as to give the student the advantage of a knowledge of the practical details of printing, and the ability to take charge of any ordinary newspaper establishment at the outset.

Fourthly. We have proposed to have a short course of general lectures on journalism proper, by some one of thorough experience and large and sound ideas, as supplementary to the general mass of instruction bearing on the whole subject.

Fifthly. It is proposed to give in addition to the baccalaureate degree, which the student may take in Literature, Arts or Philosophy, a special certificate to be known as a " Certificate in Journalism," which shall show just what the student has done with reference to his contemplated profession. These are the main features of our plan here, and they will probably indicate our views in the main. I regret that my other duties do not allow me more time, at present, than to dictate for you this hurried letter.

I remain, very truly yours,

ANDREW D. WHITE.

CHAS. F. WINGATE, Esq.

PRESIDENT'S OFFICE,
WASHINGTON AND LEE UNIVERSITY,
LEXINGTON, Va., *May* 25*th*, 1875.

DEAR SIR,

In the absence of Gen. Lee, it devolves on me to acknowledge yours of the 13th, just received.

There has never been any prescribed course of study established in this institution with the view of educating young men for the Profession of Journalism; all that has even been done was to provide for educating, on certain conditions, young men who proposed to make journalism their profession. But they were expected to pursue their studies in connection with the classes in the regular Academic Schools.

Yours truly,

J. J. WHITE,
Acting President.

Mr. CHAS. F. WINGATE,
  New York City.

NOM DE PLUMES.

Adirondack,	L. E. Chittenden
Alderman Rooney,	D. O. C. Townley
Arp Bill,	Chas. H. Smith
Alba,	Alexina B. White
Agate,	Whitelaw Reid
An American Girl Abroad,	Miss Trafton
Ariel,	S. R. Fisk
Arthur Sketchley,	Geo. Rose
Americus,	Dr. Francis Lieber
Amateur Casual,	James Greenwood
Artemus Ward,	Charles F. Browne
Asa Trenchard,	H. Watterson
Azamal Batuk,	N. L. Thieblin
A. Crowquill,	A. Forrester
Ally Sloper,	Charles H. Ross
Almaviva,	Clement Scott
Anthony Poplar,	Ed. Dublin University Mag.
Anchor,	J. Watts De Peyster
Bibliophile,	S. A. Allibone
Bard, Samuel A.,	E. G. Squier
Brick Pomeroy,	Mark M. Pomeroy
Besieged Resident,	H. Labonchere
Boz,	Charles Dickens
Burleigh,	Matthew Hale Smith
Bookworm,	Thos. F. Donnelly
Barrett Walter,	J. A. Scoville
Benedict Cruiser,	G. A. Sala
Barnacle,	A. C. Barnes
Colley Cibber,	James Rees
Competition Wallah,	Trevelyan
Cousin Nourma,	Dr. J. E. Nagle
Carleton,	C. C. Coffin
Carlfried.	C. F. Wingate
Carl Benson,	C. A. Bristed
Cantell A. Bigly,	Geo. W. Peck
Druid,	C. C. Flint
Doesticks, Q. K. Philander, P. B.,	Mort'r Thompson
Dow, Junior,	Eldridge Paige
Dunn, Brown,	Rev. Samuel Fiske
Darby, John,	J. E. Garretson
Dick Tinto,	F. B. Goodrich
Egyptus,	Dr. Jos. P. Thompson
Eusebius,	Dr. E. D. G. Prime
Estelle	Miss Eliz. Bogert
Eli Perkins	M. D. Landon
Eugene Pomeroy	T. F. Donnelly
Eleanor Kirk,	Mrs. Nelly Ames

Felix Merry	E. A. Duychinck
Fanchen,	Mrs. Laura M. Sandford
Frank Forrester,	Henry W. Herbert
Fanny Fern,	Mrs. James Parton
Father Prout,	Rev. Francis Mahony
Fat Contributor,	A. M. Griswold
Figaro,	H. Clapp, Jr.
Fleeta,	Kate W. Hamilton
Gringo Harry,	Lieut. Henry A. Wise
Gath,	Geo. Alfred Townsend
Grace Greenwood,	Mrs. S. J. C. Lippincott
Gail Hamilton,	Mary N. Dodge
"H. H.,"	Helen Hunt
Hans Yorkel,	A. Oakey Hall
Hans Breitman,	Chas. G. Leland
Horns,	G. C. Fisher
Harry Hazell,	Justin Jones
Harry Franco,	Chas. F. Briggs
Historicus,	Vernon Harcourt
Howard Glyndon,	Laura C. Redden
Ik. Marvel,	D. G. Mitchell
Irenœus,	Rev. Dr. Prime
January Searle,	Geo. S. Phillips
Jay Charlton,	J. C. Goldsmith
Joshua Coffin,	H. W. Longfellow
Jacob Omnium,	M. J. Higgins
Jennie June,	Mrs. J. C. Croly
John Phenix,	Capt. G. H. Derby, U. S. A
Josh Billings,	H. W. Shaw
John Paul,	C. H. Webb
Jugg, M. T.,	Joe Howard, Jr
Junius,	Junius H. Browne
Kirke Edmund,	J. R. Gilmore
Laertes,	Geo. A. Townsend
Laicus,	Rev. Lyman Abbott
Leone Leoni,	J. D. Osborne
Lucy Fountain,	Kate Hilliard
Marian Harland,	Mrs. M. V. Terhune
Mignonette,	Emily H. Moore
Miss Grundy,	Miss M. A. Sneed
Minnie Myrtle,	Anna L. Johnson
Mrs. Ramsbottom,	Theodore Hook
McArone	Geo. Arnold
Malakoff,	Dr. Johnson
Major Jack Downing,	Seba Smith
Mrs. Partington,	B. P. Shillaber
Mark Twain,	S. L. Clemens
Mercutio,	Wm. Winter
Miles O'Reilly,	C. G. Halpine
M. Quad,	Chas. B. Lewis
Major Muldoon,	Wm. H. Macartney
Mintwood,	Miss Mary A. E. Wager

Nym Crinkle,	A. C. Wheeler
Oliver Optic,	Wm. T. Adams
Orpheus C. Kerr,	R. H. Newell
Old Bachelor,	Geo. W. Curtis
Olivia,	Mrs. Briggs
Olphar Hamst,	Thomas Ralph
Oliver Yorke,	Ed. Frazers Mag
Onslow Yorke,	Hepworth Dixon
Old Cabinet,	R. Watson Gilder
Penholder,	Edward Eggleston
Peleg Arkwright,	D. L. Proudfit
Peter Query,	Martin F. Tupper
Paul Peebles,	Augustus Maverick
K. N. Pepper,	James M. Morris
Pisistratus Brown,	Wm. Blacks
Parsee Merchant,	Mr. J. S. Moore
Petroleum V. Nasby,	D. R. Locke
Porte Crayon,	D. H. Strother
Publicola,	W. J. Fox
Perley,	Major B. P. Poore
Philip Quilibet,	Geo. E. Pond
Paul Creyton,	J. T. Trowbridge
Parson Frank,	F. Jacox
Pylodet L.,	F. Leypoldt
Polinto,	F. B. Wilkie
Romeo,	G. W. Fellows
Saxe Holm,	Miss Rush Ellis
Sophie Sparkle,	Jennie E. Hicks
Sylvanus Urban,	Ed. Gentlemen's Mag
Sophie May,	Miss S. R. Clarke
Silverpen,	Eliza Meteyard
Susan Coolidge,	Miss Woolsey
Sentinel,	Wm. H. Bogart
Shirley Dare,	P. C. Dunning
Savid,	James Davis
Timon, John,	Donald G. Mitchell
Tom Folio,	J. E. Babson
Thomas Maitland,	Robt. Buchanan
Timothy Titcomb,	J. G. Holland
Trusta,	Eliz. Stuart Phelps
U. Donough Outis,	R. G. White
Vieux Moustache,	C. Goron
Veteran Observer,	E. D. Mansfield
Warrington,	W. P. Robinson
Warwick,	F. B. Ottarson
Whyte, Blythe Jr.,	Solon Robinson

INDEX.

Ability in Journalism, 60, 223, 242, 243, 253, 336.
Advertisements;—follow circulation, 34 ; limitation of, 34 ; Halstead's rule as to, 34 ; attractiveness of, 35 ; editorial notices of, 35 ; and reading matter, 116 ; classified, 117 ; English style of, 121 ; official, 124 ; rhetoric of, 140 ; kinds of, 188 ; puffnotices, 275 ; value of, 297 ; reading notices, 302 ; rates of, 306 ; country, 306 ; affected by circulation, 308 ; classification, 309 ; allusions to, 97, 120, 245.
Advertiser, (Boston), 63.
Advertisers, 118 ; accommodation of, 120.
American Press, 226 ; growth, 41 ; improvement in religious, 42 ; more like French than English, 94 ; extent of, 113 ; influence, 235 ; omniscience, 247 ; new era in, 250 ; improvement in, 249 ; effect of growth, 204 ; in time of Jackson and Van Buren, 291.
Anonymous Journalism, 17, 31, 136, 341.
Argus, (Albany), 130, 290.
Arnold, Edwin, 273.
Autocracy in Journalism, 17.
Bailey, J. M., 108.
Bazar, (Harper's), 257 ; history of, 258.
Beecher, H. W., 227.
Bennett, J. G., 55, 250, 275, 346 ; French mission, 12.
Bennett, J. G., Jr., 137, 287.
Best form of newspaper, 96.
Black, William, as novelist and journalist, 272.
Blair, F. P., 290.
Booth, Mary L., 253.
Bowker, R. R., 183.
Bowles, Samuel, 19, 41.
Bromley, I. H., 20.
Brownlow, Parson, 108, 291.
Bryant, W. C., 49, 226.
Bulwer-Lytton, 216.
Bundy, J. M., 185.
Business aspect of Journalism, 296, 345.
Carlyle, Thomas, 145, 328.

Censorship of the Press, 139, 237.
Chamberlain, I. B., on Greeley, 173 ; on Bennett, 282.
Cheap Newspapers, room for, 96.
Child, Mrs. L. M., 243.
Circulation, 91, 155, 171, 233, 245, 328.
Citizenship, the Press an educator in, 219.
Classification, of newspapers, 85 ; of editors, 241.
Cobbett, William, 108, 338.
Cobden, Richard, 216.
College;—men on *Tribune*, 30; Journalism, 184; in Journalism 242; training for Journalism, Appendix A.
Collegian, (New York), 184.
Commercial, (Cincinnati), 129, 197, 326, 327.
Cooper, J. Fenimore, trial of, 169.
Correspondence, 23 ; war, 94 ; anonymous, 94 ; New York, 105.
Cost of newspapers, 37, 134.
Country Press, 162.
Courant, (New England), 237.
Courier-Journal, (Louisville), 266.
Croly, D. G., 28, 84, 317, 325.
Croly, Mrs. Jennie C., 146.
Culture in Journalism, 45.
Cummings, Amos J., 109.
Curtis, Geo. Wm., 139.
Cushing, Caleb, a good journalist, 136.
Daily Journalism, 102, 289, 339.
Dana, Chas. A., 52, 75, 102, 175, 244, 278.
Deadheadism, 36, 295.
De Foe, Daniel, 248.
Delane, J. T., 267.
Dicey, Edward, 273.
Dickens, Charles, 172 ; probable success as journalist, 291.
Disraeli, Benjamin, 337.
Eagle, (Brooklyn), 188.
Editorial ;—writing, 16, 106, 108, 159 ; preparation, 16 ; value of writing, 61 ; department paramount, 78 ; qualifications, 80 ; opinion not purchasable, 119.
Emerson, R. W., on London *Times*, 273.
English Press, 11, 131.
Enquirer, (Richmond), 130, 290.
Ethics of Journalism, 326.
Evening Papers, 134, 188 ; future of, 189.

INDEX. 367

Forbes, Edw., 261, 272.
Forney, J. W., 163.
Fourth Estate, 235.
Francis, John M., 108.
Frank Leslie's, 104.
Franklin, Benjamin, 237, 248.
French and English Press, 14.
French Press, 13.
Fuller, Margaret, 243.
Future of Journalism, 36, 42, 43, 329; in direction of specialties, 57, 84, 86; evening, 189, 193, 205, 290; illustrated, 317.
Gazette, (Cincinnati), 227.
Gazette, (Pennsylvania), 237.
Globe, (Washington), 130, 277, 290.
Godkin, E. L., **208**.
Godwin, Parke, **222**.
Goethe, as an editor, 327.
Graphic, (New York), 189, 324. *See, also*, Croly, D. G.
Greeley, H., 12, 37, 56, 63, 71, **151**, 160, 167, 170, 173, 177, 180, 244, 290, 335, 338, 343.
Hale, E. E., 189.
Half-Penny Journal, (London), 350.
Hall, Basil, sketch of Journalism, 242.
Halstead, Murat, 19, 107, **113**.
Hammond, Charles, 227.
Harper's Weekly, 103, 305.
Harris, Benjamin, 236.
Hassard, J. R. G., 190.
Herald, (Boston), 327.
Herald, (New York), 11, 91, 127, 131, 134, 332; former circulation, 157; moral character, 156, 165, 239; independence, 60, 188, 196, 250, 275; news-collecting, 276, 326, 327; personality in, 333. *See, also*, Bennett.
Herald, (Utica), 107.
Hildreth, R. S., 63.
Independent Journalism, 22, 44, 77, 81, 135, 144, 163, 166, 197, 250, 280, 291; philosophy of, 48, 125; *vs.* partisan, 53.
Hill, Frank, 271.
Hill, Isaac, 242.
Hudson, Frederick, 41, 66, **130**, 174, 235; on Bennett, 283.
Humorous Illustration, 319.
Hunt, Thornton, 273.

Hyde, William, 19, 195.
Ideal Journalism, 25, 40, 79, 82, 179, 252 ; features of, 62, 256, 325.
Illustrated Journalism, 103, 317 ; *vs.* non-illustrated, 317 ; pictures desirable, 324.
Impersonal Journalism, 43, 74.
Impersonality in Journalism, 43, 63, 78, 198, 255, 266, 278, 290; pretense in London press, 13.
Independent Journalism, 22, 44, 77, 81, 135, 144, 163, 166, 197, 250, 280, 291; philosophy of, 48, 125 ; *vs.* partisan 53.
Influence of the Press, its basis, 80, 241 ; upon legislation, 219.
Intelligencer, (Washington), 130. 277.
Iron Age of Journalism, 205.
Iteration, 75.
Jackson, Andrew, Journalism in time of, 291.
Jefferson, Thomas, 235 ; opinion on the press, 224.
Jeffersonian, 152.
Jennie June. *See* Croly, Mrs. Jennie C.
Jennings, L. J., 68, 106.
Johnson, Samuel, newspaper criticism, 237.
Joint-Stock principle in Journalism, 87, 339.
Journal, Weekly, (Albany), 300.
Journalistic Conceit, 213, 246.
Journalistic Courage, 240, 245.
Journalistic Discouragements, 209.
Journalistic Training, 15, 16, 80, 109, 130, 143, 160, 183, 184, 185, 187, 195, 202, 210, 277, 327 ; Appendix A. ; *Herald's* theory of, 30; school for, 77.
Journalistic Enterprise, 131, 196.
Journalistic Qualifications, 52, 203, 223, 224, 228, 328.
Junius, 126.
Lawyers as Journalists, 338.
Ledger, (New York), 92.
Ledger, (Philadelphia), 108, 121, 128, 326, 327, 331.
Lesson of newspaper failures, 41.
Libertine Press, 141.
Libel, 58, 156.
Licentiousness in Journalism, 92, 156.
Literary ; Press, 143 ; criticism, 190, 336.
Literature and Journalism, 59, 158, 230, 238, 254, 272.
Local News, 39, 80, 99, 347; in New York, 40.
Locke, D. R., 108.

Personal Journalism, 12, 55, 91, 137, 157, 278, 291.
Perspective in Journalism, 27, 214.
Piatt, Don, 20,
Pneumatic Tubes, 23.
Police Gazette, (New York), 352.
Political *Status* of Editors, 24, 53, 73, 162, 331.
Pomeroy, " Brick," 108.
Post, Morning, (London), 273.
Power of the Press, 31, 43; how shown, 114 ; its basis, 79, 142.
Press Privileges, 36, 58, 115.
Principle in Journalism, 199.
Print, ordinary, injurious to the eye, 322.
Printing, improvement in, 319, 322.
Professional Training, 184.
Promotions, 16, 17, 31, 68.
Provincial Journalism, 107, 329.
Psychology of Journalism, 331
Public Occurrences, (Boston), 236.
Public opinion, 85 ; leading *vs.* following, 111 ; supporting the press, 141 ; newspaper influence, 159, 216 ; defined, 217, 294.
Publicity of the Press, value of, 217.
Publisher, relation to paper, 34 ; liability to libel, 156.
Publishing, principles of, 116; and editorial departments, 62, 78, 160.
Pulpit and the Press, 232.
Purification of the Press, 124.
Raymond, H. J., 46, 55, 64, 67 *et seq.*, 169, 244, 343.
Reed, Henry, 32.
Reid, Whitelaw, 19, 25, 106.
Religious Press, *vs.* Secular, 229.
Reynold's Journal, (London), 350
Reporters, 33 ; phonographic, 99.
Representative Journalism, 17.
Republic, (Brockport, N. Y.), 300.
Republican, (Missouri), 195.
Republican, (Springfield), 63.
Responsibility of the Press, 115.
Revues des Deux Mondes, (Paris), 239.
Ripley, George, 176, 191.
Ritchie, Thomas, 242, 339.
Robert, E. H., 170.
Robinson, J. R., 272.
Rochefort, Henri, 291.

Times, (London), 85, 135, 256, 273, 292, 327; strong points, 260; no city department, 100; Emerson on, 63.

Times, (New York), 44, 192, 249. *See, also*, Jennings, L. J., and Raymond, H. J.

Townsend, G. A., 20.

Trade Journalism, 84, 103.

Trade Marks, 311.

Tribune, (Chicago), 107, 197, 309, 326.

Tribune, (New York), 60, 127, 161, 171, 192, 197, 249; in anti-slavery movement, 28; and woman-suffrage, 29; under Greeley and Dana, 41; as a joint-stock company, 89; history of, 153; object in founding, 153; and Greeley, 168; on *Herald*, 284, 291. *See, also*, Greeley, H., and Reid, Whitelaw.

Tribune, Weekly, (New York), 202, 300, 306.

Triviality of the Press, 240.

Typography of Newspapers, 122.

Union, (Brooklyn), 53.

Union and Advertiser, Weekly, (Rochester, N. Y.), 300.

Van Buren, Martin, Journalism in time of, 291.

Vigilance of the Press, 140.

Walpole, Horace, 247.

Walter, John, and London *Times*, 269.

Washington and Lee University, Appendix A.

Watterson, Henry, 12, 33; a Bohemian, 107.

Webb, Charles H., Greeley's advice to, 161.

Webster, Daniel, 136.

Weed, Thurlow, 242, 343.

Weekly Journals, 103, 127.

Wheeler, A. C., (*Nym Crinkle*), 111.

White, A. D., Appendix A.

White, Horace, 19, 30, 17.

White, R. G., 90.

William, George, 55.

Winter, Wm., 100.

Women in Journalism.—Selection of topics, 146; department, 146, 254, qualification, 147; proper place, 147; salaries, 148; as correspondents, 149; training, 150, 240, fitness, 253; *status*, 254; training for, 300.

Wood, D., John, 100.

Wright, Elizur; as a paragrapher, 66.

Young, J. R., 175.

Young Men in Journalism, 31; their chances, 60.

PN 4864 .W5

	PN 4864 .W5	
AUTHOR	Wingate, Charles	
TITLE	Views and Interviews On Journalism	
DATE DUE	BORROWER'S NAME	ROOM NUMBER
SEP 28 '89	Linda Stelz 821-3781	USF Killenberg
	Dennis Hans - USF	
SEP 22 1992		
OCT 25 1992		
NOV 11 1992	Bob Dardenne USF	
JAN 10 1992		
JAN 18 1993		
FEB